# Power and Politics in Sustainable Consumption Research and Practice

With growing awareness of environmental deterioration, atmospheric pollution and resource depletion, the last several decades have brought increased attention and scrutiny to global consumption levels. However, there are significant and well-documented limitations associated with current efforts to encourage more sustainable consumption patterns, ranging from informational and time constraints to the highly individualizing effect of market-based participation.

This volume, featuring essays solicited from experts engaged in sustainable consumption research from around the world, presents empirical and theoretical illustrations of the various means through which politics and power influence (un)sustainable consumption practices, policies, and perspectives. With chapters on compelling topics including collective action, behaviour-change, and the transition movement, the authors discuss why current efforts have largely failed to meet environmental targets and explore promising directions for research, policy, and practice.

Featuring contributions that will help the reader open up politics and power in ways that are accessible and bridge the gaps with current approaches to sustainable consumption, this book will be of great interest to students and scholars of sustainable consumption and the politics of sustainability.

**Cindy Isenhour** is an Associate Professor appointed in the Department of Anthropology and in the Climate Change Institute at the University of Maine, USA.

**Mari Martiskainen** is a Research Fellow at Science Policy Research Unit (SPRU), University of Sussex, UK.

**Lucie Middlemiss** is an Associate Professor in Sustainability, and Co-director of the Sustainability Research Institute, in the School of Earth and Environment at the University of Leeds, UK.

# Routledge – SCORAI Studies in Sustainable Consumption

## Series Editors:

Maurie J. Cohen, *New Jersey Institute of Technology, USA.*
Halina Szejnwald Brown, *Professor Emerita of Clark University, USA.*
Philip J. Vergragt, *Professor Emeritus of Delft University, Netherlands.*

This series aims to advance conceptual and empirical contributions to this new and important field of study. For more information about The Sustainable Consumption Research and Action Initiative (SCORAI) and its activities please visit www.scorai.org.

Titles in this series include:

**Social Change and the Coming of Post-Consumer Society**
Theoretical advances and policy implications
*Edited by Maurie J. Cohen, Halina Szejnwald Brown and Philip J. Vergragt*

**Responsible Citizens and Sustainable Consumer Behaviour**
*Pietro Lanzini*

**Social Innovation and Sustainable Consumption**
Research and Action for Societal Transformation
*Edited by Julia Backhaus, Audley Genus, Sylvia Lorek, Edina Vadovics, Julia M. Wittmayer*

**Power and Politics in Sustainable Consumption Research and Practice**
*Edited by Cindy Isenhour, Mari Martiskainen and Lucie Middlemiss*

For more information about this series, please visit: https://www.routledge.com/ Routledge-SCORAI-Studies-in-Sustainable-Consumption/book-series/RSSC

# Power and Politics in Sustainable Consumption Research and Practice

Edited by Cindy Isenhour,
Mari Martiskainen, and Lucie Middlemiss

LONDON AND NEW YORK

from Routledge

First published 2019
by Routledge
2 Park Square, Milton Park, Abingdon, Oxon OX14 4RN

and by Routledge
52 Vanderbilt Avenue, New York, NY 10017

First issued in paperback 2020

*Routledge is an imprint of the Taylor & Francis Group, an informa business*

*British Library Cataloguing-in-Publication Data*
A catalogue record for this book is available from the British Library

*Library of Congress Cataloging-in-Publication Data*
Names: Isenhour, Cindy, editor. | Martiskainen, Mari, editor. |
Middlemiss, Lucie, editor.
Title: Power and politics in sustainable consumption research and practice /
edited by Cindy Isenhour, Mari Martiskainen and Lucie Middlemiss.
Description: Abingdon, Oxon ; New York, NY : Routledge, 2019. |
Series: Routledge-SCORAI studies in sustainable consumption |
Includes bibliographical references.
Identifiers: LCCN 2018052722 (print) | LCCN 2019001801 (ebook) |
ISBN 9781315165509 (Master) | ISBN 9781138056206 (hbk) |
ISBN 9781315165509 (ebk)
Subjects: LCSH: Consumption (Economics) | Consumption
(Economics)—Environmental aspects. | Sustainability.
Classification: LCC HC79.C6 (ebook) | LCC HC79.C6 P69 2019
(print) | DDC 339.4/7—dc23
LC record available at https://lccn.loc.gov/2018052722

ISBN 13: 978-0-367-67173-0 (pbk)
ISBN 13: 978-1-138-05620-6 (hbk)

Typeset in Goudy Oldstyle Std
by Cenveo® Publisher Services

# Table of contents

# List of figures

# List of tables

# Author biographies

**Manisha Anantharaman** is an Assistant Professor in Justice, Community, and Leadership at Saint Mary's College of California. Her research straddles the interconnected spheres of sustainability and social justice, applying participatory and ethnographic methodologies to study community-driven sustainability initiatives. She was recognised with an Early Career Scholar award by the Sustainable Consumption Research and Action Initiative (SCORAI) in 2016.

**Rico Defila** holds a law degree and is Deputy Leader of the Research Group Inter-/Transdisciplinarity and Senior Researcher at the Program Man-Society-Environment (MGU), Department of Environmental Sciences, University of Basel, Switzerland. Until 2014, he was Senior Researcher and Head of Planning and Operations at the Interdisciplinary Centre for General Ecology (IKAÖ), University of Bern. His research interests include theory and methodology of inter- and transdisciplinary research and teaching, structural organisation of interdisciplinary academic units, good life, sustainable development, and sustainable consumption.

**Antonietta Di Giulio** holds a Ph.D. in philosophy and is Leader of the Research Group Inter-/Transdisciplinarity and Senior Researcher at the Program Man-Society-Environment (MGU), Department of Environmental Sciences, University of Basel, Switzerland. Until 2014, she was Senior Researcher and Lecturer at the Interdisciplinary Centre for General Ecology (IKAÖ), University of Bern. Her research interests include theory and methodology of inter- and transdisciplinary research and teaching, good life and sustainable development, education for sustainable development, and sustainable consumption.

**Doris Fuchs** is Professor of International Relations and Sustainable Development and Speaker of the Center for Interdisciplinary Sustainability Research at the University of Muenster in Germany. A political scientist and economist by training, she focuses on (the potential for and barriers to) sustainability governance in her research, with a special interest in consumption and ideational and material sources of power. In consequence, her research addresses questions of justice, responsibility, and democratic legitimacy, in particular (https://www.uni-muenster.de/Fuchs/en/mitarbeitende/fuchs.html).

**Tobias Gumbert** is Research Fellow at the Institute of Political Science, University of Muenster in Germany. He has studied political science, sociology, ethnology and sinology in Muenster and Beijing. He is currently completing his Ph.D. in political science, focusing on issues of power, responsibility, and waste in global environmental governance.

**Jacobs Hammond** is a Ph.D. candidate in the Department of Sociology at Washington State University. His research examines how the value sets of Voluntary Simplifiers are impacted by internet use. He also examines social norms pertaining to parenting and work and explores what the experiences of individuals who live intentionally simplified lifestyles can illuminate about these facets of contemporary American society.

**Tom Hargreaves** is a Lecturer in Environmental Social Sciences in the Science, Society and Sustainability (3S) Research Group at the School of Environmental Sciences, University of East Anglia. His research focuses on the impacts of governance and innovation for sustainability on everyday life and practice. Recent research projects have explored pro-environmental behaviour change, community energy initiatives, smart homes, and diverse public engagements in energy and low carbon transitions.

**Emily Huddart Kennedy** is Assistant Professor in the Department of Sociology at the University of British Columbia. An Environmental Sociologist, her research program seeks to explain civic engagement in environmentalism. This broad focus is grounded in studies of local food initiatives, household-level sustainable consumption, as well as analyses of the ways that environmentalism can challenge or reproduce gendered and classed social structures.

**Cindy Isenhour** is Associate Professor appointed in the Department of Anthropology and in the Climate Change Institute at the University of Maine. As an economic and environmental anthropologist, her work focuses on various cultural and localised conceptualisations of global production-consumption systems, their environmental impacts and how we might regulate them—from market-based solutions to harmonised international governance.

**Sylvia Lorek** is a Researcher and Policy Consultant for sustainable consumption. She holds a Ph.D. in consumer economics based on degrees in household economics and nutrition (Oecotrophologie) as well as economics. As chair of the Sustainable Europe Research Institute Germany e.V., Sylvia Lorek is working on studies and as consultant for national and international organisations and is active in various national, regional, and global networks on sustainable consumption.

**Mari Martiskainen** is a Research Fellow at Science Policy Research Unit (SPRU), University of Sussex. She is a social scientist with a specific interest in the transition to more fair, clean, and sustainable energy systems. Her research centres around energy policy, with specific focus on the issues of developing low-energy housing, addressing energy poverty through grassroots innovation, promoting renewable energy, and examining low carbon pathways.

**Lucie Middlemiss** is Associate Professor in Sustainability and Co-director of the Sustainability Research Institute, at the University of Leeds, UK. She is a sociologist, and takes a critical approach to the intersection between environmental and social issues, with topic interests in sustainable consumption and energy poverty. She recently wrote the first textbook on Sustainable Consumption, also published by Routledge.

**Dennis Soron** is an Associate Professor of Sociology at Brock University in St. Catharines, Ontario, Canada. His primary teaching and research interests are social and cultural theory, the political economy of consumption, and the intersection of labour and environmental politics. He is currently a core member of a team working with the support of a Trillium Foundation grant to analyse poverty and evaluate the effects of anti-poverty programs in the Niagara Region.

**Anna Wesselink** gained extensive experience as a hydrologist in UK and Africa. In her subsequent Ph.D. thesis she analysed the roles of water expertise in water resources management. Since then she has continued to research processes of scientific knowledge production, policy formulation, and implementation in several research posts. She employs a critical, comparative interpretative policy analytical lens, focusing on the policy work done by those involved on framing issues through the mobilisation of discourses and expertise.

**David Wingate** is a Ph.D. candidate at the Sustainability Research Institute, in the School of Earth and Environment at the University of Leeds. David's current research looks at the history and philosophy of sustainability, with particular focus on the role of knowledge and power in environmental politics and environmentalist thought.

**Sarah Bradbury** completed her Ph.D. at the University of Leeds in 2015. She now works for the local transport charity, Sustrans.

# Introduction: Power, politics, and (un)sustainable consumption

*Lucie Middlemiss, Cindy Isenhour,*
*and Mari Martiskainen*

## Addressing power and politics in sustainable consumption research

In the context of pressing impacts of environmental deterioration, atmospheric pollution, resource depletion, and climate change, there is increased attention to and scrutiny of global consumption levels. Today there is widespread agreement that we must reduce global resource use and distribute resources more fairly to ensure that citizens of all nations and future generations are able to fulfil basic needs (Hoekstra & Wiedmann, 2014, Reichle et al., 2014). A contemporary emphasis on consumption brings welcome attention to the highly unsustainable nature of global demand for materials and carbon-based fuels. But, as the chapters in this book point out, there are significant and well-documented limitations associated with current efforts to encourage more sustainable consumption patterns across a range of scales, from informational constraints, to the demands of competition, and the highly individualising effect of market-based participation (Hobson, 2002, Isenhour, 2010).

The chapters in this collection draw attention to the role of power and politics in the construction and reproduction of contemporary consumption patterns, as well as the necessity to consider issues of equity and power at the very onset of sustainability policy and practice. By engaging in robust analyses of the role of politics and power, we explain why many initiatives have failed to bring about substantive changes in consumption patterns, and point towards more promising directions for research, policy, and practice. We argue that our work to date responds to a form of intellectual failure: the ideas dominating sustainable consumption policy and practice tend to be highly mechanistic (stemming from transitions management and systems theory) or highly individualistic (stemming from rational actor and risk theory). Both of these perspectives fail to properly account for the reality that individual consumption practices, the global distribution of resource use, and everything in between is fundamentally linked to political economic power and highly political processes of distribution on multiple scales, from the individual household to the global economy. As such, action inspired by these avowedly apolitical approaches has failed to stabilise or reverse environmental change (Bengtsson et al., 2018).

This collection, featuring chapters solicited from experts engaged in sustainable consumption research from around the world, aims to fill this gap with empirical and theoretical illustrations of the means through which power and politics influence (un)sustainable consumption. In this collection, we intend to help readers make stronger connections between systems of power and consumption. As a community of researchers and practitioners, we are increasingly mindful of the political barriers and power differentials that prevent more effective progress toward sustainability. A renewed focus on power and politics in sustainable consumption seeks to highlight and understand how power—throughout the production-consumption system, and across levels of scale—works to influence (un)sustainable consumption. The contributors to this collection draw attention to these power dynamics, as well as to the influence (and power) of deeply embedded social and economic institutions that make change so challenging.

In this introductory chapter we explore the diverse and diffuse ways that politics and power have been conceptualised in sustainable consumption research, particularly as a growing number of researchers and practitioners recognise the limits of traditionally dominant approaches to sustainable consumption (e.g., Hobson, 2013, Wilhite, 2017, Alfredsson et al., 2018). We begin by synthesising the ways in which sustainable consumption research, policy, and practice have engaged with ideas of power and politics to date, including a discussion of research that tended or tends to overlook these factors. We argue that both the study and the practice of sustainable consumption deserves greater critical scrutiny. This means challenging ideas that are taken for granted in this field but that may, without careful examination, work to reproduce or rationalise existing power relations and deeply embedded social structures that script for unsustainable consumption. We characterise the hallmarks of such an approach to understanding sustainable consumption in the section "towards a critical understanding...". Here we identify three key trends in writing in this area: 1) an attention to political economy; 2) an interest in governmentality and the notion of the subject; and 3) an attention to the politics of identity and difference. We finish by reflecting on how these ideas can be applied in policy and practice.

## The integration of "power and politics" in sustainable consumption research

While consumer culture has long been contested (Horowitz, 1985), the study of sustainable consumption emerged from the application of ecological economics and the environmental social sciences to environmental and ethical problems. In response to a growing awareness of the negative impacts of environmental damage resulting from resource intensive economies and consumer societies, policy-makers and social scientists began to problematise the effects of these forms of social organisation as "unsustainable consumption" (United Nations Conference on Environment and Development, 1992, Cohen and Murphy, 2001). Sustainable consumption first emerged as a political objective, in the context of international negotiations between the global South and North on environmental reform: when we talk about sustainable consumption, we gesture towards the responsibilities of richer nations of the global North to reduce the negative impacts that their inhabitants' consumption has on poorer nations, particularly those of the global South. If nations in the global South are to find cleaner, greener paths to wealth and development, so must nations in the global North start by reducing their total consumption levels, which are currently highly unsustainable (based on per-capita or fair shares analyses; see for instance, Hubacek et al., 2017). Sustainable consumption therefore implies a state in which the negative impacts from consumption on the environment, or on other people, might be avoided, with an implicit recognition that these impacts are not evenly distributed. As such, this field was highly political from the start.

### The absence of politics and power as an explicit locus of concern

Ironically, while research, policy, and practice are often driven by clear recognition of global inequalities, many of the solutions proposed have failed to address issues of power and politics comprehensively. For instance, the discipline of ecological economics has a dual interest in documenting environmental damage as well as the unequal distribution of these consequences in relation to personal and national wealth (Reisch and Røpke, 2004). Conceptions of the social in this work have principally been concerned with wealth inequality, however, as opposed to a broader account of the importance of power and social relations in shaping consumption.

More conservative visions abound, particularly in policy and practice. Proposed solutions to the problem of sustainable consumption typically focus on reducing the impact of consumption in affluent nations through technological improvements, market mechanisms to prevent the externalisation of environmental costs, and the encouragement of consumer choice towards more sustainable behaviours. These amount to intensely conservative responses to such a systemic problem, which tend to imagine that actors (individuals and states) would voluntarily and rationally respond as they learn about the risks of modernity (Giddens, 1990). While this way of thinking is outmoded in the research world (Middlemiss, 2018) it is alive and well in practice, as made clear by the continued emphasis on improved consumer education and awareness, "nudging", technological improvements, and market-based mechanisms as forms of intervention.

Such conservative approaches have attracted a wealth of criticism in the sustainable consumption literature as it became clear that, despite decades of rationalisation campaigns focused on efficiency gains and the encouragement of pro-environmental behaviours, sustainable consumption patterns have failed to emerge (Lorek and Fuchs, 2013, Akenji, 2014, Geels et al., 2015, O'Rourke and Lollo, 2015). For example, researchers in multiple fields have empirically documented rebound effects associated with technical- and efficiency-based approaches (for instance, Druckman et al., 2011). Some documented increased spending and consumption as a result of efficiency improvements in the home.

Others outlined how, in a highly unequal global economy, efficiency gains at the domestic level can result in total consumption growth globally as consumers drive demand for carbon intensive imports (Isenhour and Feng, 2016, Afionis et al., 2017). Similarly, research from a range of academic viewpoints has critiqued the focus on individual responsibility, pointing out that these approaches failed to recognise that not all consumers are able to choose pro-environmental options (Maniates, 2001, Hobson, 2002, Shove, 2010, Middlemiss, 2014). In short, these approaches fail to engage with a more complex politics which recognises social change as occurring due to forces beyond the economic or technological (Shove, 2010, Akenji, 2014, O'Rourke and Lollo, 2015). They also have tended to present policy recommendations as apolitical: implying both that the recommendations they put forward are logical consequences of the need for action, and that politics is somehow separate, and less important, than policy.

### Beyond the individual: Situating actors and institutions in socio-political context

Following these critiques, more recent research in sustainable production and consumption has increasingly integrated discussions of power and politics as part of a broader project to advocate an understanding of consumption patterns as the product of more than aggregate individual choice. In response to calls for rational consumers to take responsibility for environmental welfare, a diverse body of scholars pointed out the limitations of such calls (see for instance, Shove, 2010, Isenhour, 2010, Akenji, 2014). Those motivated to discuss politics and social difference have tended to point out how even well-intentioned sustainable consumption programming could reproduce inequalities by failing to recognise that not all consumers are equal in their ability to "vote with their wallets" (see for instance, Martiskainen, Chapter 7 of this volume), or indeed to ignore the fact that sustainable consumption is made possible by privilege and inequality (Anantharaman, 2018). This project has therefore included a political challenge to the idea of the all-knowing, influential choosing consumer-citizen (Maniates, 2001, Hobson, 2002, Middlemiss, 2014), putting this citizen firmly back into the political and social context that they inhabit.

More systemic understandings of sustainable consumption, which typically understand consumption as embedded in complex configurations of infrastructure, social norms and conventions, material objects, and practices are also a response to the individualisation in mainstream perspectives (Geels et al., 2015). Yet both practice (Shove et al., 2012) and transition approaches come into this category, neither of which engages consistently with ideas of power or politics (see Sayer, 2013, and Soron, Chapter 2 of this volume). These approaches, which attempt to understand how social structures produce and reproduce practices, and the potential for shifts in practices and structures over time, often explain the world in rather material terms, neglecting the importance of symbolism, narratives, and discourse. Practice approaches also tend to distance themselves from explaining change in relation to individuals, which makes it challenging to link the characteristics of individual bodies (holding gender, disability, ethnicity, etc.) to the politics of consumption.

### Inequality on multiple scales

There is also an emerging literature that represents both a broadening and tightening of focus, to consider consumption as both the product of deeply rooted global socio-economic structures and as inextricably bound to a wide array of everyday social complexities (Seyfang and Paavola, 2008). Sustainable consumption scholars with an interest in political economy and ecologically unequal exchange have begun to more explicitly link discussions about sustainable consumption to environmental justice, arguing that colonially rooted disparities and relations of exchange are at the root of unsustainable levels of production and consumption (see Isenhour in Chapter 1 of this volume, Hornborg, 1998, Rice, 2007, Anantharaman, 2018). These inequalities enable the costs of unsustainability to be externalised to societies with little capacity to resist. For these scholars, voluntary behavioural changes, efficiency gains, and market-based tweaks all address symptoms of a larger underlying problem. This is not to deprive individuals of agency or meaning or to propose a return to structural economic determinism, but rather to acknowledge that durable solutions will require social pressure and cooperation, if not social transformation. Unsustainable levels of production and consumption are fundamentally linked to inequality, implying that solutions need to tackle inequality head on (Anantharaman, 2018). While the environmental damage wreaked by contemporary societies and economies is still at the heart of this work, we also uncover a more complex set of social politics which broadens debates about social impacts beyond the relatively straightforward association of environmental damage with wealth, to include forms of marginalisation linked to identity and difference (Anantharaman, 2016; also see Hammond and Huddart Kennedy, Chapter 8 of this volume).

These inequalities can be found on multiple scales and often become painfully apparent when tracing the effects of sustainable consumption programming built on the assumption of a singular and homogenous rational actor. Differences in socio-economic status, gender, ethnicity, race, or disability shape both access to resources and the ability of individuals and groups to access more sustainable alternatives. Critical scholars have outlined how, despite the best intentions, many of the proposed solutions to unsustainable levels of consumption can reproduce or exacerbate social inequalities (Anantharaman, 2014, Kenis and Mathijs, 2014; see Anantharaman et al., Chapter 9 of this volume). Without explicit planning, even the most well-intentioned policies can unintentionally reproduce disadvantage. For example, the recent attention to degrowth represents an attempt to achieve "strong" sustainability, which, when articulated in relation to social goals, hopes to ensure less environmental damage and a more equal distribution of wealth (Lorek and Fuchs, 2013). However, many iterations of degrowth are presented as the solution to environmental (and social ills) without any critical attention to how policy might differentially affect disadvantaged and disenfranchised segments of the population (see also Cohen, 2016). A similar zeal characterises responses to a range of popular solutions in the environmental community: including, for instance, localisation and voluntary simplicity. In reality, there is limited evidence to suggest that, for instance, degrowth will result in more equal distribution of resources (Hobson, 2013), that wellbeing will result from less consumption (see Middlemiss et al., Chapter 6 of this volume), or that localisation will be a positive force for social good (Quilley, 2013, Taylor Aiken et al., 2017). The presentation of these politics as if they represent the logical solution to environmental problems, and as if they are likely to have only positive outcomes, marks a failure to engage with the complex politics of such proposed change. We argue that this engagement is necessary to ensure that sustainable consumption programming not only reduces environmental pressures, but also results in positive and fair social outcomes.

## Toward a critical understanding: Themes and organisation

We were inspired to bring this collection together to highlight the need for a shift in the literature on sustainable consumption, toward a more critical consideration of politics and power (see also Anantharaman, 2018). Many of the chapters collected here emerged from a special session on politics, power, and sustainable consumption at a Sustainable Consumption Research and Action Initiative (SCORAI) conference in Maine in June of 2016, which was designed to stimulate a broader project on politics and power. This collection, featuring chapters solicited from experts engaged in sustainable consumption research from around the world, aims to mark out recent engagement with the politics of sustainable consumption. We are delighted to offer a series of empirical and theoretical illustrations of the various means by which politics and power influence (un) sustainable consumption practices, policies, and perspectives. Increasingly, we, as a community of researchers, have come to recognise the political barriers and power differentials that prevent more effective progress toward both ecological and social sustainability. We feature chapters that help us to open up politics and power in ways that are accessible and productive, which identify entry points into these seemingly impenetrable issues, and bridge the gaps with current approaches to sustainable consumption.

In characterising this body of work, we find a varied engagement with ideas of politics and power. Given that these studies are led by scholars from a range of nations and disciplines, and that they frequently start with an empirical problem which is unpacked in relation to concepts of politics and power, a variable engagement with these concepts is not altogether surprising. Some engage directly and explicitly while others position discussion about power more obliquely in relation to the object of analysis. Some also draw directly on theorists including Sara Ahmed, Jean Baudrillard, Karl Marx, Pierre Bourdieu,

Mitchell Dean, Bent Flyvberg, Michel Foucault, Antonio Gramsci, Ian Hacking, Martha Nussbaum, Nikolas Rose, and Amartya Sen; while others more loosely engage with concepts associated with such theorists, such as governmentality, needs, hegemony, alienation, distinction, and wellbeing. We encourage readers to think more critically about the theoretical grounding of research on sustainable consumption that engages concepts of politics and power, and to continue to build collective approaches for engaging with these concepts. For now, in this book, we present a wide range of approaches and perspectives to begin what we hope will be a stronger collective process focused on power and politics and their role in (un)sustainable consumption.

The chapters in this book also tackle the concepts of power and politics at a range of scales and levels of analysis. This spans from the everyday politics of social position that shape people's access to sustainable alternatives, to the macro-level structures of the global political economy that enable unsustainable levels of consumption in some geographies and environmental destruction in others. We also find that, at times, differences in the level of analysis and theoretical engagements with power put the implications of our arguments at odds (see for instance, the contradictions between Chapters 3 and 6 in this volume). Of course, as a community of researchers, sustainable consumption scholars are not immune to politics and power, and thus the research questions we ask and the approaches we take must be reflexively and critically considered.

The chapters contained here do indeed start from a shared political position: consensus that action on sustainable consumption to date has tended to reproduce the status quo, failing to challenge or transform either from environmental or social perspectives. Critical scholars and thinkers often want to know how a problem is being defined or "problematised" (Rose, 1999). In sustainable consumption research, this emerging focus on power and politics arises from a disaffection with the rather conservative problematisations that currently dominate policy and practice: what Lorek and Fuchs would call "weak sustainability" (2013). We also share a conviction that ideas associated with the status quo (e.g., aiming for economic growth, changing marginal individual behaviours, individualising responsibility, economisation of society) have a tendency to be left unchallenged or unquestioned, and as a result to show up persistently and in unexpected places. This body of work looks for more durable, effective, and just solutions by recognising the political and distributive roots of the problems associated with unsustainable consumption levels and by tackling the politics of sustainable consumption ideology, programming, policy, and practice head on.

In addition to this shared recognition that the status quo is not sufficient, we argue that there are three additional characteristics that mark a new, more politically aware, approach to sustainable consumption research: 1) an attention to political economy; 2) an interest in governmentality and the notion of the subject; and 3) an attention to the politics of identity and difference.

We have organised the chapters in this collection to illustrate these three overlapping themes. We introduce them in turn, along with the chapters included to illustrate each:

### Section I: Attention to political economy

The emerging critical approach to sustainable consumption research takes a renewed interest in political economy. Having witnessed the failure of efforts focused on individual consumer behaviours and programs designed to rationalise both production processes and consumer choice, recent scholarship explores the links between capitalist logics, inequality on multiple scales, and consumption levels. This often takes the form of an interest in the political rationalities behind governance of the status quo (economic growth, consumer spending, liberal visions of the consumer) as well as the material dimensions that reflect and structure (un)sustainable production-consumption systems (burden shifting, ecologically unequal exchange, environmental justice). By broadening the frame and scale of analysis, these approaches encourage political actors to move beyond the realm of consumer activism to advocate for structural changes. They also encourage us to consider subjects beyond the household consumer, complementing the macro-level research that has characterised the field to think about actors and consumers in production–consumption and chains of policy consequence. Taken together, the three chapters to follow draw attention to the broadest scales—to macro-level processes—to consider the role of political economy, capitalist markets, international inequality, global finance, and state policies in shaping contemporary consumption patterns. Without recognition of these factors and the powerful interests that have a stake in their reproduction, we have very little chance but to reproduce the individualist frames that have failed practitioners and have already been heavily critiqued by the sustainable consumption research community. Lorek and Spangenberg encourage a bold approach, arguing that discussions about structural changes are necessary to draw attention to "precisely those institutions that contribute most to shaping patterns of consumption" (2014:39).

In **Chapter 1**, Cindy ISENHOUR opens the collection with a case study designed to illustrate how power operates on the broadest of scales to influence (un)sustainable production and consumption systems at the international level. Her analysis of the United Nations climate negotiations illustrates how affluent, powerful nations have resisted proposals which recognise the negative effects of a highly uneven global political economy—one which concentrates the costs of overconsumption (pollution, emissions, mitigation expense) in less powerful developing economies while the benefits (products, income, profit) are funnelled into powerful economic cores. This colonially embedded structure helps to underwrite unsustainable levels of production–consumption-disposal. Powerful nations have resisted persistent calls for structural change, rejecting proposals for alternative emissions accounting that would require wealthy nations to take partial responsibility for the emissions embedded in global trade. Proponents have argued that alternative accounting would encourage high-consuming nations to address total consumption levels and perhaps even implement domestic policies to reduce consumption as part of their mitigation strategy. Despite significant advocacy, these policies have been superseded by the recent emphasis on the apolitical, politically acceptable logics of circular economy.

Dennis SORON further emphasises the political economic approach in critical sustainable consumption theory, arguing in **Chapter 2** that while recent practice-theoretical approaches in sustainable consumption research have made great strides toward balancing concern with individual agency (consumer behaviour, purchasing decisions, energy use) against the social and political structures that shape choice (social position, political power, economic organisation), they have also unintentionally worked to reproduce individualist frames and "weak" sustainable consumption policy. Through a focus on routinised everyday social practices and their meaning, practice theory all too often limits its unit of analysis and object of intervention to the private sphere. Critical questions that are necessary to address, on different levels of scale—about hierarchy and relative influence and impact, about the structure of our political economy and the vested interests of states, governments, financial institutions, and trade conglomerates—are left unasked and unanswered. Soron's theoretical intervention thus urges sustainable production and consumption scholars to engage across scales, leaving the confines of the household, and to complement practice theoretical approaches with consideration of power as it operates in macro-level processes to reproduce unsustainable levels of production consumption and shape individual practice.

In **Chapter 3**, the final contribution in Section 1, Doris FUCHS, Sylvia LOREK, Antonietta DI GIULIO, and Rico DEFILA discuss some of the structural barriers that prevent the emergence of more sustainable patterns of production and consumption. Outlining the institutional lock in of capitalist models of production and growth, the authors illustrate how these existing structures constrain and limit the efficacy of individual consumption choices. An economic model built on the logic of mass production and consumption is dominant and vigorously defended by business interests with investments to protect. Outlining the complex politics of influence enacted through instrumental power (e.g., lobbying, campaign finance) and material power (e.g., industrial investments, jobs) the authors document how influence operates to protect growth in production-consumption systems. But Fuchs and colleagues also identify potential sources of counter-power including recent efforts to reduce the influence of money and business interests in politics. Through a combination of public pressure, the efforts of NGOs and some regulatory advances, the authors remind us that movement toward more sustainable consumption will likely need to engage actors (in a wide range of social, political, and economic positions), in more than their roles as consumers if we hope to create policies and practices with the power to generate new forms of structural power.

## Section II: Interest in governmentality and the notion of the subject

The second characteristic of this body of critical research emerging in sustainable consumption is focused at the intersection of the larger political-economic forces described in the first section and ongoing efforts to encourage more sustainable individual choice. This section draws attention to governance strategies that have been used to encourage more pro-environmental consumption behaviour. Making legible the ideologies that underlie these programs as well as the various disjunctures and forms of resistance they inspire, these chapters address pro-environmental behaviour change as social control and thus ultimately, as a political process.

Thinking critically about who the intended target of sustainable consumption practice and policy is ("the subject") can be productive. Typically, this involves asking further questions such as "what does this intervention anticipate people are motivated by?" or "how does this intervention expect people to behave?" Further, and as Rose might put it "how are people in turn shaped by these expectations?" (1999). It is also fruitful to consider what kinds of solutions are possible given the way that the subject is understood, and what is beyond the boundaries of possibility as a result of the specific subject definition.

The chapters in this section focus on unpacking the subjects of a particular type of intervention. Tom HARGREAVES, for instance, explores in **Chapter 4** the subject in the context of an initiative to shape employee behaviour. The campaign "Environmental Champions" was designed to improve environmental performance in the headquarters of a UK construction company. It draws heavily, Hargreaves argues, upon dominant "ABC" logics, which attempt to modify individual behaviours by changing: attitudes (A), behaviour (B), and choice (C) (Shove, 2010). Engaging with Foucauldian insights on the creation of environmental subjects, Hargreaves illustrates the deeply political nature of these efforts, ultimately about disciplining and governing the behaviour of employees and citizens. And yet, despite these efforts, premised on surveillance, normalising judgements, and evaluation of progress, Hargreaves finds examples of counter-conduct and the incomplete disciplining of environmental subjects.

Complementing Hargreaves's contribution, in **Chapter 5** Tobias GUMBERT draws on governmentality scholarship to critically examine contemporary strategies of choice editing as a modern exercise of political power. His analysis points to the responsibilisation of environmental subjects in an era of neoliberal reforms aimed at devolving responsibility for environmental welfare—away from the state and toward market actors. Gumbert points out that states are not governing less, but rather differently through novel techniques designed to create responsible subjects who internalise the interests of the state. Drawing on EU efforts to reduce food waste, Gumbert illustrates how these efforts, by drawing on an "ethnopolitics" seek to govern behaviour on ethical terms. Appealing to the self-evident rationality of reducing waste, these efforts operate indirectly, not through mandates or restrictions but rather through behavioural-economic and social-psychological techniques of governing choice. And yet, Gumbert argues, these apolitical approaches deflect attention away from the "systemic connections of unsustainability and the structural dynamics of competition and economic growth" (p. 119). While recognising this problem and the unbalanced power of "choice architects" to define rationality, morality, and responsibility, Gumbert sees these approaches a being likely "here to stay", necessitating that sustainable consumption research critically engage with choice editing to expose ethical issues and inform policy.

Finally, in **Chapter 6**, Lucie MIDDLEMISS, David WINGATE, and Anna WESSELINK critically examine the concept of the "double dividend"—or the idea that consumers can simultaneously protect the environment and improve life satisfaction through more sustainable consumption patterns. These authors challenge the idea of the happy environmentalist: the subject that consumes less to achieve greater wellbeing, drawing on Sara Ahmed's work on happiness, and in particular asking the question "what does happiness do?" In unpicking the logic of the double dividend, the authors reveal an individualised and rational subject, who responds to incentivisation and self-interest: choosing greater wellbeing for oneself by consuming less. In positioning individual happiness as an end goal, and in suggesting that this can be incentivised by the promise of greater wellbeing, the double dividend reproduces some key tenets of the received view of consumption (incentivisation, self-interest), and risks further embedding these as appropriate responses to the problem of sustainability. Further, in espousing this logic, the double dividend risks distracting attention from the core goals of sustainable consumption: to end environmental degradation and material inequality.

## Section III: Attention to the politics of identity and difference

The third characteristic of an emerging politically engaged scholarship on sustainable production consumption is attention to the politics of identity and difference. While early sustainable consumption research and programming operated from an ideology of a homogenous, rational consumer free to signal his or her preferences on the market, empirical and theoretical advances have drawn our attention to issues of differential access and capacity, located at the intersection of a number of social categories (e.g., gender, disability status, ethnicity, class). Not only does social position at the intersection of these various axes influence the construction of sustainability and the role of consumption in that definition, but it can also create extremely diverse experiences with problems of sustainability and with prescribed policy and practice.

For these contributions, social categories are not understood as deterministic but are recognised as products of social relations, while at the same time understood to be important in structuring people's responses. One of the key contributions of our writing here is to unpick and expose the political in all forms of policy and practice on sustainable consumption. In this section, chapters on housing policy, voluntary simplicity, and community projects illustrate how diversity articulates in dominant sustainability programming. A critical approach suggests being careful not to accept at face value attempts to "improve the way things are done" (Horkheimer, 1972). This is particularly important in sustainable consumption research, policy, and practice. We may have good intentions, but we cannot always see how our own prejudices affect our recommendations.

Mari MARTISKAINEN, through an historical examination of UK housing policy featured in **Chapter 7**, illustrates how neoliberal and austerity politics have undermined sustainability in the housing sector. While these events certainly have a significant impact on sustainability policy writ large—due to the significant impact of the built environment on energy and materials consumption—they can have an even greater impact on households' wellbeing, especially those living in fuel poverty (or energy poverty) (i.e., those unable to access inadequate energy services due to factors such as high energy bills and poor housing conditions). The UK was on course to have compulsory policies requiring all new homes to be zero carbon from 2016 onwards. However, these were removed by a Conservative government in 2015, leaving little policy support for sustainable homes in the UK. Hence, improving the sustainability of both new and existing homes is now based on voluntary measures. Martiskainen argues that the individualisation of responsibility for sustainable housing differentially affects lower income individuals who lack the resources to retrofit or weatherise their homes.

In **Chapter 8**, authors Jacobs HAMMOND and Emily HUDDART KENNEDY provide an examination of downshifting, often perceived as a voluntary movement toward reduced income and consumption— intended to improve life satisfaction. Drawing on surveys and in-depth interviews, the authors find that while serving as a positive example to others does provide satisfaction, the experience of downshifting is highly variable, depending on social location. Those with limited socio-economic-status (SES) have a difficult time achieving work-life balance relative to high SES households. This social stratification of the downshifting experience raises questions about the viability of downshifting as an effective individual strategy for sustainability given that, without social policies, it does not address issues of democracy and equity of access. Hammond and Kennedy argue that

> Downshifters cannot evade the structural parameters shaping the labor force, the home, and care work. For downshifting to offer a truly transformative contribution to the pursuit of sustainability, scholars and policy makers must address and redress the social structures currently stratifying opportunity and fulfillment in the downshifting context. (p. 175).

The authors thus conclude that while politically contentious, structural solutions more effectively target the primary drivers of unsustainable production-consumption systems than encouraging voluntary lifestyle modifications.

Finally, in **Chapter 9**, Manisha ANANTHARAMAN, Emily HUDDART KENNEDY, Lucie MIDDLEMISS, and Sarah BRADBURY clearly demonstrate how environmental governance campaigns can work to decentre discussions of politics and broader discussions about inclusion, equity, and democracy. Their comparative case study of community-based sustainable consumption projects in England, Canada, and India illustrates how those with the power to define appropriate environmental behaviours can shape programming and practice in exclusionary ways, even if unintentionally. While the consensus-based, practical, and non-political solutions these groups often advocate are seen as being feasible and inclusive (by not alienating anyone with political discussions), the opposite is often the case, as unquestioned, class-based ideologies are reproduced in ways that are compatible with the interests of the dominant class, the state, and the market. In a neoliberal age, when states are taking a back seat to non-governmental actors, the authors argue that it is even more essential to interrogate "community-based" sustainable consumption initiatives through the lens of power and politics; and to examine who has the power to define the interests of a diverse community and whose definition of sustainability is being prioritised. The authors encourage sustainable consumption researchers and practitioners to plan for inclusion to ensure that injustices are avoided, and sustainability transitions draw on the ideas and energy from a broader swath of society.

## Applying a critical understanding in policy and practice

Philosophies and theories of politics and power can appear purely academic, especially when applied to addressing the pressing issue of sustainable consumption. Indeed, given our shared political starting point (the status quo is not working), there is a tendency for scholars to try to avoid rocking the boat: to avoid destabilising the already fragile consensus of what needs to be done. As later chapters show, however, even the most convincing of solutions can, under scrutiny, reveal themselves to be based on problematic assumptions, or likely to result in undesired consequences. Policy and practice designed without considering the key elements of a "critical understanding" outlined above, risk overlooking the underlying processes of real social change and ignoring the inescapably political activity of deciding what should be done, by whom, and to what end. The chapters in this collection both show how academics can analyse power and politics in ways that are intellectually productive, and offer practitioners and policy-makers accessible entry points into these critical and socially rich ways of thinking.

In order to encourage a direct engagement with the application of these ideas, chapter authors have been asked to reflect on the practical application of their work in the course of each chapter. As a result, we engage the academic ideas presented in each chapter with more practical recommendations that policy-makers, practitioners, communities, and individuals working with or interested in sustainable consumption can take on board. This includes translating critical assessments of the status quo into visions of possible alternative, and more progressive futures.

We are also able to offer some more general thoughts on the contribution of a critical approach to power and politics of sustainable consumption. In this book we strongly counter the characterisation of sustainable consumption as a problem of individual choice, which can be solved by markets or by technological efficiency. Such a characterisation dominates mainstream understandings of sustainable consumption. For instance, most recently it has reared its head in responses to the 2018 IPCC report, and in our view merely represents an attempt to preserve the status quo (that is, not producing more sustainable consumption). The power, in such a characterisation of environmental problems and solutions, remains in the hands of the markets and industry: in this version of events, the consumer is either ignorant or choosing "wrongly" when they consume unsustainably. Note that this is a very similar critique to that which characterises such an approach as "weak" sustainable consumption, and which promotes a "stronger" interpretation: a common refrain in the sustainable consumption literature (Lorek and Fuchs, 2013, Akenji, 2014).

Instead, we would characterise the problem of unsustainable consumption as one embedded in the status quo: markets, industry, trade, and politics at multiple scales (global, regional, national, local, personal), power relations at and between these scales, as well as the cultural and social systems that these operate within, are all structures that shape the possibilities for more or less sustainable forms of consumption. Such a conception of the problem mirrors the calls by strong sustainable consumption advocates for systemic change; however, it also puts power relations and politics at the centre of an understanding of such structural constraints. This incorporates vested power exercised by industry and by the richer nations, as well as the power exercised by people who have privilege of one sort or another (middle-class, white, colonial, or male privilege).

If we are to design meaningful change, then we must do so by taking a more structural approach that is inclusive and alert to power relations and that understands how different types of politics can work for and against the goal of sustainable consumption. This, at the very least, involves moving away from policy and practice that is focused on the micro scale (individuals, communities) only. When asked to address the consumer, we would encourage policy-makers and practitioners to immediately question the kind of world that consumers inhabit, and what kind of capacity the consumer has to exercise agency (or power) to change their consumption. We would also then suggest that people wanting to act on these issues look for the social, political, cultural, and economic barriers the consumer faces in this context, and to see their role in creating sustainable consumption as removing these barriers. We would press policy-makers and practitioners, at this point, to move beyond the mainstream conception of the consumer as a rational, self-interested individual: instead to understand that people have diverse lives, identities, and engagements with ideas around environmentalism. This means that power relations, including questions of identity tied up in social categories such as gender, ethnicity, class, and disability status, for instance, play out at the micro scale, and can open or close opportunities for participation. In developing policies and programmes, practitioners and policy-makers should ask who is benefitting and to what extent, and who is disadvantaged or left behind.

## Conclusion

It has been a privilege to work with these authors to bring together such a stellar collection of chapters in this emerging field of research. We would argue that the emergence of a critical understanding of sustainable consumption is a mark of intellectual maturity of the broader domain (sustainable consumption), which in the academic world has grown from a concern of natural scientists, to one of economics, social scientists, and finally also critical scholars. Critical interest is often sparked by the performance of politics and power in public policy and decision-making processes. When critical scholars get involved in thinking about power and politics in relation to a domain of research, policy, and practice, it is usually because the domain concerned is one in which power is being exercised in interesting and more or less problematic ways. This is certainly the case in the domain of sustainable consumption, which produces divergent political opinions, and contradictory beliefs about what should be done.

As a field within sustainable consumption research, this critical approach is still very much in development. We believe there is substantial potential for further work in this field within sustainable consumption research, and hope that our characterisation of a "critical understanding" will be of value on that front. We see particular opportunities for developing the field with respect to the three sections of the book: paying attention to the political economy, focusing on governmentality and the notion of the subject, and taking into account the politics of identity and difference. We are probably missing some categories here also: we would encourage further attempts to broaden this field of research.

This youthful field has yet to establish strong theoretical or methodological traditions. This is in many ways an advantage: authors are working creatively with a range of ideas and methods to explore ways of explaining power and politics in sustainable consumption, and as a result this is a highly innovative field. Having said this, it does mean that authors cannot turn to common concepts and categories to debate ideas around politics and power with others. There is perhaps room to bring together more common approaches in the future. This might include finding ways to translate critical approaches from academic research into policy and practice in a more sustained and collaborative manner, creating opportunities for constructive critical engagement between academics, policy-makers, and practitioners.

## References

Afionis, S., Sakai, M., Scott, K., Barrett, J., & Gouldson, A. 2017. Consumption-based carbon accounting: Does it have a future? *Wiley Interdisciplinary Reviews: Climate Change*, 8.

Akenji, L. 2014. Consumer scapegoatism and limits to green consumerism. *Journal of Cleaner Production*, 63, 13–23.

Alfredsson, E., Bengtsson, M., Brown, H.S., Isenhour, C., Lorek, S., Stevis, D., & Vergragt, P. 2018. Why achieving the Paris Agreement requires reduced overall consumption and production. *Sustainability: Science, Practice and Policy* 14, 1–5. https://doi.org/10.1080/15487733.2018.1458815

Anantharaman, M. 2014. Networked ecological citizenship, the new middle classes and the provisioning of sustainable waste management in Bangalore, India. *Journal of Cleaner Production*, 63, 173–183.

Anantharaman, M. 2016. Elite and ethical: The defensive distinctions of middle-class bicycling in Bangalore, India. *Journal of Consumer Culture*, 17, 864–886.

Anantharaman, M. 2018. Critical sustainable consumption: A research agenda. *Journal of Environmental Studies and Sciences*, 1–9.

Bengtsson, M., Alfredsson, E., Cohen, M., Lorek, S., & Schroeder, P. 2018. Transforming systems of consumption and production for achieving the sustainable development goals: Moving beyond efficiency. *Sustainability Science* 1–15. https://doi.org/10.1007/s11625-018-0582-1

Cohen, M. & Murphy, J. 2001. *Exploring Sustainable Consumption: Environmental Policy and the Social Sciences*, Oxford: Pergamon.

Cohen, M.J. 2016. *The Future of Consumer Society. Prospects for Sustainability in the New Economy*. Oxford: Oxford University Press.

Druckman, A., Chitnis, M., Sorrell, S., & Jackson, T. 2011. Missing carbon reductions? Exploring rebound and backfire effects in UK households. *Energy Policy*, 39, 3572–3581.

Geels, F.W., McMeekin, A., Mylan, J., & Southerton, D. 2015. A critical appraisal of Sustainable Consumption and Production research: The reformist, revolutionary and reconfiguration positions. *Global Environmental Change*, 34, 1–12.

Giddens, A. 1990. *The Consequences of Modernity*. Cambridge: Polity Press.

Hobson, K. 2002. Competing discourses of sustainable consumption: Does the 'rationalisation of lifestyles' make sense? *Environmental Politics*, 11, 95–120.

Hobson, K. 2013. 'Weak' or 'strong' sustainable consumption? Efficiency, degrowth, and the 10 year framework of programmes. *Environment and Planning C: Government and Policy*, 31, 1082–1098.

Hoekstra, A.Y. & Wiedmann, T. 2014. Humanity's Unsustainable Environmental Footprint. *Science*, 344(6188): 1114–1117.

Horkheimer, M. 1972. Traditional and critical theory. *Critical theory: Selected essays*. New York: The Continuum Publishing Company.

Hornborg, A. 1998. Towards an ecological theory of unequal exchange. *Ecological Economics* 25(1), 127–136.

Horowitz, D. 1985. *The Morality of Spending: Attitudes toward the Consumer Society in America, 1875-1940*. Baltimore: Johns Hopkins University Press.

Hubacek, K., Baiocchi, G., Feng, K., Castillo, R.M., Sun, L., & Xue, J. 2017. Global carbon inequality. *Energy, Ecology and Environment*, 2, 361–369.

Isenhour, C. 2010. On conflicted Swedish consumers, the effort to stop shopping and neoliberal environmental governance. *Journal of Consumer Behaviour* 9(6), 454–469.

Isenhour, C. 2017. When 'gestures of change' demand policy support: Social change and the structural underpinnings of consumer culture. *Social Change and the Coming of Post-Consumer Society*. M. Cohen, H. Brown and P. Vergragt, eds. Routledge Press.

Isenhour, C. & Feng, K. 2016. Decoupling and displaced emissions: On Swedish consumers, Chinese producers and policy to address the climate impact of consumption. *Journal of Cleaner Production* 134(a), 320–329.

Kenis, A. & Mathjis, E. 2014. (De) politicising the local: The case of the Transition Towns movement in Flanders (Belgium). *Journal of Rural Studies*, 34, 172–183.

Lorek, S. 2009. *Debunking Weak Sustainable Consumption*. Finland: University of Helsinki.

Lorek, S. & Fuchs, D. 2013. Strong sustainable consumption governance–precondition for a degrowth path? *Journal of cleaner production*, 38, 36–43.

Lorek, S. & Spangenberg, J. 2014. Sustainable consumption within a sustainable economy - Beyond green growth and green economies. *Journal of Cleaner Production*, 63, s33-44.

Maniates, M.F. 2001. Individualization: Plant a tree, Buy a bike, Save the world? *Global Environmental Politics*, 1, 31–52.

Middlemiss, L. 2014. Individualised or participatory? Exploring late-modern identity and sustainable development. *Environmental Politics*, 23, 929–946.

Middlemiss, L. 2018. *Sustainable Consumption: Key Issues*. Abingdon: Routledge.

O'Rourke, D. & Lollo, N. 2015. Transforming consumption: From decoupling, to behavior change, to system changes for sustainable consumption. *Annual Review of Environment and Resources*, 40, 233–259.

Quilley, S. 2013. De-growth is not a liberal agenda: Relocalisation and the limits to low energy cosmopolitanism. *Environmental Values*, 22, 261–285.

Reichel, A., Mortensen, L., Asquith, M., & Bogdanovic, J. 2014. *Environmental Indicator Report: Environmental Impacts of Production and Consumption Systems in Europe*. Copenhagen: European Environment Agency.

Reisch, L. & Røpke, I. 2004. *The Ecological Economics of Consumption*. Cheltenham, UK: Edward Elgar.

Rice, J. 2007. Ecological unequal exchange: Consumption, equity, and unsustainable structural relationships within the global economy. *International Journal of Comparative Sociology*, 48(1), 43–72.

Rose, N. 1999. *Governing the Soul: The Shaping of the Private Self*. London: Free Association Books.

Sayer, A. 2013. Power, sustainability and wellbeing. In: Shove, E. & Spurling, N. (eds.) *Sustainable practices: Social theory and climate change*. Abingdon: Routledge.

Seyfang, G. & Paavola, J. 2008. Inequality and sustainable consumption: Bridging the gaps. *Local Environment*, 13(8), 669–684, DOI: 10.1080/13549830802475559

Shove, E. 2010. Beyond the ABC: Climate change policy and theories of social change. *Environment and Planning A*, 42, 1273–1285.

Shove, E., Pantzar, M., & Watson, M. 2012. *The dynamics of social practice: Everyday life and how it changes*. Thousand Oaks, CA: Sage Publications.

Taylor Aiken, G., Middlemiss, L., Sallu, S., & Hauxwell-Baldwin, R. 2017. Researching climate change and community in neoliberal contexts: An emerging critical approach. *Wiley Interdisciplinary Reviews: Climate Change*, 8, e463.

United Nations Conference on Environment and Development. 1992. *Agenda 21* [Online]. Available: https://sustainabledevelopment.un.org/content/documents/Agenda21.pdf [Accessed 25 July 2018].

Wilhite, H. 2017. Politics and Sustainability, in *Routledge Handbook of Sustainable Design* ed. Rachel Beth Egenhoefer (Abingdon: Routledge, 28 Jul 2017), accessed 16 Oct 2018, Routledge Handbooks Online.

# Section I

# On political economy
# and global process

# 1 A consuming globalism: On power and the post-Paris Agreement politics of climate and consumption

*Cindy Isenhour*

## Introduction: The climate mitigation gap

> National pledges will only bring a third of the reductions in emissions required to meet the climate change targets
>
> Shareen Zorba, UNEP 10/31/17

On October 31, 2017, Shareen Zorba, Head of the Science Policy Interface for the United Nations Environment program, took the stage for the press launch of the 2017 Emissions Gap Report (UNEP, 2017). Just days ahead of the United Nations climate negotiations in Bonn, Zorba sombrely revealed a significant gap between national mitigation pledges and the emissions reductions needed to stay below two degrees of warming and avoid "dangerous" climate change. As in previous years—and by design—the report spurred multiple proposals for closing the gap during the negotiations to follow.

Drawing on observation at the 23rd Conference of Parties (COP23), analyses of negotiating texts since Paris (2016–2017), and an examination of side events since 2012, this paper traces the diffusion and reception of two different proposals intended to help close the gap: circular economy and alternative emissions accounting. Both present significant mitigation potential given that they consider the emissions embedded in international production/consumption systems and reflect a growing body of research that suggests it is unlikely that Paris mitigation targets can be met without addressing absolute global consumption growth (Afionis et al., 2017; Anderson et al., 2014; Edenhofer et al., 2014; Grubb, 2013). Climate mitigation progress has been slow, despite nearly three decades of work, in part because policy has focused on decarbonising domestic energy production while neglecting growth in absolute demand for the energy and materials embodied in internationally traded goods and services (Helm, 2013; SITRA, 2018a). Nearly three quarters of all climate mitigation funding goes toward energy efficiency and renewable energy projects (UNFCCC, 2016), even though approximately 67% of global greenhouse gas emissions can be linked to a growing international materials economy (de Wit et al., 2018). While it is true that energy production has, on the whole, become less carbon intensive, society continues to use more of it each year (Jenkins et al., 2011).

To explore how climate mitigation and sustainable production/consumption policies might be mutually advanced through circular economy or alternative accounting proposals, this paper: 1) provides background, outlining how and why concerns about the emissions embedded in international production/consumption systems have grown within the UNFCCC process; 2) empirically documents and contrasts the diffusion and reception of two proposals to close the mitigation gap; and 3) illustrates that the recent preference for circular economic perspectives, rather than alternative accounting, reveals the increased influence of neoliberal governance in the UNFCCC process, the continued preference for technical solutions, and the highly political nature of discussions about global resource use and emissions. Finally, the chapter argues that, 4) because the Paris Agreement left questions about equity, power and politics unanswered, it is likely to continue to suffer from a mitigation gap until unsustainable levels of production-consumption are recognised as a political rather than a technical problem and the structural inequities underlying them are addressed. These challenges are not made apparent, nor are they addressed by the technocratic and market-based approaches that currently characterise the circular economic logics represented in the UNFCCC to date.

As a case study focused on power and politics in sustainable consumption research, the arguments presented here are intended to illustrate how international negotiations produce political contexts that ripple across geographies to help structure production-consumption policy and practice on multiple levels, from the state to the individual. In doing so, it also seeks to complement the micro-sociological studies—focused on private, household consumption—that have characterised much of the sustainable consumption literature to date (Kennedy et al., 2016; Welch and Ward, 2015). While it has long been assumed, even in sustainable consumption research, and certainly among practitioners, that unsustainable levels of consumption could be addressed through technological innovations or the aggregate effects of encouraging and nudging individual behaviour change, debates in the UNFCCC illustrate that these strategies are nested within international political contexts and power struggles with significant potential to enable *or* constrain production/consumption levels on multiple scales. The case is therefore intended to illustrate the deeply political and multi-scalar nature of unsustainable production/consumptions levels—which are linked every bit as much to consumer awareness, individual decision making, and production technologies as they are to international political struggles over the very structure of our global political economy (Geels, 2002).

The chapter endeavours to "rise above the many factors that have kept questions of power at a distance" in sustainable consumption research (Fuchs et al., 2016, p. 299) through the re-integration of political economic perspectives. Yet, by focusing on macro-level political organisation, the chapter does not intend to advance a new form of ahistorical or economistic structural determinism. It does argue that sustainable change, at the necessary order of magnitude, and with the best hope for effective and transformative change, requires that efficiency gains are supplemented by shifts in the global structures at the very heart of unsustainable levels of production and consumption (Geels, 2002; Warde, 2014). Highly unequal relations of exchange—colonially embedded and persistent in the contemporary organisation of the global political economy—allow for the costs associated with unsustainable production/consumption (e.g., pollution, labour exploitation, resource depletion, and most importantly in this chapter, *mitigation expense*) to be externalised to developing economies, further impoverishing already disadvantaged communities and making consumption artificially cheap elsewhere. Meanwhile the benefits of unsustainable production/consumption levels are concentrated among those who stand to gain the most from, and have reason to defend, the current global arrangement (Barrett et al., 2013; Ciplet and Roberts, 2017; Hornborg, 2016). The unregulated, free market form of capitalism advanced by neoliberal logics and now on display in the UNFCCC is certainly a big part of the problem, but capitalism is not a monolith (Gibson-Graham, 2000; Wolf, 1982). There is also significant productivity in imagining how alternative global political economic arrangements, based on mutually beneficial terms of trade and a fair distribution of responsibility for the associated emissions, might help to facilitate collective action to reduce global production/consumption levels and prevent dangerous climate change.

## From France to Fiji: Background and methods

> Now could be a good time to actively start considering frameworks and models that, in the end, can help to achieve the implementation of the Paris Agreement in light of equity and climate justice.
>
> Alcaraz et al., 2018, at p. 133

In the weeks following COP21 in 2015, scholars, commentators, and climate negotiators alike concluded that the Paris Agreement (PA) marked a significant step forward in international climate negotiations (Harvey, 2015; Levi, 2015). For the first time, nearly all nations had agreed to act on a universal plan for climate mitigation. Previous agreements required developed countries to act first, based on historical responsibility and capacity, but those arrangements had been disputed by several powerful, developed countries who feared that their expensive mitigation commitments would give an unfair economic advantage to rapidly developing economies not yet bound by Kyoto commitments (Bohringer, 2003).

In contrast, the Paris Agreement was based in a new arrangement which required all signatories to propose their own nationally determined contributions through a bottom-up process—in an attempt to circumvent the distributional conflicts that had long slowed negotiations (Falkner, 2016). Developing countries were persuaded to support the agreement and accept an obligation to mitigate emissions, in part, with the promise that concerns about equity would be addressed by a roadmap to climate adaptation that included financial pledges of $100 billion (US) by 2020.

The downside of the Paris model, however, was soon clear. As of August 2018, developed countries had only raised $10.2 billion of the $100 billion pledged by 2020 (Green Climate Fund, 2018). And, because many developing countries' Nationally Determined Contributions (NDCs) are contingent on sufficient financing for mitigation efforts, funding shortfalls are undermining the efficacy of the Paris Agreement (Pauw et al., 2018). Further, without clear agreements on how to formulate NDCs or how to distribute mitigation responsibility, countries interpreted their commitments in a wide variety of ways (Alcaraz et al., 2018), contributing to the now significant mitigation gap. The Ad Hoc Working Group on the Paris Agreement (APA) continues to work on NDC accounting standard-isation (Agenda Item 3), with the understanding that all parties will voluntarily increase mitigation ambition over time. Article 14 of the Paris Agreement is also designed to help increase ambition with a "global stocktake" that will examine progress relative to the remaining carbon budget and identify shortfalls every five years. While some have called the voluntary NDC and stocktake approach of the Paris Agreement an exercise in "naming and shaming" (Falkner, 2016, p. 1107) or "a giant bet on the power of peer pressure" (Plumer, 2018, p. 1), others have suggested that it presents a significant opportunity to rethink distributional issues and close the mitigation gap (Alcaraz et al., 2018).

The Paris Agreement explicitly recognised the importance of addressing the emissions embedded in the materials economy and the mitigation potential of more sustainable production and consumption (SCP) patterns, stating, "sustaina-ble lifestyles and sustainable patterns of consumption and production, with devel-oped country Parties taking the lead, play an important role in addressing climate change" (UNFCCC, 2015a, p. 1). And yet it remains to be seen how the Paris Agreement will conceptualise, track or regulate the emissions embedded in the materials economy—or whether consideration of embedded emissions will be uti-lised to help the UNFCCC reopen highly political discussions about mitigation responsibility and climate justice.

What is clear is that the focus on the emissions associated with international production/consumption systems has increased dramatically over the past dec-ade with mounting evidence emerging from three interrelated bodies of research which suggest that:

1  Technological improvements are necessary but likely insufficient: While renewable energy and energy efficiency programs are the most common miti-gation strategies outlined in submitted NDCs (Pauw et al., 2018) and receive the lion's share of climate mitigation funding (UNFCCC, 2016), a growing body of research casts significant doubt on the idea that these technolo-gies—while necessary—will be sufficient. The UNEP, which is working to develop indicators and policy for decoupling economic growth from ecolog-ical impact, has acknowledged that although "breaking the link between human well-being and resource consumption is necessary…in reality it is hardly happening"—instead, they write, "worldwide use of natural resources has accelerated, causing severe environmental damage and depletion of

natural resources" (UNEP, 2011, p. xii). With regard to GHGs specifically, research now makes it clear that the widely assumed direct and linear relationship between energy efficiency gains and emissions reductions is not well supported by empirical evidence (Alfredsson et al., 2018; Jenkins et al., 2011). This is, in part, because the savings associated with efficiency gains are often reallocated to increased production-consumption levels, resulting in rebound effects across multiple levels of scale (Barker and Rubin, 2007; Gillingham et al., 2016; Sorrell, 2018). While many point to the mitigation potential of alternative energy technologies, their development will require a significant portion of the remaining carbon budget (IRENA, 2018), and studies suggest that, to date, renewables have done very little to displace fossil fuel energy production and use (York, 2012). To rely on energy efficiency improvements and renewables to deliver solutions while consumption and production levels continue to rise is to disregard scientific evidence to date (Alfredsson et al., 2018).

2  International spill-over effects have compromised the effectiveness of mitigation efforts, essentially displacing rather than reducing emissions: Interest in the emissions embedded in production-consumption systems has also grown with awareness of the transnational spill-over effects associated with global supply chains (Benzie et al., 2016). While many developed nations have reported significant emissions reductions associated with investments in alternative energy, changes in transport infrastructure or efficiency gains— many of these countries are no longer producing carbon-intensive goods within their own borders due to structural shifts in the global economy. But while carbon-intensive production has been outsourced to developing economies where labour is cheaper and environmental regulations less stringent (Erickson et al., 2012; Peters et al., 2012; Peters and Hertwich, 2008; Sato, 2012), in most cases demand for consumer products has not diminished but is met by importing carbon-intensive finished products. The OECD and UNEP are both aware of this risk, documenting cases in Japan and Germany, for example, that suggest that domestic emissions reductions were nearly erased when indirect flows from international trade were considered (OECD, 2004). This "weak carbon leakage" enabled by inequality in the global political economy suggests that, in many cases, emissions have not been reduced but rather displaced.

3  Production-based emissions accounting frameworks present a skewed picture of mitigation responsibility and shift the burden for mitigation toward production-based economies: Carbon leakage and spill-over effects become problematic in the context of the UNFCCC which operates solely on consideration of "production-based" emissions (Liu, 2017). Parties calculate mitigation responsibility based on the emissions produced within their borders. Developing countries that have accepted international assistance and investment centred on the development of export-oriented manufacturing are left with the burden of mitigation—even when the profits accrue to foreign investors or when products are enjoyed by more affluent consumers overseas.

Investments in mitigation are expensive and often beyond the budgetary reach of developing nations, many of which need to invest a significant portion of their carbon budget to eliminate poverty. Hubacek and colleagues (2017a) have estimated that anti-poverty programs designed to move the global poor to an income level of $3–8/day would take 66% of the available two degree global carbon budget. And yet the production-oriented calculation of emissions and mitigation responsibility put export-oriented manufacturing nations at a significant disadvantage relative to post-industrial economies, leaving them with larger, more expensive mitigation responsibilities and a smaller carbon budget to address poverty.

In order to track how the emissions associated with materials production/ consumption and international trade might be addressed through the Paris Agreement, this research specifically draws upon an analysis of party submissions and working group documents for two articles of the Paris Agreement: Article 3, which sets the mandate for NDCs (Ad Hoc Working Group on the Paris Agreement, Agenda Item 3) and Article 14, which establishes the global stocktake (Ad Hoc Working Group on the Paris Agreement, Agenda Item 6). It also draws on observations at COP23 hosted by Fiji in Bonn, and an analysis of side events between 2012 and 2017. In all observations and document analyses, references to a set of key terms were tracked to measure the level of interest in and diffusion of: 1) alternative accounting (key search terms: consumption-based emissions, trade, trade-based emissions, embedded emissions, carbon footprint, emissions accounting, carbon trade balance) and 2) circular economy (key search terms: circular economy, materials economy, materials efficiency, supply chain, materials management, trade). The coming sections provide a brief background for each approach, our empirical observations related to the diffusion of these ideas, as well as an interpretation of our findings.

## Proposal I: Circular economy and technologies of efficiency

We are a key supporter of the Paris Agreement and we've committed, within that, to deliver 100 billion dollars of global climate financing by 2020… we need to make a transition to a circular economy and we need to do more, and we need to do it faster.

Jonathan Taylor, Vice-President for Climate,
European Investment Bank (11/15/2017)

Upon arrival in Bonn for the 23rd Conference of Parties, a quick review of the program made it clear that circular economy would emerge as a dominant theme (IEEP, 2018). Given the significant emissions associated with the production and consumption of materials, several scholars, nations, NGOs and industry groups planned to promote the idea through a series of side events. Circular economic models, proponents argue, have significant mitigation potential given their intent to ensure that materials and resources are utilised with durability and reuse in mind, that resources and products are utilised as long as they have value in order to offset virgin demand for new production inputs, and that waste materials are fed back into productive systems. In aggregate, these materials efficiencies can bring down emissions across the whole supply chain and significantly reduce energy consumption. A recent report from SITRA, the Finnish Innovation Fund argues:

> So far, the focus on reducing industrial emissions [has] been mainly focused on decarbonising energy intensive processes through increases in renewable energy and energy efficiency. This is not enough. Developing circularity of materials already in use could reduce emissions from heavy industry significantly.
>
> SITRA, 2018b, p. 1

The report goes on to estimate that full implementation of circular economic principles could play a "vital role" in achieving the goals of the Paris Agreement and to keep warming below 2°C. More specifically, a report published by Ecofys and Circle Economy (Block et al., 2018) estimated that circular economic strategies could reduce the emissions embedded in products by a third, essentially cutting the current emissions gap in half.

While circular economy is a dominant policy focus in many countries (most notably Finland, Luxembourg and Germany), proponents argue that it has not yet been sufficiently integrated into the formal UNFCCC process. Observation suggests this is rapidly shifting. Side events at the COP meetings are not considered part of the official negotiations but do reflect key issues being discussed and proposals that civil society thinks should be considered in the negotiating rooms. Side event listings for all conferences between 2012 and 2017 were searched to see if there were any discernible trends in the development of circular economic proposals over time. The analysis revealed a dramatic increase in events focused on circular economy principles after the Paris Agreement (see Figure 1.1). One side event was hosted by the UNFCCC itself and featured a variety of panellists, including representatives from funding agencies, intergovernmental groups, and party representatives who shared their positive experiences with circular economy projects across the world, including Kenya, China, and Laos. Maja Johannessen of the Ellen MacArthur Foundation, for example, noted that because many developing countries are already practicing circular economic strategies, there is potential to leapfrog linear lock in. In India, it has been estimated that the annual value and cost-savings of circularity could, by 2050, total as much as 30% of India's current GDP (Johannessen, 2017).

While analyses of party submissions and working group texts for Paris Articles 3 on NDCs (APA Agenda Item 3) and Article 14 on the Global Stocktake (APA Agenda Item 6) do not yet reflect these proposals, circular economy made its way into official process at the intersessional conference in May of 2018, where a Technical Expert Meeting on mitigation focused on circular economic strategies

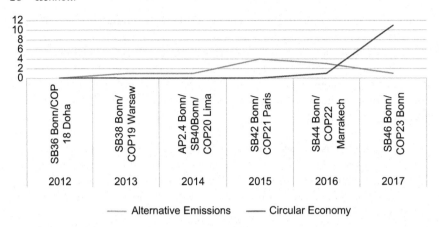

*Figure 1.1* Frequency of side events focused on emissions embodied in production/consumption systems.

including waste-to-energy and supply chain solutions. Tasked with identifying high potential mitigation strategies to boost climate action ahead of 2020, the group shared conceptualisations of circular economy as a "win-win"—good for the economy and the climate.

This dramatic increase in momentum for circular economy is linked to its compatibility with already dominant sustainability programming. Circular economy is highly consistent with the technocratic and market-based solutions that have characterised sustainability efforts to date (Hobson, 2002; Lorek and Fuchs, 2013). During COP23 four of the eleven sessions focused on circular economy were observed, all of which featured examples of CE programming around the world. Consistent with the ideology that economic growth can be decoupled from GHG emissions, every example focused on supply-side programming and policy, designed to make supply chains more resource efficient, including waste-to-energy, sustainable design, and industrial symbiosis. Fijian Minister Inia Seruiratu demonstrated the focus on supply-side approaches in his statement on the need for public-private partnerships centred on circular economy saying, "Multi-stakeholder cooperation is needed to unlock high mitigation potential opportunities... (and) create an inclusive business model for waste-to-energy and supply chain redesign" (UNFCCC, 2018).

With the climate mitigation gap figuring so prominently at COP23, circular economic approaches also presented a clear means to increase ambition by involving non-state actors through market-based mechanisms. Many non-state groups have already expressed significant commitment. Michael Bloomberg famously argued that, despite the US government's intention to withdraw from the Paris Agreement, America's Pledge—a coalition of cities, states, and businesses that collectively represent more than 50% of the US economy—should be permitted to negotiate in the government's place (Neslen, 2017). This focus on the role of non-state actors reflects not only the reality of the mitigation gap and the need to close it, but also the continued dominance and international exten-sion of market-based neoliberal governance. Drawing on more than 20 years of observations of the UNFCCC process, Ciplet and Roberts (2017) have noted a recent shift toward neoliberal principles, since the Paris Agreement. These shifts are marked by four main processes:

> Libertarian ideals of justice, in which justice is defined as the rational pursuit of sovereign self-interest between unequal parties; marketisation, in which market mechanisms, private sector engagement and purportedly "objective" considerations are viewed as the most effective and efficient forms of gov-ernance; governance by disclosure, in which the primary obstacles to sus-tainability are understood as "imperfect information" and onerous regulatory structures…; and exclusivity, in which multilateral decision-making is shifted from consensus to minilateralism."
>
> 2017, p. 148; *emphasis added*

The move toward voluntary, bottom-up national commitments—not formally linked to consideration of historical responsibilities or current capabilities—reflects the increased influence of neoliberal logics in the UNFCCC (the pro-posal coming from the United States, which has long advocated for neoliberal governance internationally). This arrangement also marked a dramatic departure from agreements prior to Paris, which were focused on top-down regulation and based explicitly on distributive justice and common but differentiated responsi-bilities (Ciplet and Roberts, 2017). Consistent with the market-based orientation of neoliberalism, the sudden and dramatic emergence of circular economic pro-posals reflects the widespread perception that the strategy presents not only a means for closing the mitigation gap, but also an opportunity for marketisation and more libertarian conceptualisations of justice. Maja Johannessen with the Ellen Macarthur Foundation, which funds a significant amount of research on circular economy, noted at COP 23 that the concept of the circular economy has been around since the 1960s but is really gaining traction now because businesses and markets see it as a key economic growth opportunity as resource depletion and climate change threaten to make inputs more expensive. She said, "The key trigger is that this agenda has been linked to business and economic opportunity. It is not about doing less, it is about doing things differently and gaining new economic opportunities" (November 15, 2017).

This sentiment was echoed by Luxembourg's Minister for the Environment, Carole Deischbourg, who opened a side event on Circular Economy, co-hosted with the European Investment Bank, with the claim that circular economy "is not an environmental issue, it is an economic issue" (November 15, 2017). The strategy is thus consistent with the current arrangement of the global political economy, and its distribution of power does not require top-down regulation or any constriction of consumer demand among the world's most affluent and provides the private sector a means to capitalise on previously wasted materi-als. Indeed, for proponents, circular economic strategies present a clear choice with multiple benefits for both emissions reductions and market-based opportunity and growth. As Jyrki Katainen, Vice President of the European Commission, remarked, "Adoption of new, circular business models based on materials reuse and improved efficiency can only bring benefits and give the European companies competitive edge...[It is]clearly THE winning strategy" (SITRA, 2018b).

## Proposal II: Emissions accounting and global political economy

Despite Vice President Katainen's declaration that circular economy is THE winning strategy, others have proposed closing the emissions gap through the development of alternative emissions accounting standards. Since the Kyoto protocol, countries have been creating inventories of domestic greenhouse gas emissions. The method for doing so is grounded in a production-based approach which accounts for emissions released within a nation's geo-political borders. Critics have argued that this system creates a false separation between fundamentally connected international production-consumption systems and is profoundly unfair given the strong division of labour in the global economy (Afionis et al., 2017; Grasso and Roberts, 2013; Liu et al., 2017; Peters and Hertwich, 2008).

Under production-based accounting regimes, emissions are the responsibility of the producing country alone, regardless of the geographical location of the associated investments, income generation, profit accumulation or where the final product is consumed. So, whether intentional or not, this system allows many high consuming, but largely post-industrial nations to indicate significant domestic mitigation progress even while shifting the mitigation burden associated with high levels of consumption entirely to the production side of international trade networks. Emissions inventories can look grossly different if calculated based on the *economic processes which induce emissions* rather than by the *act of combustion* (Davis and Caldiera, 2010), and a growing number of scholars have argued that, in the interest of increasing ambition *"in light of science and fairness,"* as mandated by Article 14 of the Paris agreement, the UNFCCC must replace or complement production-based accounting methods with alternative accounting techniques (Afionis et al., 2017; Deloitte, 2015). Proponents have suggested alternatives based, for example, on the calculation of carbon at the site of the extraction (extraction-based accounting), on the value of emissions across the supply chain, measured as improvements in earned income (income-based accounting) or based on the consumption of indirect emissions at the end of the commodity chain (consumption-based accounting) (Bergmann, 2013; Steininger et al., 2016). Csutora and Mózner (2014), for example, propose a hybrid income model, based on "beneficiary-based shared responsibility" which allocates the emissions associated with material throughput to the place of consumption while the income associated with production activities are allocated at the site of production.

Consumption-based emissions (CBE) accounting gained some reception among several parties to the convention. The United Kingdom's assessment of the emissions associated with total consumption (domestic and imported) concluded that despite domestic improvements, the UK was contributing to a net increase in global emissions due to the growing demand for imports (UKDECC, 2012). This pattern is mirrored in many other affluent nations. The European Environmental Agency (EEA) reported in 2012 that between 2000 and 2007, resource use per person increased by nearly 10% in the EU-27. This is despite improved domestic efficiencies and due largely to growing per capita consumption of indirect energy, resources, and emissions embodied in imported consumer goods (EEA, 2012). Decades of research confirms that income levels are the primary predictors of material and energy use as well as GHG emissions (Alfredsson et al., 2018; Ayres and Voudouris, 2014; Weber and Matthews, 2008; Hubacek et al., 2017b), leading advocates to make the case for an alternative distribution of mitigation responsibility toward those whose income and demand drive production-consumption levels, and toward nations with more capability to afford mitigation programs. Advocates argue that the integration of consumption-based accounting presents a promising and more effective opportunity for states to address climate footprints, using them as a scientific tool to motivate or mandate more ambitious mitigation.

At the international scale, proponents argue that alternative accounting can provide "a way to engage nations across differentiated responsibilities" given that most developed nations are net importers of embodied emissions and most developing countries are net exporters (van de Lindt et al., 2017, p. 29). Both consumption- and production-based policies are therefore necessary to ensure sufficient mitigation (Barrett et al., 2013; Crawford-Brown et al., 2016; Mir and Storm, 2016; Steininger et al., 2016). "As a starting point" Mir and Storm write:

> this requires comprehensively accounting for the total (direct and indirect) carbon pollution over global commodity chains as a whole and distinguishing between a country's production-based and consumption-based GHG emissions to enable the working out of a "fair" sharing of the responsibility between the various actors operating in the global commodity chain.
>
> 2016, p. 25, citing Andrew and Forgie, 2008; Lenzen et al., 2007

The addition of consumption-based accounting has the potential to incentivise developed nations to address domestic consumption levels and to transfer aid and environmental technologies to developing nations to reduce the carbon intensity of imports (Isenhour and Feng, 2016). Proponents also argue that CBE may also encourage developing nations to invest in low-carbon development as a means to build competitive advantage and secure trade partnerships, as carbon weighs more heavily in international economic decision-making (Wiedmann, 2009). In either case, alternative accounting standards could "enable the community to move closer toward achieving the ultimate objective of the UNFCCC of avoiding dangerous anthropogenic climate change" (Afionsis et al., 2016, p. 3).

Our findings indicate that momentum for alternative emissions proposals seemed to be building leading up to Paris (COP21) (see Figure 1.1). The number of side events focused on alternative accounting, for example, slowly increased in frequency between 2012 and 2015. While not dramatic, the increase did seem to reflect a gradual normalisation, due perhaps to the efforts of the Carbon Cap project, funded by the EU's Seventh Framework Program that ran from 2013 to 2017. Yet several countries also expressed strong support for supplementing production-based approaches with alternative accounting methods. Li Gao, Director of China's Department of Climate Change, argued ahead of Copenhagen (COP 15) that *"About 15 per cent to 25 per cent of China's emissions come from the products which we make for the world. … This share of emissions should be taken by the consumers, not the producers."* He went on to argue that the incorporation of consumption-based approaches was a *"… very important item to make a fair agreement"* (Carmondy, 2009). An observer from South Africa, Michelle Pressend of the Economic Justice Network, also argued ahead of Doha (COP 18) for the incorporation of CBE, noting that they were essential for avoiding dangerous climate change and that "looking only at territorial emissions is grossly unfair to many countries in Africa and Asia" (OHalloran, 2012). India's Minister of Environment, Prakash Javadekar, also echoed these sentiments ahead of the Lima meetings (COP 20) stating, *"It will not be rhetoric as usual at Lima. We are going to talk about not only per-capita emission, but also per-capita consumption"* (India Climate Dialogue, 2014; Yeo, 2014). More recently, as covered in an official UNFCCC press release, Gilberto Arias, a member of the Marshall Islands delegation, said he hopes that consumption-based policies can lead to an era of "collaborative, cooperative low-carbon development" (UNFCCC, 2015b).

Despite this support, in 2017, there were no side events focused on alternative accounting. Observations of working meetings on the Global Stocktake (Article 14, APA Agenda Item 6) and Accounting for NDCs (Article 3 and APA Agenda Item 3) and a review of all party submissions and notes prepared by the chairs of these two working groups since the Paris Agreement failed to reveal a single reference related to alternative accounting. While this might be explained by the relative infancy of the agreement and the basic work the APA is doing to create the rulebook for the Paris Agreement, the incorporation of alternative accounting metrics would, ideally, be introduced in the earliest stages of planning for NDCs and the accounting frameworks that will inform the global stocktake.

Indeed, alternative accounting proposals have failed to make their way into formal processes (van de Lindt, et al., 2017). Given the observations presented here, it seems that the reasons are more complex than "a range of technological and policy-related uncertainties" (Afionis et al., 2016, p. 2). Instead, observations suggest that resistance to alternative accounting is also deeply political and tied to efforts, both explicit and implicit, intentional and institutionalised, to resist efforts to reshape international relations of power in a highly unequal global economy.

Ciplet and Roberts are certainly correct that divisions among countries are no longer (or perhaps never were) as simple as the global north/developed vs. the global south/developing. However, it is largely true that alternative accounting principles have enjoyed more support from export-oriented, developing economies while opposition to these proposals has been strongest among affluent, post-industrial countries with high historical emissions and net emissions imports today. This tension has been on display in the media and negotiating rooms.

In his testimony on the House of Commons consumption-based emissions report, UK Climate Minister Greg Barker argued that the implementation of consumption-based emissions was *"politically impossible"* so much so that it would be *"well nigh impossible to negotiate"* (UKDECC, 2012). And while India expressed support for consumption-based emissions ahead of Lima, Switzerland's head negotiator and Environment Ambassador, Franz Perrez, commented in his statement to an RTCC journalist, "I'm not sure it is a serious desire of India to move towards such an approach, because it would have direct trade implications" (Yeo, 2014). This warning on trade is a common refrain among opponents of alternative accounting principles, despite a robust literature analysing the potential for WTO-compliant policies like border carbon adjustments (Boitier, 2012; Monjon and Quirion, 2011; Neuhoff et al., 2016; Sato, 2012; Steininger et al., 2016), which suggests they can help to "achieve equitable outcomes" (Steininger et al., 2016) particularly when revenues are funnelled back into clean technology transfer mechanisms that benefit developing and emerging economies (Grasso and Roberts, 2013).

Experts argued during the UNFCCC's Structured Expert Dialogue, that "in an ideal world" it should not matter which accounting method is used since total emissions are the same. From their perspective accounting methods are "apolitical tools" that "should not be used to identify responsibilities" (UNFCCC, 2015c). And yet, despite this, we found consistent evidence that parties considered the choice of accounting methods and the relative responsibilities they imply a highly political decision which, in part, helps to explain why they have not made their way into official process. Supplementing the production-based approach with consideration of the emissions embedded in trade would require some of the world's most powerful economies to accept additional mitigation responsibility (and costs) to account for high levels of indirect emissions. Holz and colleagues (2018) imagined such a scenario by dividing the remaining 1.5°C carbon budget based on an equity-based allocation framework. Contrasting this against mitigation pledges the authors found that wealthier countries' pledges currently fall far short. Proponents argue that alternative accounting can help to redistribute carbon shares in a more equitable manner, allowing space for developing countries to meet their citizens' basic needs and obliging developed nations to increase ambition by recognising indirect emissions.

### Discussion: On the hidden politics of climate and consumption

Bengtsson and colleagues (2018) identify two approaches to sustainability. The first is concentrated on improving the efficiency of existing processes—whether consumer choices, extraction, production methods, distribution channels or product design. This "efficiency" approach has long been dominant in sustainability programming. Circular economic proposals advance these ideologies by moving the focus beyond energy efficiency to also consider materials efficiencies, which, when improved, can reduce the amount of energy necessary in production/consumption systems. Circular economy also takes a more systemic approach to mitigation, considering inefficiencies across entire production-consumption-disposal chains. These are certainly steps in the right direction with significant mitigation potential.

However, despite a now considerable body of research which suggests that demand-side policies are also essential to ensure that efficiency gains are not cannibalised by rebound effects and increased production levels (Alfredsson et al., 2018; Barrett et al., 2013; Creutzig et al., 2016; Mir and Storm, 2016; Steininger et al., 2016), our findings suggest that very little of the circular economy logic on display in the UNFCCC process is focused on addressing total consumption or demand. In fact, there wasn't a single mention of demand-side policies or of production/consumption levels in any of the four side events attended.

Circle economic approaches thus fall short of Bengtsson and colleagues' second type of sustainability programming. "Systemic" approaches move beyond efficiency to consider the risk of rebound effects and consider total levels of production/consumption on a global scale. These systemic approaches are based on the argument that efficiency improvements are necessary but insufficient without parallel attention to total consumption levels and the distributional and institutional problems at the very root of unsustainable production/consumption levels.

Many advocates for systems-based approaches are influenced by research which suggests that current systems of production-consumption not only depend upon but also exacerbate inequalities between and within countries (e.g., Dabla-Norris et al. 2015; Piketty, 2013). Theory and empirical work on ecologically unequal exchanges demonstrates how the value associated with production/consumption systems is concentrated unequally across geographies (Ciplet and Roberts, 2017). Because the organisation of the global political economy is highly uneven, "conditioned by a colonial history of unequal insertion into the world economy and uneven trade relations," the benefits of high levels of production/consumption are concentrated within already wealthy nations while resources (human and natural) are extracted from less developed economies "as their societies are transformed to deliver these resources to the developed nations at lowest price" (Ibid., 2017, p. 376, citing Roberts and Parks, 2006; Cardoso and Faletto, 1979; Bunker, 1985). This ability to externalise costs enables the world's most affluent to sustain high levels of consumption which is artificially cheap. Meanwhile the costs (pollution, resource depletion, and mitigation expense) are most often borne by those least able to invest in mitigation.

Proponents of systemic approaches to sustainability recognise the need to address issues of distributional justice on moral and rational grounds. While proposals for consumption-based accounting may have recently lost steam in the UNFCCC process, literature reviews suggest that the academic and activist communities are still very much focused on alternative means through which to calculate and fairly distribute the remaining carbon budget, based on the recognition that an effective climate agreement hinges on fairness principles. Liu (2016) argues for incorporation of emissions per capita, gains from trade and horizontal allocation rules, in which "the carbon trade balance between trading partners is distributed according to their respective levels of development." Liu complements this with "vertical extending rules" that integrate historical emissions. Other equity-based frameworks for sharing the remaining carbon budget are based on these and a wide variety of additional criteria including the ability to pay and the right to development (Alcaraz et al., 2018; Mattoo and Subramanian, 2012; Pan et al., 2017).

These analyses suggest that the US and the EU have already "exceeded their fair share of entitlement to the atmosphere's ability to absorb GHGs long ago and are squatting on someone else's atmospheric space" (Mathai, 2018, p. 1). Indeed, comparisons of contemporary emissions per capita, historical emissions and levels of development against NDC ambition suggest, that as a general trend, most developed countries must greatly reduce their carbon budget relative to their current NDCs, while developing countries make use of carbon budgets that are higher than their cumulative historical emissions (Alcaraz et al., 2018).

However, the neoliberal logics reflected in the Paris Agreement de-emphasise regulatory interventions like those implied by alternative accounting frameworks. As economic anthropologists have long observed, part of the hegemonic power of neoliberal logics is the idea that the market will ultimately "benefit everyone in their economic role as consumers" (Carrier and Miller, 1999, p. 38) through markets responsive to rational demand, efficiency and thus low prices. And, as Karl Polanyi observed, "If the movement for *laissez-faire* simply argued that expanding markets would create more profit opportunities for certain firms, their arguments would have little resonance" (Block, 2008, p. 4). But advocates of neoliberal governance nonetheless frame the benefits of self-regulating markets in universal terms, hinging on a more efficient economy and freedom from bureaucratic over-regulation, including any sort of restriction on a consumer's right to choose (Wilk, 2009).

Consumer choice is seen, in many high-consuming liberal democracies, as a fundamental right (Maniates, 2002; Princen et al., 2002). In this context, governments have been hesitant to support climate mitigation policies with the potential to address total consumer demand—which is assumed to be deeply unpopular domestically. Indeed, the Paris Agreement has thus far prioritised concerns about national sovereignty and political feasibility (Alcaraz, 2017), including strategies that don't require that high-consuming nations recognise indirect emissions or address high consumption levels.

Several prominent sustainable consumption scholars have noted this persistent state-level hesitancy to confront consumption and the associated "wasteful materials and energy usage patterns" (Cohen, 2010, p. 108). Fuchs and Lorek (2005) note that "governments have, at best, limited their sustainable consumption focus to measures of weak sustainable consumption, i.e. efforts to increase the resource efficiency of products" (Fuchs and Lorek, 2005), essentially constituting an effort to make the status quo more efficient with incremental changes and reforms (Geels et al., 2015).These often take the shape of ineffective consumer education and nudging campaigns (Isenhour, 2010, see also Gumbert and Hargreaves, this collection) designed to encourage consumers to make more environmentally friendly choices.

And yet there is a clear double standard. While politicians rarely fathom limiting consumer choice in wealthy, affluent contexts, some UNFCCC programs have their very basis in limiting consumption in the interest of climate mitigation. Communities included in REDD+ programming, many of which have very little culpability for climate change, are asked to refrain from consuming forest products in the name of carbon sequestration—while the affluent consumers at the other end of the associated commodity chains evade any responsibility for the deforestation associated with extraction (Brown, 2013). Innumerable conservation programs also limit consumption, in various ways, particularly in communities directly dependent on local resources (Büscher et al., 2014; Liverman, 2009). Ironically, indirect resource user and emitters escape scrutiny.

While not often recognised in the negotiating rooms at the UNFCCC, consumption is a "mechanism of power" (Baudrillard, 1981, p. 75) that can operate across scales to reproduce patterns of unequal access to resources and atmospheric space. This mechanism becomes particularly hegemonic (Gramsci, 2005) when cloaked in the apolitical ideologies of consumer choice and market freedom—envisioned to benefit all equally—and when the mathematics of representation project an image of resource use that reproduces a false separation between fundamentally connected producers and consumers.

The international community has set some standards for minimum levels of consumption necessary to meet basic needs (e.g., Sustainable Development Goals), but has not yet seen the political will to directly challenge the consumption levels of the world's most consuming citizens. Some proposals have been advanced, beginning in the 1990s with the Scandinavian concept of "fair environmental space," which propose to address growing consumption levels. More recently "consumption corridors" (Di Giulio and Fuchs, 2014) and "doughnut economies" (Raworth, 2017) suggest the need for environmental ceilings, or maximum consumption levels that consider issues of social justice and global ecological limits.

Sceptics would likely label such proposals idealistic and politically infeasible since most people are assumed to be naturally self-interested, despite empirical evidence which indicates otherwise (Henrich et al., 2009; Thaler, 2000). However, a rapidly emerging body of research in a variety of international contexts suggests that an awareness and concern for collective wellbeing and environmental justice may be more salient and effective for encouraging behavioural change and citizen involvement (Isenhour, 2012; Lorenzoni and Hulme, 2009; Lorenzoni and Pidgeon, 2006; Zwick et al., 2007). Grasso argues that proposals like alternative emissions accounting should be politically feasible given that they are grounded in the "fairness" principle laid out by the UNFCCC process, and Bechel and Scheve (2013) argue that these fairness principles present a powerful means to build public support for ambitious mitigation.

Perhaps a greater indicator of potential feasibility is that programs designed to address total consumption, like those that might be inspired by alternative emissions accounting, do exist. Sweden, for example, was one of the first states to account for the emissions embedded in their imports (SEPA, 2008). While under

Kyoto accounting guidance, Sweden had previously reported that their emissions were significantly below 1990 levels; when using consumption-based emissions accounting, they found that their emissions were more than 20% higher than 1990 levels (Swedish EPA, 2010). This realisation encouraged the state to increase ambition through a variety of measures including international environmental technological assistance (Isenhour and Feng, 2016) and, more recently, innovative demand-side policies designed to reduce total domestic consumption levels, including a tax rebate for product repair (Orange, 2016).

CarbonCap's analysis of policies designed to address consumption in affluent nations, as a means toward climate mitigation, encourages movement beyond the consumer-choice model which has proven to be relatively ineffective (Halkier, 1999; Hobson, 2002). Their research indicates that, "consumer choice is difficult to influence when consumers have equal access to high and low carbon goods that meet the same needs"— they therefore recommend instruments that work first to "alter the range of products available, their ease of access and/or their cost" (2017, p. 43) While policies that might work to reduce total consumption in affluent contexts like carbon taxes or bans on particularly polluting products may not be politically popular, solutions that operate at higher levels of scale and apply equally to all consumers— not just an already burdened core of interested and engaged consumers—can more effectively target the key drivers of emissions, including a growing materials economy.

## Conclusion: On collective action and the climate

Both circular economy and alternative emissions accounting approaches encourage states to move beyond the nationalist orientation of the UNFCCC process, which has long suffered from power struggles as nations seek to maintain or build their ability to compete on international markets and to defend their national sovereignty. By recognising international chains of carbon, embedded in global trade, both proposals open the door for more bi- and multilateral cooperation as well as greater recognition of the highly political and uneven nature of international resource consumption and associated emissions. Indeed, the IPCC's Fifth Assessment Report concluded that:

> Effective mitigation will not be achieved if individual agents advance their own interests independently. Climate change has the characteristics of a collective action problem at the global scale because most greenhouse gases (GHGs) accumulate over time and mix globally, and emissions by any agent (e.g., individual, community, company, country) affect other agents. International cooperation is therefore required to effectively mitigate GHG emissions and address other climate change issues.
>
> 2014, p. 4

Emissions models validate this claim. Holz and colleagues (2018), for example, estimate that 1.5°C compliant mitigation is entirely impossible without large-scale international cooperation, including attention to the emissions embodied in trade. And yet cooperation and trust are dependent on an equitable distribution of responsibility (Liu, 2016).

We have argued here that because the Paris Agreement left questions about inequality, power and politics largely unanswered, it is likely to continue to suffer from a significant mitigation gap until unsustainable levels of production-consumption are recognised as a political rather than a technical problem and the structural inequities underlying them are addressed. These challenges are not made apparent, nor addressed by the technocratic and market-based approaches that characterise the circular economic logics represented in the UNFCCC to date. And while the neoliberal logics underlying the Paris Agreement seem to be contrary to efforts to implement alternative emissions accounting frameworks, the need for cooperation and collective action depends on a more equitable distribution of mitigation responsibility.

Sustainable consumption researchers and practitioners have long focused on strategies to influence culture change and individual behaviours, but current levels of materials and energy use and associated emissions do not indicate that these efforts have had a significant impact. Those concerned about sustainability can no longer afford to neglect discussions about alternative global political economic arrangements—based on mutually beneficial terms of trade and a fair distribution of responsibility for the associated emissions—and how such arrangements might facilitate collective action to reduce global production/consumption levels and prevent dangerous climate change.

## References

Afionis, S., Sakai, M., Scott, K., Barrett, J., Gouldson, A., 2017. "Consumption-based carbon accounting: Does it have a future?", *WIREs Climate Change* 8(1). https://doi.org/10.1002/wcc.438

Alcaraz, O., Buenestado, P., Escribano, B., Sureda, B., Turon, A., Xercavins, J., 2018. "Distributing the Global Carbon Budget with climate justice criteria", *Climatic Change* 149(2), 1–15. https://doi.org/10.1007/s10584-018-2224-0

Alfredsson, E., Bengtsson, M., Brown, H.S., Isenhour, C., Lorek, S., Stevis, D., Vergragt, P., 2018. "Why achieving the Paris Agreement requires reduced overall consumption and production.", *Sustainability: Science, Practice and Policy* 14, 1–5. https://doi.org/10.1080/15487733.2018.1458815

Anderson, K., Quéré, C., Mclachlan, C., 2014. "Radical emission reductions: the role of demand reductions in accelerating full decarbonization", *Carbon Management* 5, 321–323.

Andrew, R., Forgie, V., 2008. "A three-perspective view of greenhouse gas emission responsibilities in New Zealand", *Ecological Economics* 68, 194–204. https://doi.org/10.1016/j.ecolecon.2008.02.016

Ayres, R., and V. Voudouris, 2014. "The economic growth enigma: Capital, labour and useful energy?", *Energy Policy* 64:16–28.

Barker, T., Rubin, J., 2007. "Macroeconomic Effects of Climate Policies on Road Transport: Efficiency Agreements Versus Fuel Taxation for the United Kingdom, 2000-2010", *Transportation Research Record: Journal of the Transportation Research Board* 2017, 54–60.

Barrett, J., Peters, G., Weidmann, T., Scott, K., Roelich, K., Le Quere, C., 2013. "Consumption-based GHG emissions accounting: A UK case study", *Climate Policy* 13, 451–470.

Baudrillard, J., 1981. *For a Critique of the Political Economy of the Signs.* Telos Press, St. Louis.

Bechel, M. M., and Scheve, K.F., 2013. "Mass Support for Global Climate Agreements Depends on Institutional Design", *PNAS* 110(34): 13763–13768.

Bengtsson, M., Alfredsson, E., Cohen, M., Lorek, S., Schroeder, P., 2018. "Transforming systems of consumption and production for achieving the sustainable development goals: Moving beyond efficiency", *Sustain Sci* 1–15. https://doi.org/10.1007/s11625-018-0582-1

Benzie, M., Carlsen, H., Hedlund, J., 2016. "Introducing the transnational climate impacts index: Indicators of country-level exposure methodology report" (No. Working Paper 2016-07). Stockholm Environment Institute, Stockholm.

Bergmann, L., 2013. "Bound by chains of carbon: Ecological–economic geographies of globalization", *Annals of the Association of American Geographers* 103, 1348–1370. https://doi.org/10.1080/00045608.2013.779547

Block, F., 2008. "Polanyi's double movement and the reconstruction of critical theory", *Interventions in Political Economy* 38, 1–17.

Block, K., Hoogzaad, J., Ramkumar, S., Ridley, A., Srivastav, P., Tan, I., Terlouw, W., de Wit, M., 2018. "Implementing circular economy globally makes Paris targets achievable". Ecofys/Circle Economy. Available at https://unfccc.int/sites/default/files/resource/Circular%20economy%201.pdf (accessed 4.01.19).

Bohringer, C., 2003. "The Kyoto Protocol: A review and perspectives", *Oxford Review of Economic Policy* 19, 451.

Boitier, B., 2012. "$CO_2$ Emissions Production-Based Accounting vs. Consumption: Insights from the WOID Database (Lab)", ERASME, Ecole Centrale, Paris.

Brown, M.I., 2013. *Redeeming REDD: Policies, Incentives and Social Feasibility for Avoided Deforestation,* 1 ed. Routledge, London; New York.

Bunker, S. G., 1985. *Underdeveloping the Amazon: Extraction, Unequal Exchange, and the Failure of the Modern State.* Chicago: University of Chicago Press.

Büscher, B., Dressler, W., Fletcher, R., 2014. "Nature Inc.: Environmental Conservation in the Neoliberal Age", *Critical Green Engagements: Investigating the Green Economy and its Alternatives.* University of Arizona Press, Tucson.

Cardoso, F. H. and Faletto, E., 1979. *Dependency and Development in Latin America.* University of California Press, Berkeley.

Carmondy, G., 2009. "Can china change the copenhagen consultations?", *Online Opinion Australia's E-journal of Social and Political Debate*, March.

Carrier, J. and Miller, D., 1999. "From public virtue to private vice", In *Anthropological Theory Today*, Moore, ed. Blackwell Press, 24–47.

Ciplet, D., Roberts, J.T., 2017. "Climate change and the transition to neoliberal environmental governance", *Global Environmental Change* 46, 148–156. https://doi.org/10.1016/j.gloenvcha.2017.09.003

Cohen, M.J., 2010. "The International Political Economy of (Un)Sustainable Consumption and Global Financial Collapse", *Environmental Politics* 19(1): 107–126.

Crawford-Brown, D., Grubb, M., Hawkins, S., Villanueva, A., 2016. "Carbon CAP Policy Brief 2: Acceptance of Consumption-based Climate Policy Instruments and Implementation Challenges". Available at https://climatestrategies.org/publication/carbon-cap-policy-brief-2-acceptance-of-consumption-based-climate-policy-instruments-and-implementation-challenges/ (accessed 4.01.19).

Creutzig, F., Fernandez, B., Haberl, H., Khosla, R., Mulugetta, Y., Seto, K.C., 2016. "Beyond Technology: Demand-Side Solutions for Climate Change Mitigation", *Annual Review of Environment and Resources* 41, 173–198. https://doi.org/10.1146/annurev-environ-110615-085428

Csutora, M., Mózner, Z.V., 2014. "Proposing a beneficiary-based shared responsibility approach for calculating national carbon accounts during the post-Kyoto era", *Climate Policy* 14, 599–616. https://doi.org/10.1080/14693062.2014.905442

Dabla-Norris, E., Kochhar, K., Suphaphiphat, N., Ricka, F., Tsounta, E. 2015. "Causes and consequences of income inequality: A global perspective", *International Monetary Fund Staff*, Discussion Notes No. 15/13

Davis, S.J., Caldiera, K., 2010. "Consumption-based accounting of $CO_2$ emissions", *PNAS* 107(12).

de Wit, M., Hoogzaad, J., Ramkumar, S., Friedl, H., Douma, A., 2018. "Global circularity gap report", *Circle Economy/Shifting Paradigms*, January.

Deloitte, 2015. *Consumption Based Carbon Emissions*. Deloitte Access Economics.

Di Giulio, A. and Fuchs, D., 2014. "Sustainable consumption corridors: Concept, objections, and responses", *GAIA* 23(1):184–192.

Edenhofer, O., Pichs-Madruga, R., Sokona, Y., Farahani, E., Kadner, S., Seyboth, K., Adler, A., Baum, I., Brunner, S., Eickemeier, P., 2014. *Climate Change 2014: Mitigation of Climate Change. Contribution of Working Group III to the Fifth Assessment Report of the Intergovernmental Panel on Climate Change*. Cambridge University Press, Cambridge.

Erickson, P., Chandler, C., Lazarus, M., 2012. "Reducing greenhouse gas emissions associated with consumption: A methodology for scenario snalysis", (Working Paper No. 2012-05). Stockholm Environmental Institute.

European Environment Agency, 2012. *Europe's Demand for Resources Reaching Far Beyond its Borders*. European Environment Agency.

Falkner, R., 2016. "The Paris Agreement and the new logic of international climate politics", *International Affairs* 92, 1107–1125. https://doi.org/10.1111/1468-2346.12708

Fuchs, D., Di Giulio, A., Glaab, K., Lorek, S., Maniates, M., Princen, T., Røpke, I., 2016. "Power: The missing element in sustainable consumption and absolute reductions research and action", *Journal of Cleaner Production, Absolute Reductions in Material Throughput, Energy Use and Emissions* 132, 298–307. https://doi.org/10.1016/j.jclepro.2015.02.006

Geels, F.W., 2002. "Technological transitions as evolutionary reconfiguration processes: A multi-level perspective and a case-study", *Research Policy*, NELSON + WINTER + 20 31, 1257–1274. https://doi.org/10.1016/S0048-7333(02)00062-8

Geels, F., McMeekin, A. Mylan, J. and Southerton, D., 2015. "A critical appraisal of sustainable consumption and production research: The reformist, revolutionary and reconfiguration positions", *Global Environmental Change* 34:1–12.

Gibson-Graham, J.K., 2000. *A Postcapitalist Politics*. University of Minnesota Press, Minneapolis.

Gillingham, K., Rapsony, D., Wagner, G., 2016. "The Rebound Effect and Energy Efficiency Policy", *Review of Environmental Economics & Policy* 10, 68–88. https://doi.org/10.1093/reep/rev017

Gramsci, A., 2005. *Selections from the Prison Notebooks*. Lawrence and Wishart.

Grasso, M., Roberts, J.T., 2013. "A fair compromise to break the climate iMpasse: A major economics forum approach to emissions reductions budgeting", No. Policy Paper 2013-02. The Brookings Institution, Washington, DC.

Green Climate Fund, 2018. "Replenishment", *Green Climate Fund*. Electronic resource accessed August 12, 2018 at https://www.greenclimate.fund/who-we-are/about-the-fund

Grubb, M., 2013. *Planetary Economics*. Routledge, New York.

Halkier, B., 1999. "Consequences of the politicization of consumption: The example of environmentally friendly consumption practices", *Journal of Environmental Policy and Planning Banner*, 1(1), 25–41.

Harvey, F., 2015. "Paris climate change agreement: The world's greatest diplomatic success", *The Guardian*, December.

Helm, D., 2013. *The Carbon Crunch: How We're Getting Climate Change Wrong–and How to Fix It*, Reprint edition. Yale University Press.

Henrich, J., Boyd, R., Bowles, S., Camerer, C., Fehr, E., Gintis, H., McElreath, R., 2001. "In search of homo economicus: Behavioral experiments in 15 small-scale societies", *The American Economic Review* 91(2): 73–78.

Hobson, K., 2002. "Competing discourses of sustainable consumption: Does the 'rationalization of lifestyles' make sense?", *Environmental Politics* 11, 95–120.

Holz, C., Kartha, S., Athanasiou, T., 2018. "Fairly sharing 1.5: National fair shares of a 1.5° C-compliant global mitigation effort", *Int Environ Agreements* 18, 117–134. https://doi.org/10.1007/s10784-017-9371-z

Hubacek, K., G. Baiocchi, K. Feng, R. Munoz Castillo, L. Sun, and J. Xue. 2017a. "Global carbon inequality." *Energy, Ecology and Environment*, 1–9.

Hubacek, K., Baiocchi, G., Feng, K., Patwardhan, A., 2017b. "Poverty eradication in a carbon constrained world", *Nat Commun* 8. https://doi.org/10.1038/s41467-017-00919-4

Hornborg, A., 2016. *Global Magic: Technologies of Appropriation from Ancient Rome to Wall Street*. New York, NY: Palgrave Macmillian.

India Climate Dialogue, 2014. "India can't follow China's emissions pledge, says negotiator", *India Climate Dialogue*.

Institute for European Environmental Policy, 2018. "What role can circular economy play in delivering the Paris Agreement?", [WWW Document]. URL https://ieep.eu/news/what-role-can-circular-economy-play-in-delivering-the-paris-agreement (accessed 08.11.2018).

IRENA, 2018. "Global energy transformation: A roadmap to 2050", *International Renewable Energy Agency*, Abu Dhabi.

Isenhour, C. 2010, "On conflicted swedish consumers, the effort to 'stop shopping' and neoliberal environmental governance", *Journal of Consumer Behavior* 9(6): 454–469.

Isenhour, C., Feng, K., 2016. "Decoupling and displaced emissions: On Swedish consumers, Chinese producers and policy to address the climate impact of consumption", *Journal of Cleaner Production*, Special Volume: Transitions to Sustainable Consumption and Production in Cities 134, 320–329. https://doi.org/10.1016/j.jclepro.2014.12.037

Jenkins, J., Nordhaus, T., Shellenberger, M., 2011. *Energy Emergence: Rebound and Backfire as Emergent Phenomena*. Breakthrough Institute.

Johannessen, M., 2017. *Ambitious Climate Action with Circular Economy. Presentation at Side Event at COP23*. Bonn Germany (November 15, 2017).

Kennedy, E.H., Cohen, M.J., Krogman, N., 2016. *Putting Sustainability into Practice: Applications and Advances in Research on Sustainable Consumption*. Edward Elgar Pub, Cheltenham, UK.

Lenzen, M., Murray, J., Sack, F., Wiedmann, T., 2007. "Shared producer and consumer responsibility – Theory and practice", *Ecological Economics* 61, 27–42.

Levi, M., 2015. "Two Cheers for the Paris Agreement on Climate Change" [WWW Document]. *Council on Foreign Relations.* URL https://www.cfr.org/blog/two-cheers-paris-agreement-climate-change (accessed 8.9.18).

Liu, L., Wu, T., Huang, Y., 2017. "An equity-based framework for defining national responsibilities in global climate change mitigation", *Climate and Development* 9, 152–163. https://doi.org/10.1080/17565529.2015.1085358

Liverman, D.M., 2009. "Conventions of climate change: Constructions of danger and the dispossession of the atmosphere", *Journal of Historical Geography* 35, 279–296. https://doi.org/10.1016/j.jhg.2008.08.008

Lorek, S., Fuchs, D., 2013. "Strong sustainable consumption governance – precondition for a degrowth path?", *Journal of Cleaner Production, Degrowth: From Theory to Practice* 38, 36–43. https://doi.org/10.1016/j.jclepro.2011.08.008

Lorenzoni, I., Hulme, M., 2009. "Believing is seeing: Laypeople's views of future socioeconomic and climate change in England and in Ital", *Understanding of Science* 18, 383–400.

Lorenzoni, L., Pidgeon, N., 2006. "Public views on climate change: European and USA Perspectives", *Climatic Change* 77, 73–95.

Mathai, M., 2018. "In India, the discourse of environmental governance is always rooted in the future tense", *The Wire.* [WWW Document] URL https://thewire.in/environment/in-india-the-discourse-of-environmental-governance-is-always-rooted-in-the-future-tense (accessed 08.12.2018).

Maniates, M., 2002. "Individualization: Plant a tree, buy a bike, save the world?", in *Confronting Consumption.* MIT Press, Cambridge, MA, pp. 43–66.

Mattoo, A., Subramanian, A., 2012. "Equity in climate change: An analytical review", *World Development* 40, 1083–1097. https://doi.org/10.1016/j.worlddev.2011.11.007

Mir, G.-U.-R., Storm, S., 2016. "Carbon Emissions and Economic Growth: Production versus Consumption-Based Evidence on Decoupling", No. Working Paper No 41. Institute for New Economic Thinking, New York, NY.

Monjon, S., Quirion, P., 2011. "Which design of a border adjustment for the EU ETS? A quantitative assessment", in EAERE 2011 Conference. Presented at the EAERE 2011 conference.

Neslen, A., 2017. "Bloomberg demands seat at UN climate negotiating table for cities and states", [WWW Document]. *Climate Home News.* URL http://www.climatechangenews.com/2017/11/11/bloomberg-demands-seat-un-climate-negotiating-table-cities-states/ (accessed 8.10.18).

Neuhoff, K., et al., 2016. "Inclusion of Consumption of carbon intensive material in emissions trading", *Climate Strategies.*

OECD, 2004. "Indicators to measure decoupling of environmental pressure from economic growth", *Organization for Economic Cooperation and Development.*

OHalloran, J., 2012. "America and the West's dirty little secret" [WWW Document]. *Latitude News,* World Resources Institute. URL http://www.worldwatch.org/system/files/Latitude%20News%20061912.pdf (accessed 8.12.18).

Orange, R., 2016. "Waste not want not: Sweden to give tax breaks for repairs" [WWW Document]. *The Guardian.* URL http://www.theguardian.com/world/2016/sep/19/waste-not-want-not-sweden-tax-breaks-repairs (accessed 2.28.18).

Pan, X., Elzen, M. den, Höhne, N., Teng, F., Wang, L., 2017. "Exploring fair and ambitious mitigation contributions under the Paris Agreement goals", *Environmental Science & Policy* 74, 49–56. https://doi.org/10.1016/j.envsci.2017.04.020

Pauw, W.P., Klein, R.J.T., Mbeva, K., Dzebo, A., Cassanmagnago, D., Rudloff, A., 2018. "Beyond headline mitigation numbers: We need more transparent and comparable NDCs to achieve the Paris Agreement on climate change", *Climatic Change* 147, 23–29. https://doi.org/10.1007/s10584-017-2122-x

Peters, G., Davis, S.J., Andrew, R.M., 2012. "A synthesis of carbon in international trade", *Biogeosciences Discuss* 9, 3949–4023.

Peters, G., Hertwich, E.G., 2008. "$CO_2$ embodied in international trade with implications for global climate policy", *Environmental Science and Technology* 42, 1401.

Piketty, T., 2013. *Capital in the Twenty-First Century*. Harvard University Press, Cambridge.

Plumer, B., 2018. "At bonn climate talks, stakes get higher in gamble on planet's future", *The New York Times*.

Princen, T., Maniates, M., Conca, K., 2002. *Confronting Consumption*. MIT Press, Cambridge, MA.

Raworth, K. 2017. *Doughnut Economics: Seven Ways to Think Like a 21st-Century Economist*. Chelsea Green Publishing, White River Junction, VT.

Sato, M., 2012. "Embodied carbon in trade: A survey of the empirical literature", Working Paper No. 89. Centre for Climate Change Economics and Policy.

SEPA, 2008. *Konsumtionsbaserademiljöindikatorer: Underlagföruppföljningavgenerationsmålet*. Swedish Environmental Protection Agency, Stockholm.

SITRA, 2018a. *The Circular Economy – A Powerful Force for Climate Mitigation*. Finnish Innovation Fund, Stockholm.

SITRA, 2018b. "Ground-breaking analysis finds that the circular economy could make it possible to keep global warming below 2°C", *Sitra*.

Sorrell, S., 2018. "Rebound effects in UK road freight transport. Transportation Research Part D", *Transport and Environment* 63, 156–174.

Steininger, K.W., Lininger, C., Meyer, L.H., Muñoz, P., Schinko, T., 2016. "Multiple carbon accounting to support just and effective climate policies", *Nature Clim. Change* 6, 35–41. https://doi.org/10.1038/nclimate2867

Swedish EPA, 2010. *The Climate Impact of Swedish Consumption*. London: Natuvardsverket.

Thaler, R. H., 2000. "From homo economicus to homo sapiens", *Journal of Economic Perspectives* 14(1): 133–141.

UKDECC, 2012. "Consumption-based emissions reporting: Twelfth report of session 2010-12", Vol. 1: Report, together with formal minutes, oral and written evidence. *The Stationery Office*.

UNEP, 2017. *2017 Emissions Gap Report*. UNEP.

UNEP, 2011. "Decoupling natural resource use and environmental impacts from economic growth, A Report of the Working Group on Decoupling to the International Resource Panel", *United Nations Environment Program*.

UNFCCC, 2018. "Circular economies 2.0: Experts highlight innovation and best practice" | *UNFCCC* [WWW Document]. URL https://unfccc.int/news/circular-economies-20-experts-highlight-innovation-and-best-practice (accessed 8.10.18).

UNFCCC, 2016. *Biennial Assessment and Overview of Climate Finance Flows - 2016*. United Nations, Bonn, Germany.

UNFCCC, 2015a. "Paris Agreement. Report of the conference of the parties on its twenty-first session", UNFCC. (No. FCCC/CP/2015/10/Add.1).

UNFCCC, 2015b. "Accounting for emissions to consume with care: Bonn Talks Side Event", [WWW Document]. *UNFCCC*. URL http://newsroom.unfccc.int/green-urban/accounting-emissions-to-consume-with-care/ (accessed 2.7.17).

UNFCCC, 2015c. "Report on the structured expert dialogue on the 2013–2015 review", *UNFCC* (No. FCCC/SB/2015/INF.1).

van de Lindt, M., Emmert, S., Tukker, A., Anger-Kraavi, A., Neuhoff, K., Blachowicz, A., Derwent, H., Carr, A., Canzi, G., Crawford-Brown, D., 2017. "Carbon-CAP Final Report" | *Climate Strategies* (Final Report). Climate Strategies.

Warde, A., 2014. "After taste: Culture, consumption and theories of practice", *Journal of Consumer Culture* 14, 279–303. https://doi.org/10.1177/1469540514547828

Weber, C. L., and H. S. Matthews, 2008. "Quantifying the global and distributional aspects of American household carbon footprint", *Ecological Economics* 66(2): 379–391.

Welch, D., Ward, A., 2015. "Theories of practice and sustainable consumption", in *Handbook of Research on Sustainable Consumption*, Reisch L, Thøgersen J (Eds). Edward Elgar Publishing, Cheltenham.

Wiedmann, T., 2009. "A review of recent multi-region input–output models used for consumption-based emission and resource accounting", *Ecological Economics* 211–222.

Wolf, E., 1982. *Europe and the People Without History*. University of California Press.

Wilk, R., 2009. "Consuming ourselves to death", in *Anthropology and Climate Change*, S. Crate and M. Nuttall, eds., 265–276.

Yeo, 2014. "India hints at new focus on consumption-based emissions", [WWW Document]. *Climate Home - climate change news*. URL http://www.climatechangenews.com/2014/11/24/india-hints-at-new-focus-on-consumption-based-emissions/ (accessed 2.6.17).

York, R., 2012. "Do alternative energy sources displace fossil fuels?", *Nature Climate Change* 2, 441–443. https://doi.org/10.1038/nclimate1451

Zwick, D., Denegri-Knott, J., Schroeder, J., 2007. "The Social Pedagogy of Wall Street. Stock Trading as Political Activism?", *Journal of Consumer Policy* 30, 167–75.

# 2 Practice does not make perfect: Sustainable consumption, practice theory, and the question of power

*Dennis Soron*

For many environmentalists, as Park, Conca, and Finger have written, the 1992 Rio Earth Summit conjured up an enticing vision of a world in which governments were finally "starting to come together to hammer out a cooperative path toward long-term sustainability" (2008, p. 3). Unfortunately, the disappointing pace and scale of change since that heady time has done much to dispel such optimism. Given the widespread political inertia that persists in the face of deepening ecological crisis, they argue, Agenda 21 and other high-minded, non-binding action plans have effectively become "the environmental equivalent of the League Nations' resolutions against war—that is, high on political symbolism and low on policy impact" (2008, p. 3). To move beyond this troubling impasse, they assert, contemporary environmentalists must fundamentally rethink mainstream approaches to environmental reform that have in recent decades fallen "far short of the more fundamental social, political and economic changes needed to achieve true sustainability" (2008, p. 4).

Such prognostications of "the death of Rio environmentalism" (2008, p. 1) bear directly onto discussions of sustainable consumption—a goal which was itself formally placed on the international policy agenda at Rio. In spite of its initial appeal to many as a potentially far-reaching agenda linking environmental sustainability and global equity to deep transformations in the consumption-intensive lifestyles of the affluent world, even steadfast proponents of sustainable consumption have come to express doubts about the mainstream policy program that has coalesced under its banner. The "insipidness" of much current policy around sustainable consumption, Cohen asserts, not only strips the concept of its prior sense of novelty and possibility, but also attests to the abiding "hesitancy of affluent countries to forthrightly confront their wasteful materials and energy usage patterns" (2010, p. 108). Increasingly, as Geels et al. argue, the notion of sustainable consumption is associated not with broad socio-economic transformations commensurate with the daunting ecological challenges we now face, but with timid reformist measures that present "environmental sustainability as a more resource-efficient version of contemporary forms of the status quo, with incremental changes in the organization of production, institutional arrangements or daily life practices" (2015, p. 3).

In the midst of such sober acknowledgements of the limits of mainstream approaches to sustainable consumption, social practice theory has increasingly been set forth by a wide variety of thinkers as a means of intellectually and politically resuscitating the sustainable consumption agenda. In recent years, practice theory has garnered a great deal of attention and enthusiasm for its purported ability to reframe the sustainable consumption debate and to highlight promising new strategies for "intervening" into complex social processes so as to steer them in a more sustainable direction. While, as Welch and Warde argue, the task of confronting today's environmental crisis "will be a formidable, collective, political endeavour which entails a radical transformation of patterns, forms, and levels of consumption in wealthier societies," recent research inspired by theories of practice has "picked up on the near impossibility of current responses successfully resolving the problem" (2015, p. 84). Thus, they suggest, the practice turn in analyses of sustainable consumption must be understood "against the background of a highly intractable set of political difficulties upon which a new theoretical perspective offers fresh insight about the nature of the problem and its solution" (2015, p. 84).

This chapter offers an appreciative critique of the so-called "practice turn" within debates over sustainable consumption. This theoretical turn has done much to address some of the key deficiencies in previous conceptualizations of sustainable consumption within academic and policy literature. While the enthusiasm it has inspired is palpable, and its contributions to the development of a theoretically sophisticated sociology of sustainable consumption are undeniable, the practice turn remains beset by a number of unresolved problems that undercut its capacity to productively refocus the sustainable consumption agenda. Indeed, while practice-theoretical approaches often present themselves as representing a bold departure from earlier work in the field, they often recapitulate and compound many of the qualities in that work that have contributed to the current malaise of "weak" sustainable consumption. Primary among such qualities is what Fuchs et al. have identified as the "troublesome pattern of neglect of questions of power in research and action on sustainable consumption" (2016, p. 298). While applications of practice theory to sustainable consumption are not entirely incompatible with the type of "power lens" that such authors propose, their failure to more explicitly and forthrightly engage with questions of power has significantly weakened their conceptualization of the dynamics of overconsumption, the specific forces and interests that perpetuate it, and the forms of collective agency required to initiate meaningful change.

## Sustainable consumption at a crossroads

Since its inception, the discourse of sustainable consumption has been a plural and contested one, articulating a range of positions about the nature of the problem at hand and about the most viable strategies for addressing it. Although sustainable consumption has been placed firmly on the international policy map in the years since Rio, Tim Jackson has written, "consensus on what sustainable consumption actually is or should be" has been quite difficult to achieve (2007, p. 256). As Gill Seyfang argues, sustainable consumption remains a fundamentally "pluralistic concept" (2005, p. 293) that embodies unresolved tensions regarding strategies for promoting change and the very nature and scale of the changes being sought. In its most expansive sense, she believes, sustainable consumption's ambition to dramatically reduce the aggregate material consumption of affluent nations implies a "radical realignment of social and economic institutions" (2005, p. 293) away from dominant conceptions of prosperity, well-being, growth and development. Unfortunately, she holds, sustainable consumption's "definition narrowed as it became more widely accepted as a policy goal," such that its challenging and ambitious elements "became marginalized as governments instead focused on politically and socially acceptable, and economically rational, tools for changing consumption patterns such as cleaning up production processes and marketing green products" (2005, p. 293). Consequently, she asserts, the mainstream model of sustainable consumption has become largely confined to enhancing the eco-efficiency of consumer practices through market-driven technological change, the uptake of eco-friendly products, and behaviours on the part of individual consumers and households, and other unobtrusive measures holding out the "promise of an environmentally friendly future which does not threaten the political or commercial status quo" (2005, p. 297).

In much recent literature, this disillusioned awareness of the gap between sustainable consumption's initial promise and subsequent historical performance is expressed as a sense of disappointment that a "strong" model of sustainable consumption has been supplanted by a "weak" model oriented around eco-efficiency and green consumerism. For Fuchs and Lorek, sustainable consumption governance since 1992 comprises "a history of promises and failures" (2005, p. 261) in which the "strong" goals of absolute reductions and broad socio-economic transformation have been relinquished, continuing to exist "only in marginal sectors of society and research, or as a symbolic reminder in official documents" (2005, p. 263). This gravitation toward "weak" models, of course, is not simply a matter of faulty reasoning, but of an abiding reluctance to directly challenge the powerful vested interests and systemic imperatives driving consumption-intensive ways of life. Lacking support from powerful economic and political actors, Lorek and Spangenberg argue, proponents of sustainable consumption have tended to seek out a foothold in policy debates by soft-peddling their message and prioritizing "themes they suspect their prospective counterparts would consider to be 'harmless', and thus discussable topics" (2014, p. 39). While this pragmatic strategy, they suggest, is often presented as a "promising entry point into a broader debate," in practice it has tended to foreclose discussion of the structural changes required to achieve sustainability, and to direct public concern away from "precisely those institutions that contribute most to shaping patterns of consumption" (2014, p. 39).

In this regard, the "narrowing" and "weakening" of sustainable consumption is perhaps a telling reflection of the broader ways in which the sustainability agenda as a whole has been gradually reshaped and brought into alignment with dominant political-economic imperatives. As Bailey et al. argue, environmental problems in recent decades have increasingly "come to be framed as issues that are politically, economically and technologically solvable within the context of existing institutions and power structures and continued economic growth" (2011, p. 683). In suit, as some have argued, the sustainable consumption agenda has been reshaped over time so as to defuse its lingering radical and countercultural elements, and to buttress the legitimacy of governing institutions in the context of mounting ecological crises. Long before sustainable consumption was placed on the international policy agenda at Rio, Matthew Paterson has asserted, critiques of overconsumption had tended to be associated with "radical challenges to the basic logic of capitalist societies" (2008, p. 110). As sustainable consumption has become institutionalised, it has retained a vicarious association with such radical critiques even as it has gradually accommodated itself to the foregone necessity of profit-driven economic expansion, ever-escalating demand and consumerist lifestyles. By orienting solutions to "the consumption problem" toward market-driven techno-fixes, production-side efficiency gains and the rationalization of individual- and household-level consumption behaviours, mainstream sustainable consumption provides a response to the environmental crisis that attempts to allay public concerns while remaining aligned with the very economic, political and cultural prerogatives driving that crisis. This, as Paterson argues, reflects the degree to which sustainable consumption governance "has been shaped to respond to the legitimization requirements of capitalist societies and away from a serious analysis of the role of consumption in environmental degradation" (2008, p. 123).

Knitting together and giving sharp focus to many such recent critiques, Fuchs et al. (2016) have recently argued that a clear and forthright engagement with questions of power has been the key "missing piece" within extant research and action around sustainable consumption. The enormous collective challenge of achieving significant net reductions in aggregate material consumption within affluent regions, they argue, is "inextricably tied up with questions of power—the power to initiate change in service of sustainability and long-term human prosperity and the power to blunt such changes by entrenched interests and institutions" (2016, p. 299). In spite of this fact, they continue, "the dominant story of academic and policy foci on sustainable consumption is largely one of avoidance—of dodging any sustained and systematic analysis of and confrontation with power" (2016, p. 299). This story, in turn, is of a piece with the broader depoliticization that has afflicted environmentalism over the past generation—expressed variously in the decline of mobilised social movements, the rise of scientific and managerial sustainability discourses, popular preoccupations with lifestyle and identity issues, and the widespread entrenchment of neoliberal ideals of limited government, the self-regulating market, and individual responsibility.

In the latter case, sustainable consumption's disengagement from questions of power is particularly evident in the abstract, highly individualistic models of consumer behaviour it has incorporated from influential fields such as economics, psychology, and marketing. The methodological individualism of much work on sustainable consumption has tended to go along with an "individualization of environmental responsibility" which, as Maniates has argued, places undue burdens upon ordinary consumers and leaves "little room to ponder institutions, the nature and exercise of political power, or ways of collectively changing the distribution of power and influence in society" (2002, p. 45). When individuals are saddled with such inflated obligations, Warde asserts, the state and other powerful interests are effectively "relieved of responsibility...Governments do not need to articulate or mobilise concerted political will, nor are they required to develop policies which challenge vested interests or upset powerful corporations or organizations" (2013). Another related reason for the neglect of power within sustainable consumption research and policy, as Fuchs et al. (2016) compellingly suggest, arises from the very complexity of aggregate "consumption" itself, whose origins and drivers appear so intricate, diffuse, and murky that the determinative power and agency of specific actors is sometimes hard to fully ascertain or pin down. Whatever its origin, this pattern of neglect has undercut the viability of the models of social change implicitly accepted by many proponents of sustainable consumption, which have underestimated the systemic forces arrayed against environmental reform, and have placed unrealistic hopes upon the transformative potential of appealing to the good will of political leaders, exhorting and educating consumers, promoting new technologies and consumer products, and so on. "If research on sustainable consumption is to reach its potential as a field of inquiry and action capable of fostering absolute reductions," they conclude, "it must rise above the many factors that have kept questions of power at a distance" (2016, p. 299).

## The "practice turn" and sustainable consumption

As noted above, a wide range of thinkers have increasingly availed themselves of the conceptual resources of social practice theory to reinvigorate the sustainable consumption agenda and to rectify many of the weaknesses that have hampered its success in recent decades. This process of theoretical renewal has acquired an added sense of urgency in a context in which our failure to adequately confront the historical challenges posed by climate change and other ecological threats is becoming ever more troublingly evident. In the face of such crises, Shove and Spurling argue, "social theories of practice provide an important intellectual resource for understanding and perhaps establishing social, institutional and infrastructural conditions in which much less resource intensive ways of life might take hold" (2013, p. 1).

Taken as a whole, social practice theory is a diverse, complex, contentious, and sometimes contradictory field of academic debate that resists easy summation. To this extent, Warde suggests, perhaps the best way to understand what is distinctive about social practice theories is to consider "that which they oppose and which they seek to minimize when offering explanations" (2014, p. 285). In the first instance, practice-theoretical approaches have sought to directly oppose and minimize the influence of the methodological individualism that has characterised much sustainable consumption research and policy since Rio. Indeed, Walker asserts, such approaches have represented a concerted effort to reorient discussions of sustainability by dislodging the "dominant and pervasive 'behavioural' understanding of the dynamics of resource consumption that centres on individuals and their attitudes, values and choices" (2015, p. 45). As diverse as they may be, Evans et al. write, theories of practice are held together "by the ontological premise that practices—as opposed to individuals, social structures or discourses—are the basic unit of social analysis" (2012, p. 116).

In the broadest sense, practices themselves can be conceptualised as routinised patterns of behaviour whose conditions of existence are furnished by a complex nexus of interconnected social, material, technological, ideational, and affective elements. To the extent that the social world is definitively comprised of social practices, individuals are best seen not as autonomous agents driven by their own values, intentions, preferences, and choices, but as "carriers" or "practitioners" of diverse, collectively orchestrated practices that are enacted and reproduced within the ambit of their everyday lives. Similarly, the "consumption" of goods and services should no longer be regarded as a discrete, intentional action undertaken by individual consumers, but as an embedded moment in the routine performance of social practices shaped by their own conventions and standards and grounded in the constraints and affordances of particular social and material contexts. As Hargreaves argues, to the extent that practices (rather than individuals or encircling social structures) are the basic unit of analysis, "anti- or pro-environmental actions, and more or less sustainable patterns of consumption, are not seen as the result of individuals' attitudes, values and beliefs constrained by various contextual 'barriers', but as embedded within and occurring as part of social practices" (2011, p. 82).

In their efforts to address the flaws of methodological individualism, and of the individualised models of environmental responsibility that typically flow from it, proponents of practice theory have contributed to the development of a theoretically sophisticated and nuanced sociology of (un)sustainable consumption. Although current debates over consumption and the environment have much to gain from sociological lines of analysis, the sociology of consumption itself has remained, until relatively recently, curiously disengaged from environmental concerns. Indeed, as Evans and Jackson argue, while sociological insights add a welcome sophistication to our understanding of the web of influences that escalate material demand and lock in ecologically destructive consumption patterns, "sociological theories of consumption—with a few notable exceptions—have tended to shy away from an explicit concern with 'sustainability', eschewing in particular its normative agenda" (2008, p. 4). Although the expansion of this subfield has coincided with an upsurge in popular, governmental, and academic discourses surrounding overconsumption, Shove and Warde assert, "few sociologists of consumption have taken account of the environmental impact of practices they describe" (2003, p. 1).

While this pattern of evasion is unfortunate, it is also understandable in some respects. Given its foundational need to establish the legitimacy of consumption as an object worthy of close scholarly attention, much work in this field has been infused with a heightened defensiveness toward reductive macro-sociological approaches that regard consumption practices as a barometer of the pathological aspects of contemporary capitalist society or as a secondary expression of its underlying political-economic logic. The so-called "practice turn" within the sociology of consumption has enabled a deeper engagement with previously unaddressed questions of sustainability by excising any lingering trace of moralism and structural determinism from its sociological account of environmentally significant consumption. As Warde (echoing Schatzki) puts it, "practice theories are neither individualist nor holist; they portray social organisation as something other than individuals making contracts, yet are not dependent on a holistic notion of culture or societal totality" (2017, p. 85). For Schatzki and others, practice theory is associated with a "flat" or "horizontal" conception of social life in which diverse practices are composed of the same basic elements, variously intersecting and reciprocally constituting themselves without any macro-social logic ordering them as a whole or shaping their course from "above." In this manner, Schatzki asserts, practice theories "present pluralistic and flexible pictures of the constitution of social life that generally oppose hypostatised unities, root order in local contexts, and/or successfully accommodate complexities, differences and particularities" (in Warde, 2017, pp. 80–81).

Steering a course between "individualism" and "holism," practice-theoretical approaches to sustainable consumption have sought to establish a "middle-level" model for conceptualizing the complex interplay of structure and agency within routine everyday social practices. As a routinised pattern of action with considerable inertia and regularity, a social practice is an objectivated "entity" that coordinates and constrains individual behaviour, and yet this entity can only take shape and persist across time and space through the "performances" by which individuals enact and modify it in various local settings. In this sense, Evans et al. assert,

> A focus on practices as entities draws attention to a range of relatively stable elements that configure (at a macro-level) blocks and patterns of action, while a focus on practices as performances draws attention to the (micro-level) production and reproduction of the "doings" of daily life. It is in this recursive interaction (between entity and performance) where the dynamics of reproduction and change are located. (2012, p. 117).

While allowing some scope for the agency and reflexivity of "practitioners," proponents of practice theory have been at pains to challenge the voluntaristic assumptions underlying deliberative and expressive models of consumer action. As Warde and Shove emphasize, the world of "relatively individualized consumer behaviour involving the selection of discrete and visible commodities" accounts for only a small portion of environmentally consequential consumption, the majority of which continues to arise from a "muddier world of embedded, interdependent practices and habits" (1998, p. 6). The inconspicuous, mundane, habitual, routinised, and unreflexive nature of much consumption is given little credence within culturalist approaches that focus primarily on the spectacular, symbolic, and identity-oriented dimensions of consumer behaviour. To this extent, they suggest, developing viable strategies for promoting sustainability will require us to fundamentally "shift attention away from an intellectual obsession with the glamorous aspects of consumption towards its more routine, pragmatic, practical, symbolically neutral, socially determined, collectively imposed, jointly experienced, non-individualised elements" (1998, p. 13).

In view of their emphasis on the "socially determined" and "collectively imposed" nature of environmentally damaging consumption patterns, practice-inspired approaches point beyond the simplistic models of social change embedded in much literature and policy surrounding sustainable consumption. "Bringing about pro-environmental patterns of consumption," Tom Hargreaves states, "does not depend upon educating or persuading individuals to make sustainable decisions, but instead on transforming practices to make them more sustainable" (2011, p. 83). Transforming practices, in turn, requires directing our critical attention toward the complex matrix of material infrastructures, socio-technical arrangements, cultural conventions, shared understandings, routines, and other factors that are integral to their ongoing performance. Taking practices, as opposed to individual actors, as the site of intervention, Evans et al. write, "immediately shifts away from thinking about single types of intervention that are targeted at isolated activities or single elements. Instead, the emphasis is on simultaneously addressing the elements that coordinate any practice as an entity and the way it is performed" (2012, p. 14).

This basic shift, for many thinkers adopting practice-based approaches, hearkens toward a model of environmental reform and socio-technical change that is practical in application and potentially far-reaching in its effects. For many thinkers, practice-theoretical approaches to sustainable consumption present themselves as a useful resource or tool-kit for progressive "policy-makers" as they attempt to strategically reorient and strengthen a range of sustainability interventions. For Geels et al., practice theory provides the foundation for a broader approach to sustainable consumption that mediates between "reformist" efforts that do little to challenge the consumerist status quo, and an overweening "revolutionary" approach that "argues for wholesale changes to the organization of society but offers little insight into the governance of processes that could facilitate such a revolution" (2015, p. 5). Their preferred "reconfiguration" approach, as they call it, does not rely upon obtrusive measures to reconfigure individual behaviour or somehow uproot the social totality, but upon practical, "economically viable and socially acceptable" means of promoting "the transformation of socio-technical systems and daily life practices in domains such as mobility, food, and energy provision and use" (2015, pp. 7; 5). Even in the absence of widespread or disruptive change, as Evans et al. underline, "interventions in the institutional organization of practices…can have important and positive implications for the resource-intensity of everyday life" (2012, p. 123).

## Practice, power and social change

Proponents of practice theory generally claim that it provides not only the theoretical means to deepen our understanding of the complex social dynamics of (un)sustainable consumption, but the pragmatic ability to reorient sustainability interventions away from weak and ineffective "behaviour change" initiatives. Insisting on the incompatibility of practice-inspired and behavioural approaches, Elizabeth Shove asserts that "[o]n all the counts that matter, social theories of practice on the one hand, and of behaviour on the other, are like chalk and cheese" (2010, p. 1279). The insights of practice theory, as Evans et al. argue, "signal an altogether different approach to sustainable consumption," offering a welcome opportunity to fundamentally "re-think and re-frame the entry points, scope and orientations of policy initiatives" (2012, pp. 115–116). Such claims notwithstanding, ample grounds exist for questioning the degree to which practice-theoretical work represents a departure from the status quo in mainstream sustainable consumption policy and research. While the practice-based approach to sustainable consumption claims to have transcended the much-maligned behavioural model and established the basis for a bold new environmental program, Jackson pointedly argues, its "understanding of the dynamics of social practice, of the ways in which social practices evolve, and of the interaction between policy and social practice is as yet so limited that it would be difficult to see how policy could make use of this position—beyond taking social norms a bit more seriously as influences on behaviour" (2005, p. 63).

Indeed, as newfangled as it may seem, much recent practice-theoretical work draws its primary empirical examples from the existing behaviour-change policy repertoire, and—as with Tom Hargreaves—values practice theory because it "offers a more holistic and grounded perspective on behaviour change processes as they occur in situ......[and] offers up a wide range of mundane footholds for behaviour change, over and above individuals' attitudes or values" (2011, p. 79). While asserting the "altogether different" quality of practice-oriented approaches to sustainable consumption, Evans et al. effectively employ the language of practice theory to re-describe a range of established behavioural initiatives, emphasizing that "durable behaviour change" requires "the re-ordering of the multiple elements that configure practices as entities alongside sufficient numbers of practitioners performing these such that they 'stick' as normal and appropriate" (2012, p. 125). In these and other instances, the distinction between a "holistic" approach to promoting "behaviour change" and what Evans et al. call "encouraging recruitment and defection from variously sustainable practices" (2012, p. 123) can often seem more semantic than substantive. Lacking a sufficient empirical base to support their claims about the transformative potential of practice-inspired policies and actions, practice-oriented analyses often fall back on a restricted range of over-used examples (the Cool Biz initiative in Japan, for instance), which can be readily explained in conventional policy language and which fall dramatically short of the "formidable, collective, political endeavour" that Welch and Warde believe is required to confront today's ecological crisis.

While social practice theory has helped to address some of the key deficiencies of extant work on sustainable consumption, lending it a renewed sense of political urgency and infusing it with a new degree of sociological depth and complexity, it has also recapitulated many of the most disabling qualities of the very work it criticizes. In this regard, perhaps the most significant shortcoming in the practice-based approach to sustainable consumption to date is its perpetuation of what Fuchs et al. identify as sustainable consumption's historical habit of "dodging any sustained and systematic analysis of and confrontation with power" (2016, p. 299). While, as Geels et al. argue, the prospect of bringing about "sustainable reconfigurations" across a wide range of social practices will inevitably require significant financial and political resources and demand a concerted collective effort to reorient state priorities, transform the embedded norms and expectations of consumer culture and challenge vested economic interests, "politics, power and political economy are, so far, noticeably absent" from practice-theoretical approaches (2015, p. 10). Indeed, as Keller, Halkier, and Wilska suggest, such approaches more characteristically give rise to "detailed studies of everyday performances" in which "questions of power and ideology dissolve into the background" (2016, p. 83). Despite the seeming "intellectual radicalism" of practice theory, Matt Watson argues, its failure to develop an explicit account of power that forthrightly addresses powerful agents such as governments and corporations, large-scale social structures and processes, hegemonic ideologies, and so on, means that it "is typically conservative in terms of its practical implications" (2017, p. 169).

This "conservative" leaning is to some extent reflected in the specific sites of consumption and scales of activity that practice-inspired approaches address. As the discourse of sustainable consumption has increasingly become influenced by theories of social practice, Kennedy, Cohen, and Krogman argue, it has largely retained the "emphasis on consumption that takes place in the private sphere, or household" (2015, p. 12) that was evident in earlier behaviour-change approaches. In this respect, the key locus of environmental "intervention" and change implicitly remains a relatively restricted range of routinised everyday behaviours in which ordinary people engage—showering, commuting, cooking, and so on—conceptually sequestered from other ecologically significant sites of institutional consumption and other spheres of practice (corporate, governmental, organizational) in which concentrated types of power are exercised with little popular awareness or accountability. By continuing to focus narrowly upon a circumscribed realm of everyday consumption activities, Sayer asserts, and to deflect its analytical attention away from crucial questions of economic and political power, the practice approach "might be said to accommodate and merely qualify rather than challenge the tendency to load all the responsibility onto individuals" (2013, p. 178).

At one level, this neglect of highly consequential business and governmental practices, and of the broader systemic imperatives driving ecologically destructive consumption patterns, is merely a continuation of earlier "weak" versions of sustainable consumption and their commitment to relatively "harmless," "politically and socially acceptable" environmental positions that don't tread on the prerogatives of the powerful. At another level, it also speaks to the peculiarities of practice theory itself, which provides us with a model of the social in which it can be quite difficult to critically address the distinctive role played by powerful agents and institutions such as corporations and the state, the determinative effects of large-scale structures and processes, the supra-practice influence of hegemonic ideologies and discourses, and so on. In its effort to account for the complexities of social reproduction and change, Watson argues, "practice theory is inevitably tackling processes that are shot through with power" (2014, p. 1), and yet its account of power has largely remained implicit or "unspoken" to date. This relative silence, Watson suggests, reflects in part "the difficulty of analytically grasping what we take for power in a way that is consistent with the ontological commitments of practice theory" (2017, p. 169). Consistent with its view of social life as composed first and foremost of diverse practices (rather than social structures, institutions, purposive agents and so on) "power must be understood as an effect of performances of practices, not as something external to them. Power only has reality insofar as it is effected—and made manifest—in moments of human action and doing" (2017, p. 171). This view of power—as something constituted in and through moments of human action an interaction—lends itself well to close analysis of localised everyday practices, but not so well to other "observable phenomena in the social world – powerful institutions, patterns of domination, the reproduction of social elites and of hegemonic ideologies—[which] demand some means of understanding if practice theory is indeed an account of the social" (2017, p. 173).

Striving to avoid the reductive tendencies of "holistic" or mono-causal theoretical frameworks, practice theory presents us with a contingent and heterogeneous social field in which power is ubiquitous and diffuse, and no privileged agent or structure decisively shapes action from "above." As Watson and others have noted, this "flat" view of social life can make it difficult to account for questions of hierarchy and scale, or to adequately comprehend how practices in particular locales—like governments, corporations, international financial institutions, trade bodies and so on—have a disproportionate ability to influence and orchestrate practices in a range of other dispersed locales. In the case of debates over sustainable consumption, maintaining this "flat" understanding of social life can result in the bracketing off of everyday consumption activities from other key locales that systematically shape and enable them.

In particular, as Welch and Warde acknowledge, most practice-theoretical research "has engaged in micro-sociological studies of everyday life to the neglect of the sphere of economic production" (2015, p. 11). In the first instance, this neglect is significant because the production process itself is an extremely significant site of material "consumption," accounting for up to 70 percent of the materials consumed in capitalist economies today (Renner, 2004, pp. 101–2). To this extent, Paterson underlines, the lopsided focus on domestic and household consumption within sustainable consumption discourse not only dodges crucial questions about the decisive influence of private economic power under capitalism, but "misses the bulk of consumption understood as aggregate throughput" (2008, p. 122). While the sphere of production does not (as many practice theorists are quick to point out) in any simple or direct sense "determine" prevailing patterns of consumption, the interests and imperatives embedded within the capitalist economy do obviously play a crucial role in driving unsustainable forms of growth premised on ever-rising volumes of material consumption, and in perpetually ratcheting-up established consumer norms and expectations. While private economic interests cannot ultimately command all consumption-related practices from on high, they nevertheless exert a significant degree of power over what is produced and how it is produced, packaged, distributed, marketed, and rendered available for use in the context of a wide variety of everyday social practices. All of these private decisions have a significant impact upon the material-intensity of everyday life, and reinforce Sayer's point that practice-theoretical approaches must more directly and explicitly reckon with "the power and responsibilities of business" (2013, p. 178).

Sayer's call for practice theory to engage with political economy goes beyond simply entreating it to pay attention to the business world, its doings and its societal responsibilities. Even if practice theory were to turn toward a close analysis of business practices and their various effects, Sayer argues, it risks failing "to grasp the particular capitalist economic logic (in the form of the rule of exchange-value, money, cost and profit) that drives and shapes them" (2013, p. 171). Any focus on large-scale or overarching systemic "logic" tends to dissipate in the "flat ontology" of practice theory, which—as Welch and Warde write— holds that "there is no macro-level beyond the realm of social practices, which are not merely 'sites' of interaction but are, instead, ordering and orchestrating entities in their own right" (2015, p. 8). Within the language of practice theory, Warde asserts, concepts such as "practice bundles" and "practice complexes" can provide a clumsy way to theoretically "ramp up" from the minutiae of everyday performances to large-scale systems, institutions and processes involved in supra-practice patterning and configuration (2014, p. 296). In this respect, he adds, "practice theories may need supplementing with other frameworks, particularly to capture macro-level or structural aspects of consumption. This does not mean a return to the old economism, but probably entails some recovery of political economy and rearticulation of the link between consumption and economic production" (2014, p. 297).

The question that arises is whether practice theory can simply "supplement" itself with political economy and other macro-level frameworks without violating its own underlying premises. Theories of political economy, Watson highlights, could not perform the type of analysis they do "if they refused to reify power relations and if instead power relations were always analysed through the multiple practices from which they are an effect" (2017, p. 180). This is a theoretical conundrum that is largely left unresolved by otherwise compelling recent works such as Harold Wilhite's *The Political Economy of Low Carbon Transformation: Breaking the Habits of Capitalism* (2016). Wilhite's environmentally attuned account of the "habits of capitalism" presumes that a wide array of everyday practices in contemporary society are configured in ways that reflect and serve the overarching imperatives of the capitalist system. While provocative and original, Wilhite's argument does not appear to be fully compatible with the idea (voiced most strongly by Schatzki) that there is no "vertical" dimension to social life, that social practices are "ordering and orchestrating entities in their own right," rather than the determined outcome of higher-order systems and structures. To a certain extent, Wilhite's analysis hearkens back to an older brand of "everyday life critique" (associated with Henri Lefebvre and other Marxist thinkers) in which, as Kossoff et al. argue, "both the details and general structure of everyday life were connected back to the macro-structures of society" (2015, p. 14). While focused centrally on the composition and reproduction of everyday life, they argue, social practice theory "tends not to address its general, dysfunctional structure, nor the forces that have fostered this" (2015, p. 14). For this reason, they continue, the notion of sustainability tends to be viewed within a utilitarian frame, "primarily seen as a matter of conserving resources through developing more efficient practices" rather than radically transforming the broader power relations structuring everyday life (2015, p. 14).

While many proponents of practice theory agree that concerted collective action will be required to transform the environmentally "dysfunctional" aspects of everyday life, practice theory's model of "distributed governance" runs contrary to this vision of social change in some key respects. To the extent that social life is "flat," the power to "shape and direct" it is not concentrated in a single locus of governing power, but is widely distributed across a range of "governors." Given the dispersed nature of governance, and the contingency and complexity of social life, Schatzki argues, "movement toward sustainability will neither result from all-powerful governors nor take the form of distinct large-scale shifts," but will arise instead from "the efforts of innumerable would-be governors, distributed through the practice–arrangement plenum, to foster appropriate developments in their specific domains of governance" (2015, p. 26). In this ecumenical spirit, he calls on a wide array of governors—everyone from transnational corporate CEOs to politicians, local officials, activist groups, neighbourhood associations, parents and even children—to "foster sustainable development" by doing whatever they can in their particular domains of influence (2015, p. 27). In this manner, Schatzki's conceptualization of distributed governance downplays if not entirely dissolves the unequal distribution of social, cultural, economic, and political power, along with the widely disparate capacities of individuals and institutions to shape and direct the constitution and reproduction of environmentally significant practices. By entreating individuals to assume equal responsibility for global environmental challenges within their own delimited "domains," without considering how power differentially structures the influence and scope of such domains, his practice-theoretical approach effectively recapitulates problems associated with the "individualization of environmental responsibility" noted at the outset of this chapter.

In this instance, Schatzki's model of distributed governance is based upon a conflicted relationship to state power that is shared, in different ways and to different degrees, by other proponents of practice-theory. Schatzki's rejection of the "heroic" policy actor and the potential of top-down political action to reorganize social life by fiat seems to blend a Hayek-style paranoia about the latently totalitarian quality of progressive state action with a conventional conception of the state's supposed impotence in the era of globalization. His scepticism about the ability of the state to initiate and effect large-scale, systemic change toward sustainability perhaps needs to be tempered by greater acknowledgement of the degree to which the state is already crucially involved in the perpetuation of environmentally damaging practices (through its subsidies, economic and social policies, provision of infrastructure, policing of social conflicts, and so on), and in forms of governance (such as the negotiation of corporate-friendly international trade agreements) that restrict our collective capacity to curtail them. In other cases, the problem with practice-theoretical approaches is not so much their emphasis on the powerlessness of the state as an underestimation of its intractability. For all of its wariness toward deliberative individualism, much recent work on sustainable consumption is premised on a highly voluntaristic view of well-meaning and disinterested "policy-makers" who, once they have cast off the blinders of conventional behaviour models and accepted the tenets of practice theory, set forth to "intervene" into the organization of social practices to promote sustainability. This view is given particularly sharp expression in the stilted dialogue Shove (2014) stages between a fictional social scientist, intent on parlaying the insights of practice theory, and a fictional policy-maker who gradually warms to their strategic implications. Such idealistic schemas, in which wide-ranging social change is initiated by earnest policy-makers without regard to institutional or systemic constraints, call out for a more thorough and nuanced account of state power and environmental governance under neoliberalism—and under capitalism, more generally.

The persistence with which the abstract and idealised figure of the sustainability-inducing "policy-maker" appears in recent literature on sustainable consumption reflects a fairly widespread conceptualization of socio-technical change that is bloodless, impersonal, and divorced from the messy process of popular contestation and mobilization. As Fuchs et al. put it, dramatic reductions in resource use,

> ...will not arrive spontaneously, nor simply on the basis of more data, better models and greater understanding of impacts. Nor will they occur solely due to better arguments and more pleading by and to policymakers. Real sustainable consumption—consumption at levels that reversed the depletion of natural capital, repair the rapid unraveling of the global biosphere, and produce more prosperity at lower levels of overall consumption—will only emerge through collective action, adroit organizing and the focused exertion of influence; in short through the dynamics of power. It will arise when particular agents, working alongside or within established organizations or across institutions, deliberately change behaviours, prevailing norms, institutional structures, arenas of choice, and the boundaries of rational policymaking.

This work of creating conditions that initiate and accommodate real net reductions in consumption in planned and just ways is thus inextricably tied up with questions of power—the power to initiate change in service of sustainability and long-term human prosperity, and the power to blunt such changes by entrenched interests and institutions (2016, pp. 298–299).

In some ways, the "policy-maker" in practice-theoretical work serves as a convenient stand-in for politics more generally, bypassing a more detailed discussion of social, political and cultural struggle, collective agency and the development of the popular will for significant environmental reform. The implication often seems to be that systemic change, far from relying on mass mobilization and struggle to transform state policy, economic institutions and the norms and values of consumer culture, can be better initiated and "diffused" by a technocratic policy elite who set about incrementally redesigning the everyday life of "practitioners" whose consent or input is otherwise not required.

In this light, as Warde and Welch underline (2015, p. 8), Shove's own examination of the diffusion, transformation, and disappearance of ordinary, routinised practices is premised on a pronounced scepticism about the ability of popular environmental and anti-consumerist commitments, and other forms of public contestation and debate, to shift the dynamics of everyday life and to contribute to enduring social change. As they argue, the practice-theoretical approach has tended to neglect "the role of collective social and political projects, ideologies and cultural discourses. This is ironic given that sustainable consumption was initiated as a purposive project, promoted by powerful collective actors and expressed via a cultural, reflexive discourse" (2015, p. 12). In this respect, the practice turn's rejection of so-called culturalist approaches has perhaps gone too far, ignoring not only the power of hegemonic cultural discourses perpetuated through the mass media, advertising, and so on, but also the important role that cultural struggle can still play in problematizing and politicizing existing consumption patterns, dislodging our entrenched sense of what is "normal" and desirable, defamiliarizing the routine and habitual, and promoting alternative views of sustainability conjoined to a positive vision of post-consumerist ways of life.

This chapter has offered a somewhat truncated account of some of the ways in which practice theory, while doing much to intellectually reinvigorate the field of sustainable consumption research and policy in recent years, has remained beset by certain conceptual problems that perpetuate rather than challenge this field's "troublesome pattern of neglect of questions of power." Ultimately, as Fuchs et al. argue, if "research on sustainable consumption is to reach its potential as a field of inquiry and action capable of fostering absolute reductions, it must rise above the many factors that have kept questions of power at a distance" (2016, p. 299). While it is unlikely that practice theory—whether through internal refinement or external "supplementation"—can facilitate this process of its own accord, it nevertheless (as Watson writes) "has distinctive contributions to make as part of a range of related strategies that shed light on how power exists as an effect of collective activity and its consequences" (2017, p. 180).

# References

Bailey, I., Gouldson, A. and Newell, P. (2011). 'Ecological modernisation and the governance of carbon: a critical analysis', *Antipode* 43(3), pp. 682–703.

Cohen, M. (2010). 'The international political economy of (un)sustainable consumption and the global financial collapse', *Environmental Politics*, 19(1), pp. 107–126.

Evans, D., McMeekin, A. and Southerton, D. (2012). 'Sustainable consumption, behaviour change policies and theories of practice', in Warde, A. and Southerton, D. (eds.) *The habits of consumption - Collegium: studies across disciplines in the humanities and social sciences* 12, pp. 113–129. [online] Available at: https://helda.helsinki.fi/bitstream/handle/10138/34226/12_07_evans-southerton-mcmeekin.pdf;sequence=1

Evans, D. and Jackson, T. (2008). 'Sustainable consumption: perspectives from social and cultural theory', *RESOLVE*, Working Paper 05-08. [online] Available at: http://www.surrey.ac.uk/resolve/

Fuchs, D., Di Giulio, A., Glaab, K., Lorek, S., Maniates, M., Princen, T. and Ropke, I. (2016). 'Power: the missing element in sustainable consumption and absolute reductions research and action', *Journal of Cleaner Production* 132, pp. 298–307.

Fuchs, D. and Lorek, S. (2005). 'Sustainable consumption governance: a history of promises and failures', *Journal of Consumer Policy* 28, pp. 261–288.

Geels, F., McMeekin, A., Mylan, J. and Southerton, D. (2015). 'A critical appraisal of sustainable consumption and production research: the reformist, revolutionary and reconfiguration positions', *Global Environmental Change* 34, pp. 1–12.

Hargreaves, T. (2011). 'Practice-ing behaviour change: applying social practice theory to pro-environmental behaviour change', *Journal of Consumer Culture* 11(1), pp. 79–99.

Jackson, T. (2005). *Motivating Sustainable Consumption: A Review of Evidence on Consumer Behaviour and Behavioural Change*. Report to the Sustainable Development Research Network. [online] Available at: http://www.sustainablelifestyles.ac.uk/sites/default/files/motivating_sc_final.pdf

Jackson, T. (2007). 'Sustainable Consumption' in Atkinson, G., Dietz, S. and Neumayer, E. (eds.) *Handbook of Sustainable Development*. Northampton (MA): Edward Elgar, pp. 254–268.

Keller, M., Halkier, B. and Wilska, T. (2016). 'Policy and governance for sustainable consumption at the crossroads of theories and concepts', *Environmental Policy and Governance* 26, pp. 75–88.

Kennedy, E., Cohen, M., and Krogman, N., eds., 2015. Social practice theory and research on sustainable consumption. In *Putting Sustainability into Practice: Applications and Advances in Research in Sustainable Consumption*. Northampton (MA): Edward Elgar, 3-21.

Kossoff, G., Tonkinwise, C. and Irwin, T. (2015). 'Transition design: the importance of everyday life and lifestyle as a leverage point for sustainability transitions. Paper presented at the STRN Conference (Sussex). [online] Available at: https://www.academia.edu/15403946/Transition_Design_The_Importance_of_Everyday_Life_and_Lifestyles_as_a_Leverage_Point_for_Sustainability_Transitions_presented_at_the_STRN_Conference_2015_Sussex_

Lorek, S. and Spangenberg, J. (2014). 'Sustainable consumption within a sustainable economy – beyond green growth and green economies', *Journal of Cleaner Production* 63, pp. 33–44.

Maniates, M. (2002). 'Individualization: plant a tree, buy a bike, save the world?' in, Princen T., Maniates M. and Conca, K. (eds.) *Confronting Consumption*. Cambridge: MIT PRESS, pp. 43–66.

Park, J., Conca, K. and Finger, M. (2008). 'The death of rio environmentalism' in Park, J., Conca, K. and Finger, M. (eds.), *The crisis of global environmental governance: towards a new political economy of sustainability*. New York: Routledge, pp. 1–12.

Paterson, M. (2008). 'Sustainable consumption? Legitimation, regulation, and environmental governance. In Park, J., Conca, K. and Finger, M. (eds) *The crisis of global environmental governance: towards a new political economy of sustainability*. New York: Routledge, pp. 110–131.

Renner M. (2004). 'Moving a less consumptive economy', in The Worldwatch Institue (ed) *State of the World 2004. The Special Focus: The Consumer Society*. Norton: New York; 96–119.

Sayer, A. (2013). 'Power, sustainability and well being: an outsider's view' in Shove, E. and Spurling, N. (eds.) *Sustainable practices: social theory and climate change*. New York: Routledge, pp. 167–180.

Schatzki, T. (2015). 'Practices, governance and sustainability' in Strenger, Y. and Maller, C. (eds.) *Social practices, intervention and sustainability: beyond behaviour change*. New York: Routledge, pp. 15–30.

Seyfang, G. (2005). 'Shopping for sustainability: can sustainable consumption promote ecological citizenship?', *Environmental Politics* 14(2), pp. 290–306.

Shove, E. (2010). 'Beyond the ABC: climate change policy and theories of social change. *Environment and Planning* 42, pp. 1273–1285.

Shove, E. (2014). 'Putting practice into policy: reconfiguring questions of consumption and climate change. *Contemporary Social Science* 9 (4), pp. 415–429.

Shove, E. and Spurling, N. (2013). 'Sustainable practices: social theory and climate change' in Shove, E. and Spurling, N. (eds.) *Sustainable practices: social theory and climate change*. New York: Routledge, pp. 1–13.

Shove, E. and Warde, A. (1998). 'Inconspicuous consumption: the sociology of consumption and the environment'[online]. Available at: http://www.lancaster.ac.uk/fass/resources/sociology-online-papers/papers/shove-warde-inconspicuous-consumption.pdf

Walker, G. (2015). 'Beyond individual responsibility: social practice, capabilities and the right to environmentally sustainable ways of life' in Strenger, Y. and Maller, C. (eds.) *Social practices, intervention and sustainability: beyond behaviour change*. New York: Routledge, pp. 45–59.

Warde, A. (2013). 'Sustainable consumption and behaviour change', *Discover Society* (Oct 1). [online] Available at: http://discoversociety.org/2013/10/01/sustainable-consumption-and-behaviour-change/

Warde, A. (2014). 'After taste: culture, consumption and theories of practice', *Journal of Consumer Culture* 14(3), pp. 279–303.

Warde, A. (2017). *Consumption: a sociological analysis*. London: Palgrave Macmillan.

Watson, M. (2014). 'Placing Power in Practice Theory', *Demanding Ideas*, Working Paper 6. [online] Available at: http://www.demand.ac.uk/wp-content/uploads/2014/07/wp6-watson.pdf

Watson, M. (2017). 'Placing power in practice theory' in Hui, A., Schatzki, T. and Shove, E. (eds) *The nexus of practices: connections, constellations, practitioners*. New York: Routledge, pp. 169–182.

Welch, D. and Warde, A. (2015). 'Theories of practice and sustainable consumption' in Reisch, L. and Thorgersen, J. (eds.) *Handbook of Research on Sustainable Consumption*. Cheltenham: Edward Elgar, pp. 84–100.

Wilhite, H. (2016). *The political economy of low carbon transformation: breaking the habits of capitalism*. New York: Routledge.

# 3 Sources of power for sustainable consumption: Where to look

*Doris Fuchs, Sylvia Lorek, Antonietta Di Giulio, and Rico Defila*

## Introduction

A number of positive trends in the sustainability of consumption can be recognized, especially when considering individual consumer motivations and choices. Taking a look at the bigger picture, however, reveals that the overwhelming number of trends point in the opposite direction. Numerous examples for a worsening of the environmental and social impacts of consumption can be identified. Overall, increasing numbers of scholars note that, indeed, consumption by the global consumer class[1] is the major cause behind humanity's overstepping of planetary boundaries (e.g., Akenji and Chen 2016; Cohen, Brown, and Vergragt 2017; Defila, Di Giulio, and Kaufmann-Hayoz 2012; Fuchs 2017; Hirschnitz-Garbers et al. 2016)[2]. Unfortunately, this agreement has frequently led practitioners and scholars to focus solely on the role of the individual consumer (Akenji 2014). Yet, such a reduction of complexity neglects broader structural forces driving overconsumption and thus severely limits the ability of society to pursue a transformation towards sustainability in consumption (Lorek and Vergragt 2015). In this chapter, we aim to highlight these broader structural forces, drawing particular attention to structural ideational and material power dynamics creating barriers to sustainable consumption. We also want to identify potential sources of counter power, that is, of power for sustainable consumption. Specifically, we point out a promising alternative and already existing ideational paradigm as well as corresponding tendencies of shifts in material institutions that hold the potential to foster sustainable consumption.

In our argument, we proceed from the assumption that ideational and material structures, cognition and action, go together, reinforce each other, and cannot really be distinguished in practice. Narratives provide the epistemic fabric for how the material dimension of society is perceived, assessed, and shaped and thus go hand in hand with structural material forces (e.g., Malone et al. 2017). They provide explanations and are thus part of individual and collective knowledge, and knowledge in turn informs individual and collective problem framing, the setting of priorities, the questions that are asked, and the options and pathways that are considered (Stirling 2014). Narratives are supported in their stability and diffusion by material structures. Thus, it is important to identify both—the relevant ideational structures in the form of narratives or paradigms[3] underlying socio-economic, political, and cultural practices of (unsustainable and sustainable) consumption, and the corresponding material structures (see also Isenhour 2017).

## Towards unsustainable consumption

For more than four decades, scholars have alerted us to the limits to growth (Meadows et al. 1972). Over the past 30 years, sustainable development (integrating environmental, economic, and social aspects) has been promoted as a pathway to a better "common future" (Brundtland 1987). We have seen decades full of hope, of World Summits, and their declarations (United Nations 1992, 2002, 2015), the rise of civil society and environmentalism, as well as increasing academic engagement with social and environmental justice (Martinez-Alier et al. 2014). Step by step, awareness of how vulnerable ecosystems are and how environmental degradation might affect human health and security permeated public discourse as well as national and international politics (Rockström et al. 2009; Steffen et al. 2015). This trend is reflected in research on individual attitudes and consumption. Studies consistently report significant levels of environmental concern among consumers in many countries (European Commission 2014). Sustainable fashion labels have emerged; fair trade labels have gained additional ground; the number of consumers choosing organic food or even vegetarian or vegan lifestyles has increased; insulation of buildings has improved; sales of electric vehicles have risen; and evermore people are participating in car-sharing schemes or other sharing initiatives, to name just a few examples (Fuchs 2017).[4] In sum, concerns about the environmental and social impacts of human activities and the effects of environmental changes on humans seem to have diffused in society and to have become part of what has to be considered in daily business.

Still, a look at one of the most prominent indicators of global environmental development, the Ecological Footprint, shows that the situation is worsening continuously. The related "Earth Overshoot Day"[5] reveals that humanity fails miserably and, indeed, increasingly so when it comes to living in a fair balance with nature as its provider of natural resources. In 2017, by August 2, humanity was no longer living on nature's "interest" but rather by depleting the "stock" of "natural capital" (see Figure 3.1).

As this data show, indications of trends towards sustainable consumption tell only part of the story. The other part seems to be gloomier. Sales in electric vehicles are more than trumped by sales in SUVs, and life cycle assessments of electric vehicles show that they do not unconditionally save resources (Hawkins et al. 2013). People may be using more efficient household appliances, but they are also using more of them, as well as bigger ones (EEA 2015). In communications technology, people replace equipment at faster rates than ever before in order to stay on top of technological developments and maintain their ability to participate (Wieser 2016). The visible pollution of bodies of water may have diminished, but non-visible inputs of substances originating from medicines, nutrients,

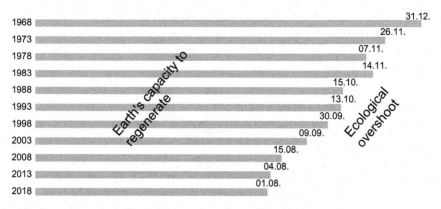

*Figure 3.1* Development of the "Earth Overshoot Day".

Source: Global Footprint Network. *Past Earth Overshoot Days* 2018 [cited 01.10.2018. Available from https://www.overshootday.org/newsroom/past-earth-overshoot-days].

or nano-particles have increased (Frimmel and Niessner 2014). Overfishing is also more prevalent (Zaneveld et al. 2016). Combined, pollution and overfishing have led to a decrease of global fish stocks (Essington et al. 2015). In many countries, single dweller households (which tend to be less resource efficient than households with multiple members), cars, kilometers or miles traveled, flights taken, space used for settlement, and road systems all continue to grow (Eurostat 2017). Affluent nations may have reduced $CO_2$-emissions and pollution, but they have done so largely by outsourcing resource-intensive stages of production and the disposal of hazardous waste to poorer nations. Next to sustainable fashion labels, retail chains branded on selling the cheapest clothes are still spreading, and plantation and slaughterhouse workers continue to be exploited for the sake of cheap food products.[6] Even some high-tech companies have been associated with slavery-like working conditions (Ngai and Chan 2012). In sum, the positive trends reported above seem to be vastly overshadowed by negative ones.

Why is this the case—after more than 40 years of discussions about the depletion of resources and the risks of irreversibly damaging the environment, and after more than 25 years of research and debate on sustainable consumption?

This question has been debated extensively inside and outside of academia. As noted above, many scholars today view consumption by the global consumer class as the main problem. The ever-growing and accelerating demand for renewable and non-renewable natural resources, the rising amount of waste, and the continuing emission of substances harming ecosystems and inducing climate change can be causally attributed to patterns of consumption associated with high material throughput all over the world (Lorek 2014). Taking this as the starting point, it seems natural to focus upon the individual consumer and his/her behavior, thus blaming individuals for unsustainable consumption and an unreasonable use of resources: if only he/she would make the effort to consume sustainably, everything would be fine—or at least much better. Doing so leads researchers and practitioners to investigate issues such as how knowledge about the environmental impacts of consumption could be transformed into action, how young people have to be educated to be sustainable grown-ups, or whether incentives are more effective in changing individual behavior or regulations. The dynamics that have been investigated, in this context, include the rebound effect, the attitude-behavior gap, and the behavior-impact gap (Csutora and Zsóka 2016). These are, no doubt, important issues, but we are convinced that they will not lead us to a comprehensive answer because they neglect the broader structural forces driving overconsumption (see also Akenji 2014; Fuchs et al. 2016; Maniates 2001, 2014).

Accordingly, the following section seeks to offer a complementary answer to the questions: what is going wrong and why are good intentions and trends towards sustainable consumption hitting barriers? It will do so by showing that these intentions and trends towards sustainable consumption are being overpowered, if not subverted, by forces aiming in the opposite direction.

## Drivers of (over)consumption and barriers to change

Looking for the broader picture leads us to look at the set-up of the global politico-economic system and, more precisely, at the ideational as well as material forces embodied and exerted within this system and their relation to consumption (Lorek and Vergragt 2015). From this perspective, we see, for instance, material forces in the form of existing infrastructure and product supply, causing constraints on individual consumption choices (such as the necessity of replacing appliances because they cannot be repaired or taking the car because no public transport is available or having to use smartphones produced with the help of slave labor). Such forces establish lock-in effects and make it extremely difficult for individuals to significantly reduce their individual environmental impact and to avoid contributing to global social injustice in production processes. With regard to strong ideational forces, we see, for instance, that wellbeing is measured by GDP per capita and thus in terms of added (economic) value, although the shortcomings of GDP as a means to measure wellbeing have been known for decades (Costanza et al. 2014; Lorek and Spangenberg 2014). In addition, we see countless reports (in newspapers and issued by governments) providing statistics about consumer spending, travel to trendy destinations, or growth in car sales, for example. These, in turn, generate and reinforce societal narratives informing and shaping individual and collective value systems based on the quantity of tangibles; for individuals it is almost impossible to escape this material culture. The broad picture thus shows strong overarching forces pushing what might be summarized as overconsumption. It also highlights the necessity of identifying specific, targeted exercises of power fueling these forces and the various actors involved.

Governance research has documented that business actors gained enormous power and influence as political actors, especially in the context of globalization and associated capital concentration trends, but also due to their strategic political mobilization since the 1970s and 1980s (Fuchs 2007, 2013). The vast share of today's global economy, in turn, is built on the model of mass production and mass consumption and continues to neglect fundamental environmental and social considerations. Business actors exercise discursive power and bombard the public with thousands of messages every day aimed at generating the desire for certain products and lifestyles. The promotion of certain lifestyles in these messages, in turn, can contribute to individuals' disinclination to question what kind of consumption really benefits their wellbeing. These messages vary from explicit to subtle. They range from recognizable commercials to the sponsorship of media personalities and content. Frequently, they are not easy to recognize as promotional activities, which actually may render them more powerful. Do viewers of movies or TV/network series question the presence of certain products in what they are watching, for instance, or do they consume the promotion of such products unaware?[7] In a similar manner, readers probably do not ask why newspapers tend to include a section on car sales on weekends but not, let us say, on volunteering. In addition, business actors use instrumental power (via lobbying, campaign finance, political sponsorship, or revolving doors, for example) as well as structural material power (e.g., the threat of moving investments and jobs to other countries) to influence policy decisions in the direction of more production and consumption rather than environmental and social concerns. Such activities may target: political subsidies or tax breaks resulting in lower prices of certain products; standards prescribing the possession or use of certain goods or services (for instance, in the form of regulations requiring new safety devices); the liberalization of opening hours in the retail sector; or the prevention of governmental regulations that would hurt sales opportunities (e.g., restrictions on advertising or environmental or social standards raising the costs of certain products). In addition, self-regulation in the form of private standards, for instance, is often used to change market structures, influence prices, and prevent more stringent public regulation. The power of investor-interests and profit motives to obfuscate environmental and social consequences might become most visible in the cooptation of challengers. Organic food production and retailing has become corporatized, for instance (Gumbert and Fuchs 2018 in press). Likewise, the last years have witnessed the rise and subsequent commercialization of sharing schemes.[8] In exercising their power to foster mass production and mass consumption, business actors draw on material as well as on ideational sources of power. Corporate actors invest millions of dollars in advertising and the funding of public/political relations departments, for instance. One strong ideational source of power is the paradigm of "consumer sovereignty", that is, the assumption that consumers have the power to rule the market and indirectly control production. This idea, rooted in economic liberalism, is frequently used by politicians and business actors in claims to protect the power of consumers, when, in fact, it intends to delegitimize state intervention. Another is the equation of individual wellbeing with the possession of consumer goods and of prosperity with a growing economy and flourishing business (Fuchs 2007; Jackson 2009).

Alongside business actors, governments also tend to equate economic growth with improvements in collective wellbeing, and consequently aim to increase collective wellbeing by increasing consumer spending. This can result in efforts to improve national wellbeing via consumer subsidies, as happened during the financial crisis in Germany in 2008, when the government provided a scrappage bonus to consumers replacing their old cars with new ones. Accordingly, and in the interest of satisfying their electorate as well as powerful business actors, governments have, at best, limited their sustainable consumption focus to measures of weak sustainable consumption, that is, efforts to increase the resource efficiency of products (Fuchs and Lorek 2005). They have aimed to "boost markets" with environmentally friendlier products (European Commission - DG Health and Consumers 2012). Yet, measures addressing levels and fundamental patterns of consumption, and thus aiming at strong sustainable consumption, are lacking in governmental efforts (Fuchs and Lorek 2005). As a result, consumers get the impression that sustainability is something one can buy or perhaps even something one has to buy. Consequently, sustainable consumption is sometimes perceived as being a luxury, not as being a necessity. This is reflected in the (frequently heard) remark "I can't afford sustainability", a remark that, by the way, hides the fact that the less affluent consumer segments most often are not the biggest problem anyway (Moser and Kleinhückelkotten 2017). Moreover, it reveals the lack of recognition that not buying something may in many cases be the most sustainable choice. Furthermore, governments tend to attribute responsibility for the sustainability of consumption to business actors and, most of all, to individual consumers. In doing so, governments also draw on and tout the paradigm of "consumer sovereignty" while simultaneously banking on the necessity of freely acting business actors. Again, we can also recognize ideational foundations of such perceptions resulting, for instance, from economists arguing that "domestic consumption" is an important basis of and stabilizer for economic growth or pushing exports (i.e., consumption elsewhere), for similar purposes. In compliance with this idea, policy actors follow and promote the narrative of growth, which most of the time translates into the firm belief that consumer spending has to grow for societies to flourish (Keynes 1936).

Finally, next to initiatives such as transition towns, local sharing circles, or degrowth communities actively trying to downshift and reduce consumption, many institutionalized civil society organizations also draw on and promote paradigms similar to those identified above, that is consumer sovereignty and freedom. Consumer organizations lobby for more consumer protection and better consumer information, but in the interest of supporting and facilitating consumption. Although they also advise consumers on the sustainability of products and services, primarily and in most cases, they advise consumers on how to purchase the same goods or services for less, thus making price a highly important, if not the most important quality. Automobile clubs lobby for regulations and infrastructure investments promoting and facilitating the use of automobiles. Even environmental organizations have rarely asked the public to substantially reduce consumption in the past, but instead bank on environmentally friendlier products and/or fair trade products, for example. As a result, they contribute to the diffusion of the idea that sustainable consumption is primarily to be equated with buying certain kinds of products. Last but not least, consumers also are powerful actors, and they often protest attempts to limit their consumption levels and choices. Ideas such as lower speed limits on the German Autobahn or vegetarian days in public cafeterias supposedly have cost the Green party in Germany substantial shares in votes, when they were part of an election program.

All these forms and exercises of power feed what might be called a "consumer culture", defined by a specific value system, specific norms and rules, and by how individuals perceive and construct their own identity and the identity of others. Following the Cambridge dictionary, a consumer society is "a society in which people often buy new goods, and that places a high value on owning things: In a consumer society, there may be no better measure of how people feel than what they buy" (Cambridge University Press 2017). This captures the underlying dynamics well. In consumer societies, wellbeing is equated with possessing products, that is, the more products one owns the higher one's wellbeing. This, in turn, leads to dynamics such as competitive consumption, the "keeping up with the Jones's" or "keeping up with 'Friends'" effect.[9] In a consumer society, satisfying needs via material consumption is very common, be they needs for leisure, status, or belonging. Of course, many other ways to satisfy needs exist as well. But the prominence of the turn to material consumption when looking for satisfiers is a core characteristic of consumer societies. Correspondingly, those providing products claim to, and frequently are seen to, provide wellbeing and thereby gain political power, in a consumer society (Fuchs 2007, 2013).

It is difficult to recognize the quality and extent of power dynamics involved in developing and in maintaining cultural value systems and norms, in particular because these values and norms are so ingrained in everyday life, that is, in self-perception, in rules to follow, in behavior, and in assessing what other people do. Their force is often not visible but opaque, diffuse, and embodied in material and ideational structures. This is one reason why it is so hard to change the relevant values, norms, and rules. In addition, what is societally accepted or even "the norm" depends on joint understandings and cannot be changed by individual action. An individual may challenge values, norms, and rules and try to resist them in individual life choices, but that individual will still be surrounded by others who do not share his or her concerns and reproduce those exact values, norms, and rules and expect their friends, family members, or colleagues to do the same. Dropping out of the system, here, can carry real costs for the individual.

Interestingly enough, even the actors trying to foster sustainable consumption—including researchers—often draw on the same narratives instead of challenging or counteracting the forces behind unsustainable consumption. This sums up, for instance, in promotional campaigns communicating small and easy steps—or even the 50 to 100 easy steps—to live a sustainable lifestyle. While those sending out such messages might intend to pave the way for further steps in the direction of sustainability, consumers may well stop after these first steps, assuming their lifestyle is much more sustainable now. Indeed, communicating the big points is often completely missing (Bilharz and Schmitt 2011). The spill-over effect from smaller to bigger steps of sustainability in consumption, which many governments, civil society organizations, and scholars have expected, appears to be a myth (Mont et al. 2013; WWF-UK 2009). Furthermore, NGOs, in their attempt to professionalize their activities, increasingly adopt a marketing approach in their exchanges with their audience and, in doing so, sometimes strengthen extrinsic motivations instead of enforcing intrinsic ones. Arguing, for example, for investments in renewable energy on the basis of individual opportunities for benefitting from public subsidies meets its limits at the very moment that the subsidies disappear. In contrast, activities motivated by environmental objectives, the common good of the community, etc., tend to be more stable under changing framework conditions (WWF-UK 2009).

This picture of the multiple, diverse, and pervasive forces pushing unsustainable consumption converges in a rather bleak outlook for the future. It must seem like there is no hope, that there is no force pushing in the opposite direction. We are convinced this is not the case, however. In the following section, we will therefore look for foundations of an alternative picture. Specifically, we will try to identify potential sources of power for strong sustainable consumption.

## Power for sustainable consumption

As long as the stage is defined by structural ideational and material forces such as the narrative of economic growth and policies and business strategies fueling increasing mass consumption, fundamental change will not be achievable. As pointed out above, paradigms and narratives provide society's epistemic fabric and are closely intertwined with its material structures. In order to redefine the stage for sustainable consumption, it is therefore necessary to look for an ideational source of power strong enough to replace the narrative of growth, respectively "the more the better", and for corresponding material structural sources of power. In the first part of this section, we will argue that such a paradigm, suited to create societal momentum for sustainable consumption exists. In its second part, we will name material sources of power that are consistent with this paradigm.

### On "A Good Life and Justice"—A narrative strong enough to provide a paradigm for sustainable consumption

Identifying a narrative offering an ideational source of power for sustainable consumption depends first on defining sustainability in consumption. Proceeding from arguments developed in an inter- and transdisciplinary research program, we suggest that assessing the sustainability of consumption is not about assessing single products or the acts of consumption per se, but about assessing the impacts and intentions behind acts of consumption (Fischer et al. 2012). Accordingly, acts of consumption are defined to be sustainable if they foster the objectives of sustainable development, that is, to secure for all humans living now and in the future the possibility to live a good life, in intention and impact (op. cit., p. 73).

In terms of intention, this implies a non-individualistic mentality and a distinction between wellbeing and consumer goods (products, services, infrastructures). With respect to impact, this definition implies also the consideration of collective responsibilities, due to the social and structural embedding of individuals' acts of consumption as well as the complexity of intended and unintended impacts (op. cit., p. 77). In other words, the responsibility to attain sustainability in consumption is neither attributed solely to the individual, nor solely to the community. This definition of sustainable consumption draws attention, first, to the pivotal role of the notion of a good life with regard to sustainability. Secondly, by making the achievement of a good life for everybody the dominating goal, this definition of sustainable consumption points to justice as a driving factor of sustainability. And thirdly, it emphasizes the necessity of distinguishing human needs from the satisfiers used to satisfy these needs, and from the natural and social resources necessary to provide satisfiers and thus needs satisfaction (Di Giulio et al. 2012; Di Giulio, Defila, and Kaufmann-Hayoz 2010).

An ideational paradigm providing a societal source of power for sustainable consumption has to be compatible with this definition of sustainability in consumption. Therefore, the first question to ask is whether a good life and justice actually are normative foundations of societies, and whether they offer components of a narrative powerful enough not only to challenge and deconstruct existing messaging but also to provide an alternative to currently dominant narratives.[10] There is promising evidence for both.

The importance for individuals to lead a life they value is, by and large, uncontested. Whether this is called "good life", "quality of life", "wellbeing", "happiness", or "life satisfaction" does not matter, nor does it matter whether the theory adopted is based on psychological wellbeing (Ryff 1989), capabilities (Nussbaum 1992), or needs (Doyal and Gough 1991). One of the most important research objectives in this field is the identification of conditions leading to or hindering individual wellbeing (e.g., Dolan et al. 2008). Such research proceeds from the assumption that it is not only possible, but necessary, to distinguish human needs from satisfiers (Costanza et al. 2007; Max-Neef, Elizalde, and Hopenhayn 1991; Robeyns and van der Veen 2007). Research inquiring into the conditions of individual wellbeing shows:

> ...that the more people focus on financial and materialistic goals, the lower their well-being. This result has been confirmed both in developed countries such as the United States and Germany (…) and in less economically developed nations such as Russia and India (…). Furthermore (…) studies suggest that, whereas progress toward intrinsic goals enhances well-being, progress toward extrinsic goals such as money either does not enhance well-being or does so to a lesser extent (Ryan and Deci 2001, p. 153f).

This leads to the conclusion that wellbeing can be distinguished from consumer goods. It also suggests that focusing on this distinction has the potential of seriously challenging the narrative of growth, especially if it is combined with drawing attention to what Max-Neef, Elizalde, and Hopenhayn (1991) in their typology of satisfiers called "violators or destroyers" (they impair need satisfaction), "pseudo-satisfiers" (they give a false sense of satisfaction), and "inhibiting satisfiers" (they satisfy one need but curtail need satisfaction with regard to other needs), in contrast especially to "synergic satisfiers" (they contribute to the fulfilment of several needs) (op. cit., p. 31ff).

The notion of justice is, in turn, ingrained in the value system of human beings and also part of the normative foundations of societies. This has been demonstrated by the still authoritative cross-cultural investigation into human values by Schwartz (1994). In comparing data from 44 countries, he showed that potentially universal values exist:

> The answer to the question of the title—Are there universal aspects in the structure and contents of human values?—was foreordained to be negative, if only because of statistical error and the limitations of methodology. Nonetheless, there is support for the near universality of the four higher order value types (…). Moreover, there is considerable evidence that, when they think about the importance of their values, many people, across contemporary societies, implicitly recognize the ten value types and the postulated conflicts and compatibilities among them. (op. cit., p. 42)

The four "higher order value types" and the ten corresponding "value types" are: (1) openness to change (composed of the value types hedonism, stimulation, and self-direction); (2) self-transcendence (composed of the value types universalism and benevolence); (3) conservation (composed of the value types conformity, tradition, and security); and (4) self-enhancement (composed of the value types power, achievement, and hedonism, hedonism belonging to both self-enhancement and openness to change). According to the results found by Schwartz, the goal of the value type "universalism" is expressed by single values such as "social justice", "equality", "world at peace", or "protect environment" (op. cit.). In other words: the aim of enhancing others and transcending selfish interests, as expressed by the value type "universalism", is basic to "the nature of the human condition" (op. cit, p. 42), and it entails the value "social justice". This does not imply, of course, that justice is an important value for every single human being or that this value is stronger than other forces influencing human behavior, but it indicates that justice seems, indeed, to be deeply rooted in human nature and thus can be a normative foundation of societal cohesion. These findings are backed by a recent study showing that individuals, in their role as citizen, actually do not primarily think in dimensions of self-interest but adopt a non-individualistic mentality showing their aim of transcending selfish interests when assessing and deciding upon environmental policies (Defila, Di Giulio, and Schweizer 2018).

To show that a narrative integrating the ideas of a good life and justice is a suitable ideational source of power for sustainable consumption, there is one last point to address: the role of the natural environment. One might object that drawing on a narrative of "Good Life and Justice" might, in the end, depreciate the importance of nature and of planetary boundaries. The contrary is true: there is, first, a growing awareness in different societies across the world of the importance of the natural environment for human wellbeing (not only in the distant future, but also in the present). Secondly, not only sustainability scholars, but also scholars working in the field of human wellbeing are convinced that the two go and even belong together (e.g., Ryan and Deci 2001, p. 161). Thirdly, empirical findings show that in assessing and deciding upon environmental policies, individuals in their role as citizen consider both the natural environment and wellbeing and social justice (Defila, Di Giulio, and Schweizer 2018).

In sum, a narrative linking the ideas of a good life and justice actually exists and could, if supported and reinforced by relevant material structures and coherent action, serve as a societal source of power for sustainable consumption. This narrative has the potential of appealing to many humans because it corresponds to what most humans are seeking. At the same time, it is part of what could turn out to be a "culture of sustainability" (Ruesch and Di Giulio 2016). According to Ruesch and Di Giulio (op. cit.), a set of four values can be indicative for such a culture: good life, intergenerational justice, intragenerational justice, and common good.

### Corresponding structural material sources of power

As we said above, cognition and action cannot really be distinguished, and in order to redefine the stage, we need both an ideational source of power for sustainable consumption and corresponding structural material sources of power (see also Isenhour 2017). Thus, the question is whether there are such material sources of power that are coherent with the narrative delineated above. There is promising evidence for this as well, that is, material forms of power drawing on and reinforcing the paradigm of "a good life and justice".

Policies and practices do not only draw on narratives; they also reinforce narratives and transform them into legislation and other forms of structural power (e.g., Briggs and Feve 2013; Malone et al. 2017). The consensus that GDP is not a good indicator to measure and assess the welfare of nations has grown and received renewed attention in the last decade (e.g., the report of the so-called "Stiglitz-Sen-Fitoussi Commission" (Stiglitz, Sen, and Fitoussi 2009)). National, transnational, and supranational actors are starting to use complementary indicators—while not replacing GDP so far (see above)—to capture wellbeing. Interestingly enough, all these reports and endeavors, as different as they are in detail and in terms of the theory they adopt, proceed from the notion of a good life. They name it differently, such as "quality of life", individual and/or societal "flourishing", "wellbeing" of individuals and communities, or "happiness", but it amounts to the same thing: they all draw on the assumption that measuring the welfare of nations means measuring how people are doing, whether (or to what extent) individuals have the possibility of living a life they value. Moreover, many of these indicators address issues of social justice (although limited to justice within societies). This increasing interest in alternative ways to conceptualize and assess wellbeing on the national level (e.g., Bhutan, Canada, France, Germany, Switzerland, UK) as well as on the international level (e.g., the World Happiness Report 2017, or the EU's Statistics on Income and Living Conditions) is a clear indication of the growing importance attributed to a good life as a crucial goal for societies on the national and international level (Dolan, Layard, and Metcalfe 2011). Given the current momentum, it is becoming increasingly conceivable that GDP eventually will be replaced by indicators measuring the possibility of leading a good life of individuals and thus reporting on the quality of life and on justice instead of reporting on economic growth. And this, in turn, will lead to or further reinforce corresponding governmental and non-governmental strategies and action plans.

Simultaneously, the messaging suggesting that accumulating material goods leads to life satisfaction needs to be marginalized. This can, for instance, be done by constraining the exercise of discursive power transporting this message in advertisements. Indeed, there is precedent for restrictions on harmful advertising; in many countries, restrictions on advertising exist with respect to drugs such as tobacco and alcohol. Likewise, it is often forbidden to make false statements and promises in advertising comestibles such as dietary supplements. Nuances in tone and message are harder to regulate, of course, but regulators are forced to weigh questions all the time regarding what is obscene or discriminatory. Where to draw the line in advertising is an issue constantly negotiated in societies, as can be observed in public debates about the image of women conveyed in advertisements. Overall, we notice a rising awareness with regard to the influence of advertising and an increasing willingness to regulate it. This momentum could be broadened to address the harm of advertisements transporting the notion "more is better" and to, subsequently, marginalize if not ban this kind of messaging. Such a ban might seem far-fetched, at this point. Yet, progressively more subtle and intrusive strategies in advertising, including, for example, sponsoring in kindergartens and schools and the need for advertising-free public spaces, are increasingly becoming a topic of societal debate.

In addition, policies supporting consumer choices of "environmentally friendlier" and/or "fairer" products as well as research (funding) and infrastructures in support of such weak sustainable consumption governance would need to be complemented by policies, research (funding), and infrastructures targeting consumption that serves wellbeing while allowing for absolute reductions in ecological and social resources. Again, some developments in this direction are noticeable, especially in terms of research and research funding. In the scientific community, we observe a renewed interest in linking sustainable consumption, a good life, and justice, in investigating how to relate needs, satisfiers, resources, and societal as well as natural impacts of acts of consumption to each other. Thus, a growing number of scholars are asking other questions and exploring alternative options of societal development (e.g., Brand-Correa and Steinberger 2017; Fleurbaey and Blanchet 2013; Gough 2017; Syse and Mueller 2015). These scholars will eventually provide knowledge in terms of theories and empirical evidence disentangling wellbeing and growth. At the same time, some (often non-governmental) funding agencies are reinforcing this trend by funding research investigating how fundamental changes in the systems of consumption and production can be generated, rather than just research trying to find better and better ways to motivate individuals to buy more "sustainable products".

Likewise, the influence of business interests on political processes needs to be dramatically reduced. Today, money plays an enormous role even in supposedly democratic political processes (Fuchs 2007, 2013), and politicians and parties can choose to benefit from material support by business actors (including private media outlets). These conditions create barriers to serious policy efforts in the direction of strong sustainable consumption, as Section 3 delineated. Yet, efforts to disentangle politics and business are noticeable on various levels of governance.[11] Transparency efforts requiring the documentation and publication of lobbying activity, donations, and ancillary incomes are being implemented by national governments as well as at the supranational level (e.g., the European Union). NGOs such as Transparency International, Corporate Watch, or Democracy Now are creating publicity and thereby pressure in this direction. These regulatory efforts currently focus on limiting the influence of money and business actors in policy processes. There is still a long way to go to allow for a real disentanglement of political and business interests. But the existing efforts, as small as they are, indicate that the political realm is trying to achieve this disentanglement and—due to increasing public pressure—being forced to regain room for maneuver independent of and against business interests, if necessary.[12]

Finally, we are witnessing an increasing number of actors searching for alternative forms of living and consuming that correspond with the paradigm of "Good Life and Justice". Current trends show an exponential growth in civil society initiatives and individual practices such as transition towns, food sharing, urban gardening, fair trade, sustainable clothing initiatives, dumpster-diving, or zero waste lifestyles. While a number of these initiatives have been around for a while, recent developments, fueled perhaps by the convergence of multiple crises (ecological, financial, economic), appear to have further enhanced participation in such initiatives and the uptake of such practices. Moreover, increasing possibilities of virtual communication and exchange are strengthening the potential for learning across borders. All these initiatives demonstrate that different civil society actors are searching for alternative ways of consumption, allowing both living a good life and respecting planetary boundaries and social justice. Each of them may be imperfect or difficult to scale up, but they nevertheless testify to a common search based on broadly shared goals. It would be wrong to marginalize or ridicule such activities. On the contrary, they should be encouraged in their experiments, and approaches facilitating societal learning from their experiences should be developed and implemented (Blättel-Mink et al. 2013, p. 117ff). Looking at civil society actors advocating environmental or social issues, issues of human rights and justice, as well as consumer interests shows, moreover, additional potential for these actors to act in concert, due to the compatibility of their individually specific agendas with the paradigm of Good Life and Justice. More collaboration and leveraging of synergies would strengthen the material forces and has the potential to further shift the balance in support of this paradigm.[13] Similarly, transdisciplinary coalitions and networks promoting ideas and reforms matching the narrative "Good Life and Justice" exist, which create further synergies for the development and diffusion of relevant knowledge. Here, too, we are currently witnessing an increasing number and reach of initiatives, such as "Hot or Cool", SCORAI(-Europe), Future Earth, or the Degrowth network. Strategic collaboration between these initiatives in research and especially communication, highlighting common ideational foundations while emphasizing complementary aspects, holds the potential for creating a strong epistemic community and thus for further increasing power for sustainable consumption in political processes (Haas 1992; Hastie 2007). Importantly, the resilience of networks and coalitions supporting sustainable development, in general, also is increasing. Trump's announcement that the US will leave the Paris Agreement, for instance, only led to declarations of stronger commitment to it by other countries and especially by US American cities and states (see also Isenhour, this collection).

In sum, we recognize a number of promising tendencies in structural ideational and material power for sustainable consumption. Clearly, these tendencies may appear rather weak compared to the forces against sustainable consumption discussed in Section 3, but they do offer a chance to push for real change if they are taken up and reinforced.

## Conclusion: Taking up and reinforcing power for sustainable consumption

In the previous sections of this chapter, we delineated power against, but also power for, sustainable consumption. We argued, in particular, that dominant ideational and material structures, which shape actor interests and frequently are stabilized by powerful actors, currently create a politico-economic system poised against real advances in the sustainability of consumption. We also pointed out developments suggesting a potential for increasing power for such advances. Specifically, we argued that an integrated narrative "Good Life and Justice" holds huge promise as a common basis and vision in support of consumption that increases individual and societal wellbeing. Such a narrative exists; that is, it does not have to be invented or constructed. It draws on the distinction between human wellbeing and satisfiers. It does not fuel the narrative of growth; it does not equate sustainable consumption with buying environmentally and/or socially improved consumer goods, and it does not explicitly or implicitly perceive economic actors as being the core providers of wellbeing. We pointed out how current developments in material structures as well as actor-specific activities correspond with this paradigm, thus reinforcing it.

The last question we have to address in this chapter is the question of how the power for sustainable consumption could be further enhanced. To this end, we want to point out three pathways that correspond with the manifestations of power for sustainable consumption we identified in Section 4.

*Firmly link wellbeing and justice to sustainable consumption, but disentangle human needs and satisfiers.* A concept that is suited to inform sustainable consumption governance compatible with the identified paradigm and material changes is the concept of (Sustainable) Consumption Corridors (Blättel-Mink et al. 2013; Di Giulio and Fuchs 2014; Fuchs and Di Giulio 2016). This concept integrates social justice, planetary boundaries, and wellbeing and proceeds from three assumptions: the first assumption is that there are some essential needs of humans, which they need to be able to satisfy in order to lead a meaningful and fulfilled life—although notions of what a good life consists of in detail differ both across time and culture and between different members of the same society living in the same period of time. The second assumption is that humans need satisfiers/resources in order to satisfy their needs. Based on these assumptions, one can conclude that individuals worldwide require access to a minimum level of satisfiers/resources in order to be able to achieve a good life. The third assumption is that consumption by individuals can impair the ability of other human beings living now or in the future to have access to this minimum of satisfiers/resources and thus be able to live a life they value. Consumption Corridors would be defined by minimum standards that allow every individual to live a good life, and by maximum standards for every individual's use of satisfiers/resources that guarantee access to sufficient satisfiers/resources (in terms of quantity and quality) for others, both in the present and the future. Minimum and maximum consumption standards create a space, and this is the corridor of sustainable consumption. Consumption Corridors ensure that all individuals are able to live a fulfilling life according to their own preferences, because the space between the upper and the lower boundary is the space where individuals have the freedom to design their lives according to their individual notions of a good life. The concept of Consumption Corridors does not assume that it is possible or desirable to prescribe specific patterns of consumption and ways of living. It does not question the existence of needs; it questions how needs are satisfied, and it questions subjective desires. It does not question individual freedom but defines limits to individual freedom by taking justice into the equation. The concept of Consumption Corridors thus offers a promising basis for initiating societal and political awareness of the purpose of consumption and the need to differentiate between human needs and satisfiers. Engaging with this concept, in turn, can take place within a broad variety of approaches and venues adapted to different national situations and possibilities.

*Develop cross-sectional, cross-party networks of actors resilient against forces towards unsustainable consumption and joining forces towards sustainable consumption.* There is a need to develop policies for sustainable consumption and implement them to challenge current power structures. This will necessitate courage and mutual support in a joint effort of actors, at all levels of society. Single actors will not be able to achieve much, and if they, nevertheless, were to try, the costs to them might be too high. In order to further support and strengthen the building of resilient networks of actors, approaches are needed that facilitate coalition building, specifically on comprehensive and far-reaching policies, outside of the public "political stage". An appropriate measure is to create spaces where different societal actors, be they governmental actors or civil society actors (including scholars), can explore and debate such policies as well as look for allies before official and public policy processes start (Blättel-Mink et al. 2013, p. 47f). The suggestion is not to create a space for clandestine collusion, but to provide a protected space for factual discussion. It goes without saying that even then, developing, adopting, and implementing appropriate policies will not be easy, but this does not mean that it should not be attempted.

*Empower civil society and foster participatory policy development.* As we showed in Section 3, the different ideational and material forces and the power exerted by different actors build a complex web of interrelations fostering unsustainable consumption. It would be wrong to blame an abstract "they" for the resulting trends, because it is possible to uncover specific power dynamics and actors reinforcing these trends. At the same time, it would also be wrong to point at one single actor and to blame this actor for unsustainable consumption. Rather, all societal actors, be they governmental or civil society actors, have to contribute to and assume responsibility for the development of institutions and policies for sustainable consumption, according to their expertise and power (Blättel-Mink et al. 2013, p. 103ff). Citizens and consumers are part of that; that is, participatory policy development must include individuals in their dual role of consumer and citizen. Participatory approaches to policy development in turn depend on processes guaranteeing representativeness, fairness, transparency, and accountability, and—in consequence—require the empowerment of weaker societal actors, in particular. To that end, special attention will also need to be paid to questions of political education.

It might seem, and surely is, a long way to achieve sustainable consumption, and we certainly need to explore and understand the structural forces creating barriers to progress. But we are convinced that it is worthwhile and promising to look not only at the ideational and material power against sustainable consumption, but also at the power for sustainable consumption. This includes, first, identifying sources of such power. What we did in this chapter is, of course, no more than a first step. It includes, secondly, exploring and understanding how these sources of power can be strengthened. In this respect, there is a lot of work to do—so let us tackle it!

## Notes

1. According to the World Watch Institute, "… 1.7 billion people worldwide now belong to the 'global consumer class,' having adopting the diets, transportation systems, and lifestyles that were once mostly limited to the rich nations of Europe, North America, and Japan" (http://www.worldwatch.org/node/3816, accessed September 30, 2018).

2. Obviously, there are individuals living on this planet who need to consume more rather than less. So when we talk about unsustainable consumption we are referring to consumption by the global consumer class.

3. In this chapter, we use the terms "paradigms" and "narratives" synonymously.

4. https://www.independent.co.uk/extras/indybest/fashion-beauty/womens-clothing/best-sustainable-fashion-brands-women-clothing-ethical-eco-friendly-affordable-london-luxury-a7982316.html;
https://wfto.com/about-us/history-wfto/history-fair-trade;
https://www.soilassociation.org/certification/trade-news/2018/organic-has-reached-its-highest-sales-ever-at-over-22b/,
https://www.ifoam.bio/sites/default/files/press-release-world-2017-english.pdf;
https://www.statista.com/statistics/562911/global-sales-growth-of-the-vegan-market-by-country/;
https://www.statista.com/statistics/415636/car-sharing-number-of-users-worldwide/, all accessed September 30, 2018.

5. Calculated on the basis of the global Ecological Footprint, the "Earth Overshoot Day" marks the day, within one calendar year, that humanity has exhausted nature's budget of renewable resources for the year. For the remainder of the year, the global population is drawing down resource stocks and accumulating carbon dioxide in the atmosphere.

6. https://www.nature.com/articles/s41558-017-0058-9;
https://cdn.businessoffashion.com/reports/The_State_of_Fashion_2018_v2.pdf;
https://www.mckinsey.com/business-functions/sustainability-and-resource-productivity/our-insights/style-thats-sustainable-a-new-fast-fashion-formula;
https://www.theguardian.com/business/2017/nov/07/primark-sales-leap-high-street-spending-fasion-marks-spencer;
https://www.theguardian.com/commentisfree/2013/jan/31/agribusiness-exploitation-undocumented-labor;
https://www.oxfamamerica.org/press/new-campaign-exposes-widespread-abuses-of-workers-in-americas-poultry-industry/;
https://www.oxfamamerica.org/explore/research-publications/lives-on-the-line/;
https://viacampesina.org/en/wp-content/uploads/sites/2/2018/07/2017_Annual_Report_EN-2_lowres.pdf, all accessed September 30, 2018.

7. Other examples are advertorials (i.e., advertising in newspapers that has the form of a regular article) and lifestyle products promoted via their use by celebrities and social media personalities.

8. The best-known example is probably Airbnb, which started as an online platform for helping travelers find accommodations and house/flat owners to make use of their otherwise empty houses/flats. In less than ten years, Airbnb became the fourth most valuable venture-backed tech company worth 30 billion US$, however, creating negative impacts on the traditional hospitality industry, rents in attractive city areas, as well as governmental tax income (Farrell and Bensinger 2016).

9. This effect has become more worrisome over the years, as studies indicate that consumption is not just driven by upward comparisons, but that individuals also tend to overestimate what the next wealthier income groups own, due to media representations (Schor 1998).

10. Narratives do both: offer a positive story ("alternative narratives") and deconstruct and challenge messaging that takes place ("counter-narratives") (e.g., Briggs and Feve 2013; Eser Davolio and Lenzo 2017).

11. Again, such changes in material structures correlate with challenges to ideational structures, of course. In this case, they draw attention to the question of the societal purpose of the economy and the need not to equate the well-being of the economy with the well-being of society, or society's economic goals and sustainability with the interests of business (Di Giulio 2004, p. 323f).

12. Corresponding efforts to protect the political room for maneuver are a result of the economic crises starting in 2007/2008 and the wish that governments are not forced into supporting single businesses because they are "too big to fail" and governmental requirements for better safety mechanisms on the side of business, especially banks.

13. An interesting example for an initiative strategically trying to create and use synergies—across faiths for now—is the Multi-Faith Simple Living Initiative (http://www.livingwitness.org.uk/files/Multi-Faith%20Sustainable%20Living%20Initiative%20Nov%202017.pdf).

# References

Akenji, L. 2014. "Consumer scapegoatism and limits to green consumerism." *Journal of Cleaner Production* no. 63:16–23.

Akenji, L., and H. Chen. 2016. "A Framework for Shaping Sustainable Lifestyles." *United Nations Environment Programme: Nairobi, Kenya.*

Bilharz, M., and K. Schmitt. 2011. "Going big with big matters. The key points approach to sustainable consumption." *GAIA-Ecological Perspectives for Science and Society* no. 20 (4):232–235.

Blättel-Mink, B., B. Brohmann, R. Defila, A. Di Giulio, D. Fischer, D. Fuchs, S. Gölz, K. Götz, A. Homburg, R. Kaufmann-Hayoz, E. Matthies, G. Michelsen, M. Schäfer, K. Tews, S. Wassermann, and S. Zundel. 2013. *Konsum-Botschaften - Was Forschende fur die gesellschaftliche Gestaltung nachhaltigen Konsums empfehlen.* Stuttgart: Hirzel.

Brand-Correa, L.I., and J.K. Steinberger. 2017. "A Framework for Decoupling Human Need Satisfaction From Energy Use." *Ecological Economics* no. 141:43–52.

Briggs, R., and S. Feve. 2013. "Review of programs to counter narratives of violent extremism." London: Institute for Strategic Dialogue.

Brundtland, G.H. 1987. *Our Common Future: World Commission on Environment and Development:* Oxford University Press Oxford.

Cambridge University Press. 2017. "Consumer Society." In *Cambridge Advanced Learner's Dictionary & Thesaurus.* Cambridge University Press. http://dictionary.cambridge.org/de/worterbuch/englisch/consumer-society.

Cohen, M.J., H.S. Brown, and P.J. Vergragt. 2017. *Social Change and the Coming of Post-consumer Society: Theoretical Advances and Policy Implications:* Taylor & Francis.

Costanza, R., Fisher B., S. Ali, C. Beer, L. Bond, R. Boumans, N.L. Danigelis, J. Dickinson, C. Elliott, J. Farley, D. Elliott Gayer, G.L. MacDonald, T. Hudspeth, D. Mahoney, L. McCahil, B. McIntosh, B. Reed, S.A. Turab Rizvi, D.M. Rizzo, T. Simpatico, and R. Snapp. 2007. "Quality of life: An approach integrating opportunities, human needs, and subjective well-being." *Ecological Economics* no. 61:267–276.

Costanza, R., I. Kubiszewski, E. Giovannini, H. Lovins, J. McGlade, K.E. Pickett, K.V. Ragnarsdóttir, D. Roberts, R. De Vogli, and R. Wilkinson. 2014. "Time to leave GDP behind - Comment." *Nature* no. 505:283–285.

Csutora, M., and Á. Zsóka. 2016. Breaking through the behaviour impact gap and the rebound effect in sustainable consumption. Paper read at Sustainable Consumption and Social Justice in a Constrained World, at Budapest, Hungary, August 29-30, 2016.

Defila, R., A. Di Giulio, and R. Kaufmann-Hayoz (eds). 2012. *The Nature of Sustainable Consumption and how to Achieve it.* München: Oekom.

Defila, R., A. Di Giulio, and C.R. Schweizer. 2018. "Two souls are dwelling in my breast: Uncovering how individuals in their dual role as consumer-citizen perceive future energy policies." *Energy Research & Social Science* no. 35:152–162.

Di Giulio, A. 2004. *Die Idee der Nachhaltigkeit im Verständnis der Vereinten Nationen - Anspruch, Bedeutung und Schwierigkeiten*. Münster, Hamburg, Berlin, London: LIT Verlag.

Di Giulio, A., B. Brohmann, J. Clausen, R. Defila, D. Fuchs, R. Kaufmann-Hayoz, and A. Koch. 2012. "Needs and consumption - a conceptual system and its meaning in the context of sustainability." In *The Nature of Sustainable Consumption and How to Achieve it. Results from the Focal Topic "From Knowledge to Action - New Paths towards Sustainable Consumption"*, edited by R. Defila, A. Di Giulio and R. Kaufmann-Hayoz, 45–66. München: Oekom.

Di Giulio, A., R. Defila, and R. Kaufmann-Hayoz. 2010. "Gutes Leben, Bedürfnisse und nachhaltiger Konsum." *Nachhaltiger Konsum, Teil 1. Umweltpsychologie*. no. Jg 14 Nr. 2(27):10–29.

Di Giulio, A., and D. Fuchs. 2014. "Sustainable Consumption Corridors: Concept, Objections, and Responses." *GAIA* no. 23 (1):184–192.

Dolan, P., R. Layard, and R. Metcalfe. 2011. *Measuring Subjective Wellbeing for Public Policy: Recommendations on Measures*. London: Centre for Economic Performance.

Dolan, P., T. Peasgood, and M. P. White 2008. "Do we really know what makes us happy? A review of the economic literature on the factors associated with subjective well-being." *Journal of Economic Psychology* no. 29:94–122.

Doyal, L., and I. Gough. 1991. *A Theory of Human Need*. Basingstoke: Macmillan.

EEA. 2015. *The European environment — state and outlook 2015*. Copenhagen: European Environment Agency,.

Eser Davolio, M., and D. Lenzo. 2017. Hintergrundrecherche: Gegennarrative und alternative Narrativen.

Essington, T.E., P.E. Moriarty, H.E. Froehlich, E.E. Hodgson, L.E. Koehn, K.L. Oken, M.C. Siple, and C.C. Stawitz. 2015. "Fishing amplifies forage fish population collapses." *Proceedings of the National Academy of Sciences* no. 112 (21):6648–6652.

European Commission - DG Health and Consumers. 2012. "A new European Consumer Agenda – Boosting confidence and growth by putting consumers at the heart of the Single Market." Brussels: European Commission. Available at http://europa.eu/rapid/press-release_IP-12-491_en.htm (accessed 4.01.19).

European Commission. 2014. Attitudes of European Citizens towards the Environment. In *Special Eurobarometer 416*.

Eurostat. http://ec.europa.eu/eurostat/en 2017.

Eurostat. 2018. European Union statistics on income and living conditions. https://ec.europa.eu/eurostat/web/microdata/european-union-statistics-on-income-and-living-conditions, accessed September 30, 2018

Farrell, M., and G. Bensinger. 2016. "Airbnb's Funding Round Led by Google Capital." *Wall Street Journal*.

Fischer, D., Michelsen G., Blättel-Mink B., and Di Giulio A. 2012. "Sustainable consumption: How to evaluate sustainability in consumption acts." In *The Nature of Sustainable Consumption and How to Achieve it. Results from the Focal Topic "From Knowledge to Action - New Paths towards Sustainable Consumption*, edited by Defila R., Di Giulio A. and Kaufmann-Hayoz R., 67–80. München: Oekom.

Fleurbaey, M., and D. Blanchet. 2013. *Beyond GDP: Measuring welfare and assessing sustainability*: Oxford University Press.

Frimmel, F.H., and R. Niessner. 2014. *Nanoparticles in the water cycle*: Springer.

Fuchs, D. 2007. *Business Power in Global Governance*. Boulder: Lynne Rienner Publishers.

———. 2013. "Theorizing the power of global companies." In *The handbook of global companies*, edited by J. Mikler, 77–95. Hoboken: Wiley-Blackwell.

Fuchs, D. 2017. "Consumption Corridors as a Means for Overcoming Trends in (Un-) Sustainable Consumption." In *International Conference on Consumer Research 2016: The 21st Century Consumer: Vulnerable, Responsible, Transparent?*, edited by C. Bala and W. Schuldzinski. Düsseldorf: Verbraucherzentrale NRW. DOI 10.15501/978-3-86336-918_13.

Fuchs, D., and A. Di Giulio. 2016. "Consumption corridors and social justice: Exploring the limits." In *Sustainable Consumption and Social Justice in a Constrained World*, edited by S. Lorek and E. Vadovics. SCORAI Europe Workshop Proceedings, August 29-30, 2016, Budapest, Hungary. Sustainable Consumption Transitions Series, Issue 6.

Fuchs, D., A. Di Giulio, K. Glaab, S. Lorek, M. Maniates, T. Princen, and I. Ropke. 2016. "Power: What's missing in consumption and absolute reductions research and action." *Journal of Cleaner Production* no. 132 298–307.

Fuchs, D., and S. Lorek. 2005. "Sustainable Consumption Governance - A History of Promises and Failures." *Journal of Consumer Policy* no. 28:261–288.

Global Footprint Network. *Past Earth Overshoot Days* 2018 [cited 01.10.2018. Available from https://www.overshootday.org/newsroom/past-earth-overshoot-days].

Gough, I. 2017. *Heat, Greed and Human Need - Climate Change, Capitalism and Sustainable Wellbeing, Books*. Cheltenham: Edward Elgar.

Gumbert, T., and D. Fuchs. 2018 in press. "The Power of Corporations in Global Food Sector Governance." In *Handbook of the International Political Economy of the Corporation*, edited by A. Nölke and C. May. Cheltenham: Edward Elgar.

Haas, P.M. 1992. "Introduction: Epistemic communities and international policy coordination." *International organization* no. 46 (1):1-35.

Hastie, J. 2007. *The role of science and scientists in environmental policy, Sage Handbook on Environment and Society*. London: SAGE Publications.

Hawkins, T.R., B. Singh, G. Majeau-Bettez, and A.H. Strømman. 2013. "Comparative environmental life cycle assessment of conventional and electric vehicles." *Journal of Industrial Ecology* no. 17 (1):53–64.

Hirschnitz-Garbers, M., A.R. Tan, A. Gradmann, and T. Srebotnjak. 2016. "Key drivers for unsustainable resource use–categories, effects and policy pointers." *Journal of Cleaner Production* no. 132:13–31.

Isenhour, C. 2017. "When "gestures of change" demand policy support. Social change and the structural underpinnings of consumption in the United States." In *Social Change and the Coming of Post-consumer Society: Theoretical Advances and Policy Implications*, edited by M.J. Cohen, H.S. Brown and P.J. Vergragt. New York: Routledge.

Jackson, T. 2009. *Prosperity without growth*. London: Earthscan.

Keynes, J.M. 1936. *The General Theory of Employment, Interest, and Money*. New York: Hartcourt, Brace.

Lorek, S. 2014. "Dematerialisation." In *Degrowth: Vocabulary for a new era*, edited by G. D'Alisa, F. Demaria and G. Kallis, 83–85. New York: Routledge.

Lorek, S., and J.H. Spangenberg. 2014. "Sustainable consumption within a sustainable economy – beyond green growth and green economies." *Journal of Cleaner Production* no. 63:33–44. doi: http://dx.doi.org/10.1016/j.jclepro.2013.08.045

Lorek, S., and P. Vergragt. 2015. "Sustainable consumption as a systemic challenge." In *Handbook on Research in Sustainable Consumption*, edited by L. Reisch and J. Thøgersen, 19–32. Cheltenham: Edward Elgar Publishing.

Malone, E., N.E. Hultman, K.L. Anderson, and V. Romeiro. 2017. "Stories about ourselves: How national narratives influence the diffusion of large-scale energy technologies." *Energy Research & Social Science* no. 31:70–76.

Maniates, M. 2001. "Individualization: Plant a tree, buy a bike, save the world?" *Global Environmental Politics* no. 1 (3):31–52.

———. 2014. "Sustainable consumption–Three paradoxes." *GAIA-Ecological Perspectives for Science and Society* no. 23 (3):201–208.

Martinez-Alier, J., I. Anguelovski, P. Bond, D. DelBene, F. Demaria, J.-F. Gerber, L. Greyl, W. Hass, H. Healy, and V. Marín-Burgos. 2014. "Between activism and science: Grassroots concepts for sustainability coined by Environmental Justice Organizations." *Journal of Political Ecology* no. 21:19–60.

Max-Neef, M., A. Elizalde, and M. Hopenhayn. 1991. "Development and Human Needs." In *Human scale development: Conception, application and further reflections*, edited by A.M. Max-Neef, 13–54. London: Zed Books.

Meadows, D.H., D.L. Meadows, J. Randers, and W.W. Behrens III. 1972. *The limits to growth: A report to the club of Rome (1972)*: Universe Books, New York.

Mont, O., E. Heiskanen, K. Power, and H. Kuusi. 2013. *Improving Nordic Policymaking by Dispelling Myths on Sustainable Consumption*, TemaNord. Copenhagen: Nordic Council of Ministers Secretariat.

Moser, S., and S. Kleinhückelkotten. 2017. "Good Intents, but Low Impacts: Diverging Importance of Motivational and Socioeconomic Determinants Explaining Pro-Environmental Behavior, Energy Use, and Carbon Footprint." *Environment and Behavior* no. First Published June 9, 2017.

Ngai, P., and J. Chan. 2012. "Global Capital, the State, and Chinese Workers - The Foxconn Experience." *Modern China* no. 38 (4):383–410.

Nussbaum, M.C. 1992. "Human functioning and social justice: In defense of Aristotelian essentialism." *Political Theory* no. 20 (2):202–246.

Robeyns, I., and R.J. van der Veen. 2007. *Sustainable quality of life: Conceptual analysis for a policy-relevant empirical specification*. Bilthoven, Amsterdam: Netherlands Environmental Assessment Agency and University of Amsterdam.

Rockström, J., W. Steffen, K. Noone, Å. Persson, F.S. Chapin, E.F. Lambin, T.M. Lenton, M. Scheffer, C. Folke, H.J. Schellnhuber, B. Nykvist, C.A. de Wit, T. Hughes, S. van der Leeuw, H. Rodhe, S. Sörlin, P.K. Snyder, R. Costanza, U. Svedin, M. Falkenmark, L. Karlberg, R.W. Corell, V.J. Fabry, J. Hansen, B. Walker, D. Liverman, K. Richardson, P. Crutzen, and J.A. Foley. 2009. "A safe operating space for humanity." *Nature* no. 461 (24 September 2009).

Ruesch, C., and A. Di Giulio. 2016. "Nachhaltigkeitswerte: Eine Kultur der Nachhaltigkeit? Sekundäranalyse der Daten aus der StabeNE-Erhebung 2008." *SOCIENCE, Journal of Science-Society Interfaces* no. 1 (1):91–104.

Ryan, R.M., and E.L. Deci. 2001. "On Happiness and Human Potentials: A Review of Research on Hedonic and Eudaimonic Well-Being." *Annual Review of Psychology* no. 52:141–166.

Ryff, C.D. 1989. "Happiness Is Everything, or Is It? Explorations on the Meaning of Psychological Well-Being." *Journal of Personality and Social Psychology* no. 57 (6):1069–1081.

Schwartz, S.H. 1994. "Are there Universal Apects in the structure and Contents of Human Values?" *Journal of Social Issues* no. 50 (4):19–45.

Schor, J. 1998. *The Overspent American: Why We Buy What We Don't Need*. New York: Basic Books.

Steffen, W., K. Richardson, J. Rockström, S.E. Cornell, I. Fetzer, E.M. Bennett, R. Biggs, S.R. Carpenter, W. de Vries, and C.A. de Wit. 2015. "Planetary boundaries: Guiding human development on a changing planet." *Science* no. 347 (6223).

Stiglitz, J.E., A. Sen, and J. Fitoussi. 2009. Report by the Commission on the Measurement of Economic Performance and Social Progress.

Stirling, A. 2014. "Transforming power: Social science and the politics of energy choices." *Energy Research & Social Science* no. 1:83–95.

Syse, K.L., and M.L. Mueller. 2015. *Sustainable Consumption and the Good Life: Interdisciplinary Perspectives*: Routledge.

United Nations. 1992. *Agenda 21; Results of the World Conference on Environment and Development*. Vol. UN Doc.A/CONF.151/4. New York: United Nations.

———. 2002. Johannesburg Plan of Implementation. In *World Summit on Sustainable Development*, Johannesburg.

———. 2015. "Transforming our world: the 2030 Agenda for Sustainable Development." *New York: United Nations General Assembly*. Available at https://sustainabledevelopment.un.org/post2015/transformingourworld (accessed 4.01.19).

Wieser, H. 2016. "Beyond planned obsolescence: Product lifespans and the challenges to a circular economy." *GAIA* 25 (3):156–160.

World Happiness Report. 2017. edited by J.F. Helliwell, R. Layard and J. Sachs.

Worldwatch Institute. 2004. "Chapter 1: the State of Consumption Today". http://www.worldwatch.org/node/3816, accessed September 30, 2018.

WWF-UK. 2009. *Simple and painless? The limitations of spillover in environmental campaigning*. Surrey, UK: WWF.

Zaneveld, J.R., D.E. Burkepile, A.A. Shantz, C.E. Pritchard, R. McMinds, J.P. Payet, R. Welsh, A.M. Correa, N.P. Lemoine, and S. Rosales. 2016. "Overfishing and nutrient pollution interact with temperature to disrupt coral reefs down to microbial scales." *Nature communications* no. 7.

# Section II

# On governmentality and the notion of the subject in sustainable consumption

# 4 Pro-environmental behaviour change and governmentality: Counter-conduct and the making up of environmental individuals

*Tom Hargreaves*

## Introduction

It is now widely recognised that efforts to bring about more sustainable patterns of consumption demand considerable changes to contemporary ways of life and associated resource consumption (e.g., Shove 2010). As part of this challenge, a core preoccupation of sustainable consumption research and policy is focused on understanding and improving attempts to change people's behaviour (Shwom and Lorenzen 2012). At the same time, however, and as this collection is attempting to address, much sustainable consumption research has been reluctant to engage with the inevitable questions about power and social change that such challenges unavoidably pose (Maniates 2014). For Maniates, part of the reason for this is methodological. The dominant disciplines focussed on changing behaviour (economics, psychology, marketing, etc.) embrace a focus on individuals as the core unit of analysis and thus shy away from more challenging questions about structural inequality and change in society. Indeed, most attempts to understand pro-environmental behaviour, and certainly most policy measures, have drawn on a wide range of economic or psychological models of individual decision-making, each emphasising the different intrinsic and/or extrinsic factors said to influence behaviour (see Jackson 2005 for an extensive review). Despite the many specific differences between these models, all are premised on the basic assumption that behaviour follows, in an essentially linear and more or less rational fashion, from an individual's cognitive dispositions—and particularly, his/her attitudes or values. By implication, unsustainable consumption is assumed to stem from faulty decision-making, whereas sustainable consumption can be encouraged by the prior spread of sustainable and pro-environmental attitudes or values among the population—a task that UK policy-makers have attempted through a range of mass media information campaigns (DEMOS 2003) or, more recently, through more carefully targeted 'social marketing' and 'nudge' initiatives (e.g., Barr 2008; DEFRA 2008; Dolan et al. 2010; see also Gumbert, this collection).

This basic approach, which Shove (2010) derisively terms the 'ABC framework'—'this being an account of social change in which "A" stands for attitude, "B" for behaviour and "C" for choice' (Shove 2010, p.1274)—has been widely criticised for its scientific realist understanding of 'the environment', for its rationalist conception of behaviour, for its excessive and voluntarist individualism, and for its over-simplistic linearity (see, for example: Harrison and Davies 1998; Maniates 2002; Shove 2010). These critiques, and many others, are by now well-known and well-rehearsed and do not require further elaboration here. Despite their strength and veracity, however, the ABC framework still holds fast as the foundation of policy-making in this vital area. One potential reason for this, and as this chapter will begin to unpick, is that whilst many have critiqued the power of the ABC framework itself (e.g., Maniates 2002; Shove 2010) relatively few studies have actively examined how power operates within and through this framework (although see Webb 2012; Jones et al. 2013; Dilley 2015). Indeed, despite over 20 years of critique, there have been very few studies that have examined what actually happens when the ABC approach plays out on the ground in specific circumstances, or that have empirically examined its internal workings. Whilst critics have attacked the realism, individualism, and a-contextual nature of the ABC approach (Harrison and Davies 1998), for example, they have so far failed to show how power operates in specific behaviour change interventions to construct the 'sustainability' or 'the environment' in particular ways or to shape and define individual agency, responsibility, and subjectivity in particular ways (although see Hobson 2002 and Bulkeley et al. 2015 for rare examples). This is important because a focus on how power operates in pro-environmental behaviour change initiatives shifts the focus such that the significance of such interventions lies not solely in the environmental savings they may generate, but also in the ways they open up and generate new spaces for the formation of environmental subjects.

The central aim of this chapter is to explore and demonstrate the workings of power in a specific pro-environmental behaviour change initiative—Environment Champions—as it operated in the head offices of a UK construction company called Burnetts[1]. To do this, the chapter employs Michel Foucault's thinking about 'governmentality' (Foucault 2007) as analytics of government (Dean 2010) to explore the means and mechanisms through which environmental problems get constructed in particular ways in specific settings and how behavioural changes undertaken by environmentally aware individuals become their seemingly self-evident solution. The next section briefly introduces governmentality analytics before Section 3 introduces the case study methodology that was employed, which has particular value because the vast majority of work in this field focusses on domestic settings and practices rather than on the world of business and work. Section 4 empirically explores the internal workings of the Environment Champions initiative at Burnetts. Specifically, it details and demonstrates the forms of political rationality and governmental technology that attempted, respectively, to render the environment thinkable, and to 'make up' (Hacking 1986) environmental subjects willing to take action upon it. Section 5 concludes the chapter by reflecting on the implications of this case study for future research and practice in the area of pro-environmental behaviour change and sustainable consumption.

## Environmental governmentality

Bröckling et al. observe that Foucault himself used the notion of governmentality in a 'double sense' (2011, p.7). On the one hand, he used it to refer to the specific historical emergence of liberal government in the 18th century. On the other hand, in a much broader sense, he used it to refer to the general emergence of an 'independent art of government'. Koopman and Matza (2013) develop this double sense of governmentality by drawing a distinction between Foucaultian 'concepts' and 'analytics'. For them, governmentality is a concept—that is, a specific formulation that has emerged out of Foucault's detailed and situated historical enquiry. By contrast 'analytics' refer to the methods Foucault developed, such as genealogy or archaeology. Whilst Koopman and Matza classify governmentality as a concept, Bröckling et al. recognise that it has mostly been interpreted and employed as an 'analytic perspective' (2011, p.11). This chapter draws on governmentality as an analytic perspective to help explore the operation of power in a pro-environmental behaviour change initiative.

As an analytic perspective, governmentality (Foucault 2007) refers to the strategies and tactics used by political authorities—including but not limited to the State—to shape the interests and practices of their subjects to align with their own governmental ambitions. It is helpful, here, to understand society as a 'field of power' (Darier 1996a) comprising multiple heterogeneous agents and elements. The analytical approach of governmentality then seeks to understand the ways and means by which this heterogeneous field is made to align in particular ways. Rather than focussing solely on those who make the rules, such as the Sovereign or the State, for example, governmentality directs us to explore the micro-level relationships and practices at work between all the elements in the field that make them align in particular ways (Rouse 2005).

Governmentality suggests that individuals are not oppressed or constrained by power, but are rather enrolled in particular alignments, come to accept them as 'normal', and thus enforce particular relations of power upon themselves and each other. As Rose and Miller put it: 'power is not so much a matter of imposing constraints upon citizens as of "making up" citizens capable of bearing a kind of regulated freedom' (Rose and Miller 1992, p.174). The challenge for the researcher is then to understand the many and various ways in which subjects are 'made up' (Hacking 1986) such that they come to perceive, understand, and act in the world in a particular and predictable manner.

As an analytical approach, therefore, governmentality seeks to understand how power operates 'beyond the state' to control action at a distance through a range of what Rose and Miller (1992) term '*political rationalities*'—ways of understanding, representing, and problematising the world—and '*governmental technologies*'—ways of intervening to generate alignments in the field of power. Perhaps the central point to take from Foucault's analysis is that:

> To understand modern forms of rule…requires an investigation not merely of grand political schema, or economic ambitions, nor even of general slogans such as state control, nationalization, the free market and the like, but

of apparently humble and mundane mechanisms which appear to make it possible to govern: techniques of notation, computation and calculation; procedures of examination and assessment; the invention of devices such as surveys and presentational forms such as tables; the standardization of systems of training and the inculcation of habits; the inauguration of professional specialisms and vocabularies; building design and architectural forms—the list is heterogeneous and is, in principle, unlimited. (Miller and Rose 1990, p.8)

In this view, then, understanding the power and politics of sustainable consumption demands that attention is not paid only to sustainability or environmentalism as forms of 'grand political schema'. Rather the focus should be on the specific, grounded, and often quotidian techniques that serve to constitute various forms of (un)sustainability or (anti-)environmentalism and which operate through (rather than over) everyday practices.

In his own work, Foucault (2007) described the operation of a range of different arrangements of political rationalities and governmental technologies—what he termed 'dispositives'—as they emerged and took hold in different times and places through history. Raffnsøe et al. identify three different 'prototypical dispositives' (2016, p.280) in Foucault's work: law, discipline, and security. As Raffnsøe et al. describe them, the dispositive of 'law' serves to differentiate between the forbidden and the permitted; 'discipline' distinguishes between the preventive and the productive or the unwanted and the wanted; and 'security' serves not to deter or prevent but *'conductively* aim[s] to *facilitate* the self-regulation of a *population'* (Raffnsøe et al. 2016, p.280, original emphasis). Crucially, whilst these different dispositives have been more or less dominant at different periods, Foucault observes that new dispositives never simply erase and replace those that came before them but rather, connect with them in particular ways. As such, it is important to emphasise that dispositives, or what Rose (1993) refers to as governmental machines, are never all-encompassing. As machines, they are 'more Heath Robinson than Audi, full of parts that come from elsewhere, strange couplings, chance relations, cogs and levers that don't work' (Rose 1993, p.287). They thus generate unintended effects as often as intended ones. Individual agents can resist the relationships and practices of power operating upon them—either by following those of other dispositives instead, or by locating occasional 'cracks' in the machines in which forms of autonomous self-definition, or ways of making up oneself, are possible (Darier 1996b).

Despite the explicit focus of governmentality on 'the conduct of conduct' (Dean 2010), there have so far been relatively few attempts to develop a governmentality approach to understand dispositives that seek to bring about sustainable consumption or pro-environmental behaviour change. Those that have begun this endeavour (see Darier 1996a, Slocum 2004; Rutland and Aylett 2008; Paterson and Stripple 2010; Webb 2012; Dilley 2015) have made great strides but have too often stopped their analysis at the level of programme managers or policy-makers. Only a handful of studies have attempted to take the next step and explore how dispositives of sustainable consumption or pro-environmental behaviour change play out and are accepted, rejected, resisted, and re-negotiated in specific situations (e.g., Hargreaves 2014; Bulkeley et al. 2015). In other words, whilst much has been done to understand the design and development of dispositives that variously promote or inhibit pro-environmental behaviour, significantly less work has explored the 'messy actualities' (O'Malley et al. 1997) of these governmental projects and how they give rise to forms of counter-conduct.

The challenge, then, for a governmentality-inspired understanding of pro-environmental behaviour change is to explore empirically the dispositives of behaviour change interventions and their reception in specific settings. This demands that attention is paid to how these dispositives make use of different governmental rationalities to construct the environment as in crisis and how, simultaneously, various technologies of government are employed to 'make up' (Hacking 1986) subjects that are willing to accept and are capable of acting upon these problematisations. The rest of this chapter attempts to begin this process through a detailed ethnographic case study that explores the dispositives employed in a single pro-environmental behaviour change initiative called 'Environment Champions'.

## Environment Champions at Burnetts

Environment Champions (EC) is a behaviour change initiative operated by the environmental charity Global Action Plan (GAP). GAP's general approach to behaviour change, involving auditing and measurement processes and supportive group discussions to plan lifestyle changes, has received a relatively large amount of academic attention (e.g., Staats et al. 2004; Hargreaves et al. 2008), but the majority of this work has been conducted in domestic rather than workplace settings, and none of this work has explored the internal workings of these programmes using a governmentality analytic. The EC programme is designed to operate as a bottom-up, participant-led initiative. The first step is to recruit a team of volunteer Champions, before a GAP programme manager assists them in auditing their organisation's environmental impacts across a range of areas that they choose to focus on (e.g., energy and water use, waste generation, transport, etc). Next, a series of meetings or group discussions are held to plan changes intended to reduce environmental impacts. A campaign is then run to encourage all employees to adopt pro-environmental behaviours before a second audit is performed to reveal any savings achieved. This chapter focuses on a single example of the EC programme as it played out in the head offices of a UK construction company called Burnetts between January and November 2007.

Burnetts recruited a team of 16 Champions (eight men and eight women, aged from mid-20s to late-50s, drawn from different departments around Burnetts and of differing degrees of seniority). The initial audit was conducted in January/February; planning meetings commenced in April; a campaign to engage all employees who used the head office site (n≈300) was conducted between May and September; and the second audit was conducted in October/November. During this time, I conducted an ethnography of the initiative involving nine months of participant observation around the office site involving participating in and observing all Champions meetings and related events and conducting 38 semi-structured interviews with the Champions and other employees identified as relevant to the programme or who had been targeted by it. The field diary (FD) and interview transcripts were initially analysed using a constructivist grounded theory method (Charmaz 2006), and during this process, several themes emerged that drew out the importance of a focus on the operation of power within EC. As a result, the data were subsequently re-analysed using governmentality as an analytic. While Foucault himself did not use ethnographic data or methods, Koopman and Matza note that, unlike his concepts, Foucaultian analytics 'are much more portable in their original form' (2013, p.825), meaning that, so long as care is taken, 'one can legitimately pick up Foucault's analytics and put them to work in ways that Foucault never could have anticipated' (2013, p.829). Tamboukou and Ball argue that ethnography is well-suited to Foucaultian analysis precisely because 'It focuses on the micro-operations of power, being sensitive to local struggles and the achievement of local solutions' (2003, p.4). This is how I have attempted to use the ethnographic data in this chapter, drawing on the interviews and observations as texts which describe the techniques and practices used in the EC initiative and how they were received around the site (cf. Fadyl and Nicholls, 2013).

The rest of this chapter develops this analysis by exploring: i) the forms of political rationality employed in the EC initiative, that appeared to change how the environment was represented and understood in relation to everyday working practices: ii) the governmental technologies, and specifically a disciplinary dispositive, that sought to integrate pro-environmental behaviours into previously unquestioned actions; and iii) the ways in which this particular and localised dispositive was variously accepted or gave rise to forms of counter-conduct among employees.

## Governing environmental behaviour

### Developing pro-environmental political rationalities

Miller and Rose define political rationalities as 'the particular technical discourses of writing, listing, numbering, and computing that render a realm into discourse as a knowable, calculable, and administrable object' (1990, p.5). Several such techniques were used in the EC initiative to make 'the environment' knowable, meaningful, and manageable in the context of working practices at Burnetts. First, as in all of GAP's programmes, an audit was conducted to identify the environmental impacts of existing working practices. The specific aim of the audits is to make the previously invisible impacts of everyday practices visible so that they may be addressed and acted upon. Thus, for three weeks, the Champions stayed late after work to sort and weigh the waste generated at the offices and to take energy meter readings. GAP then compiled these raw data to reveal that the site annually emitted 297 tonnes of carbon dioxide and produced 57.4 tonnes of solid waste.

These results were presented to the Champions at an early meeting. The Champions expressed shock and surprise at the scale of these previously invisible environmental impacts, but also a sense of motivation to take action on them. GAP include audits in all of their programmes as a means, albeit often quite crude, of problematising 'the environment', rendering it visible and thinkable to the Champions and all employees at Burnetts in a way it had not previously been. A point Clare communicated very clearly:

> When you actually did that audit and…when you saw everything that could be recycled and you had that little tiny bit left in the middle…, gobsmacked, you know, you're completely shocked by it. (Clare[2])

In interviews, several of the Champions also highlighted the importance of the 'objective' numbers the audit produced as offering 'verifiable facts and truths…not wish lists' (Graham). Numbers represented a form of discourse that was already highly valorised in the commercial setting and was therefore a powerful means of linking the audit results with existing political rationalities at the offices.

Whilst the audit results were significant for the Champions themselves, they still faced the challenge of spreading them more broadly across the head office site to connect them up with and question their colleagues' normal working practices. In his work on discipline (Foucault 1977), Foucault argues that new ways of thinking about and ordering space and time represent the bedrock for new kinds of power and control.

Through the EC initiative, the Champions attempted to introduce new spatialities and temporalities that served to highlight environmentally relevant features of office life and thus to spread pro-environmental political rationalities more widely. From the outset, for example, the EC initiative 'enclosed' (Foucault 1977, p.141) the head offices, separating them off from the rest of Burnetts's working practices, to which they were closely tied on a daily basis, in order to treat them as a 'test case' about which new knowledge could be developed. Further, having enclosed the head offices, the Champions set about 'partitioning' (Foucault 1977, p.143) the site, dividing it up into different sections to make it more manageable. Foucault argues that: 'disciplinary space tends to be divided into as many sections as there are bodies or elements to be distributed' (Foucault 1977, p.143). Accordingly, in the EC initiative, the head offices were first divided into different areas—corresponding either to parts of the building (e.g., 'Duplex First Floor') or to relatively self-contained departments (e.g., 'Design and Wages'), and each was assigned its own 'area mentor'. These areas were then further sub-divided into individual offices or, in open plan areas, individual 'bays'. Whilst these forms of partition pre-existed the EC initiative, the novel elements of the Champions' partitioning focussed on a very fine-grained level, by identifying the specific light switches, bins, plug sockets, printers, etc., that sat within the different parts of the office. As such, the Champions did not need to start from scratch in their partitioning, but rather worked within the already individualised spaces of the existing disciplinary grid at the head offices. Specifically, the Champions' new pro-environmental political rationalities needed only to emphasise the particular features of the offices that were deemed environmentally salient (such as light switches, bins, printers, etc.). Through this process of partitioning, the Champions thus sought to spatially disaggregate the 'environmental crisis' contained within the audit results around the head office site and represent it in ways that made sense to employees.

A similar process occurred with the re-programming of time around the offices, as the Champions divided up existing temporalities to highlight the moments of the working day or week that appeared most environmentally relevant. According to an environmental rationality, therefore, their attention was focussed especially on moments of entry and exit from the offices at the beginning and end of each day and at lunch times. These are the moments when lights and electrical equipment are switched on or off, and when things tend to be taken out to be used or tidied up and thrown away. One of the first things the team agreed upon was to produce a 'Shutdown Checklist' (FD:54 and see Figure 4.1) to detail exactly what steps should be taken when leaving the office to ensure everything was switched off. Further still, the initiative focussed on particular times of the week; for example, the Champions sent a series of emails to all staff late on Friday afternoons to remind them to switch equipment off over the weekend. The team thus focussed their efforts on specific times when they felt they could have most impact. Whilst these observations may seem insignificant, what is important is that, just as they had with space, the Champions were introducing new environmentally salient ways of thinking about and structuring the passing of time in the offices. Notably, these moments of entry to and exit from the offices were the precise moments of the working day that are typically the most informal, disorganised, and undisciplined (Nippert-Eng 1996). In other words, these are the times that tend to escape conventional forms of workplace discipline.

---

**Extract from an Email to all Staff – sent at 16:46 on a Friday Afternoon**

'Choosing to act positively, even in a small way, we can make a significant difference, together!

If you are leaving early or staying later, don't forget you do have time to switch off your.................
> PC
> Power transformer
> Docking Station
> Screen
> Plug (- sometimes easier to switch everything off at the wall)
> Gang socket (that little LED on the end uses about 0.3Watts)
> Phone Charger
> Printer
> Lights—if you're in a shared office, who is going to turn out the lights when you go?
> Is there a photocopier near you? Does that need to be left on? – one copier uses
> enough power when on standby at night to print one thousand five hundred copies!'

---

*Figure 4.1* Shutdown checklist.

In summary, whilst the audit process first rendered the environment visible, by re-thinking space and time around the offices, highlighting those aspects that are most environmentally relevant yet which conventionally escape workplace management and control, the Champions introduced specifically pro-environmental political rationalities into the offices at Burnetts. 'The environment' was thus translated from having been an invisible, confusing, and undifferentiated mass, into something that was both in crisis, and also intimately connected to parts of the head offices and to particular working practices. In this process, the environment was also individualised (Darier 1996a) by being made into something that each and every employee should be aware of, care about, and take action upon whilst at work. Of course, these new environmental political rationalities were not necessarily accepted and acted upon by all employees at the head office site. Rather, and as Section 4.3 develops, they became objects of debate and counter-conduct as at least some employees refused to adopt the new pro-environmental subject positions. Before this could happen, however, the Champions first had to employ a range of governmental technologies to spread their new pro-environmental rationalities and convert them into action.

### The governmental technologies of pro-environmental behaviour change

> If political rationalities render reality into the domain of thought… 'technologies of government' seek to translate thought into the domain of reality, and to establish 'in the world of persons and things' spaces and devices for acting upon those entities of which they dream and scheme (Miller and Rose 1990, p.8).

Having introduced a range of political rationalities that rendered the environment into the 'domain of thought', as the EC initiative proceeded, the Champions subsequently employed a number of subtle governmental technologies to try and make their colleagues internalise the new rationalities and begin to act upon them in their daily working practices. The techniques the Champions employed, as well as the ways in which they were discussed in interviews, closely followed the 'means of correct training' (Foucault 1977, pp.170-194) that Foucault identifies as central to disciplinary dispositives. Foucault himself identified three such technologies: *hierarchical observation*, in which new forms of surveillance observe conduct; *normalising judgement*, whereby a 'norm' is constructed amid a previously disordered mass, and judgements are made against it; and *the examination*, in which subjects are constantly tested and trained to measure up with the norm. All three of these governmental technologies were widely used in the EC initiative. This section will outline each in turn.

For Foucault, understanding the field of visibility—who or what gets seen and who casts the 'gaze' upon them—is a crucial mechanism of power. The EC initiative served to introduce a new form of *hierarchical observation* to the head offices that cast a gaze upon aspects of routine everyday practice that were deemed to be environmentally salient. Throughout the EC initiative there were countless examples of the Champions, as well as their colleagues, starting to look in new places and to see things in new ways. For example, throughout the audit process and in a series of lunchtime and after-work 'spot checks', the Champions cast a judgemental gaze over previously inconspicuous and normal activities. Employees started to notice lights being left on or waste in the wrong bin and think that it 'looks weird' (Sally). Further, colleagues began to put on performances of what might be called 'conspicuous environmentalism' to one another, showing off their environmental credentials when recycling, photocopying double-sided, or switching computers off (see Hargreaves 2016). Finally, in interviews, metaphors of visibility were regularly used to describe the EC initiative. For example, the language of 'big brother', being in 'glass houses', forms of 'monitoring', or having 'eyes and ears' were common, and would appear to indicate the nature of the new gaze being cast over everyday practices.

> It's like the big brother is watching you attitude. …You can't get away with things, it's like a police force (laughs). It sounds a bit harsh…but you have somebody monitoring you. (Graham)

> When you're in the public gaze then if you're not doing what you say then, you suffer accordingly…people in glass houses isn't it really. (David)

As these quotations indicate, hierarchical observation was one of the Champions' principle governmental technologies, and as employees began to perform to one another, watch over one another's behaviour, and impose the new gaze upon themselves, it became to some extent inescapable.

The gaze cast by the EC initiative also introduced a form of *normalising judgement* around the site. The concept of normalisation is central to Foucault's thinking about power (2007, p.44–7). Whilst Foucault distinguished between three types of normalisation (the legal norm, disciplinary normation, and the normalisation of security technology—Bröckling et al. 2011, p.5), in the EC initiative, disciplinary forms of normalisation were very apparent. Disciplinary normalisation develops a prescriptive norm that serves to set standards for conduct that people can then be judged against (useful/useless; normal/abnormal, etc.). By isolating a particular characteristic of individuals or their behaviour from the chaotic and unruly mass of bodies and activities, norms are created against which all can be judged. The novelty of disciplinary normalisation is that, rather than introducing an absolute sense of right (as with legal norms) or wrong behaviour, it produces a relative sense of rightness or wrongness. The EC initiative was filled with examples of normalising judgement, from GAP programme managers judging Burnetts's environmental performance against that of other companies, to employees judging their colleagues by whether or not they switched their computers off or printed double-sided. Here, I will highlight two linked forms of normalising judgement used by the Champions.

The first is a staff survey that the Champions devised and circulated to all of their colleagues at the beginning of the initiative. This posed a series of questions in which employees had to state whether they *Never, Hardly Ever, Sometimes, Usually,* or *Always* performed a series of pro-environmental acts at work, like recycling aluminium cans or re-using plastic cups. These kinds of scales and surveys are a common feature of environmental psychological work on pro-environmental behaviour and, whilst they might be seen as a neutral means of gathering data on an objective reality, they also play a more active and productive role in isolating the environmental aspects of behaviours and constructing them as something one should have an attitude about or act upon (Corral-Verdugo 1997). As Rose and Miller put it:

> making people write things down…is itself a kind of government of them, urging them to think about and note certain aspects of their activities according to certain norms. (1992, p.200)

By filling in the survey, therefore, employees were being asked to reflect upon and internalise environmental issues and to judge their own behaviour in relation to them.

The second example is the creation of a 'league table' in which different parts of the head office site were compared with one another against environmental criteria. Although the available data were never better than patchy—and thus the league table was never comprehensively produced—the basic principle of disciplinary normalisation is obvious. In an email sent by the Champions to all staff during the campaign (see Figure 4.2), this normalising intent was communicated widely. These messages thus allowed areas of the office such as the 'Duplex Building First Floor' and 'Design and Wages' to feel a sense of satisfaction that they were doing well, but also quietly warned them that lapses in performance would be noted. As such, this normalising judgement also served to reinforce the hierarchical observation introduced by the Champions, indicating to all employees that they might be being watched and judged at any time.

---

'There has been another audit of energy usage across the site at the end of last week…The audit was to see what percentage of electrical items had been left on after the working day and people had left the office.
The results were quite varied in different areas of the site. There was an outstanding performance from both the Duplex Building First Floor and Design & Wages with only 4 & 5% of items left switched on.
In other areas, there is probably room for improvement, with one area registering up to 48% of electrical items being left on—including a number of Air Conditioning units, which would have proceeded to cool down or heat up an empty office from Friday evening until Monday morning.'

---

*Figure 4.2* A pro-environmental league table.

Foucault's final means of correct training is *the examination,* which he situates 'at the heart' of procedures of discipline (Foucault 1977, p.184). The purpose of hierarchical observation and normalising judgement is to gather knowledge of individuals such that action can be taken in accordance with it. In the examination, these two mechanisms are combined. Again, the EC initiative provided numerous examples of examination, including not only the staff survey and audits as previously mentioned, but also extending to spot-checks and 'mentoring chats' around the offices. Further, these forms of examination became ever more constant as the initiative progressed such that, by the end of the initiative, interviewees, whether Champions of non-Champions, regularly stated that they frequently examined their own or their colleagues' conduct according to its environmental credentials.

A key aspect of such procedures of examination is to educate and train subjects so they internalise the new political rationalities, act upon them, and thus conform more closely to the new norm (Darier 1996a). As the following quotation illustrates, the Champions regularly and repeatedly examined their colleagues working practices, with just such training in mind:

> We're [the Champions] like little piranhas (laughs) at people's ankles. Don't give up. Erm and you don't shout and rage at them or anything like that to belittle them. They might do it to you initially, but it's not even a war of words, you can turn them around with words…You have a suspicion that as soon as you walk out the door they're just going to go back to normal, so you go back and repeat it the next day and the next day, and the next day, and the next day. It will get there in the end. They'll get the idea you are not going to go away. (Graham)

This emphasis on the constant repetition of messages was echoed by many of the Champions as part of a sense that the more often messages were repeated, the stronger they would become.

As with hierarchical observation and normalising judgement, the presence of forms of examination in the EC initiative is impossible to deny. The key aspect of the examination for Foucault, however, is its joining of the creation of knowledge with the application of power (1977, p.187). Whilst the level of documentation and administration falls short of the ideal examples Foucault found in French prisons, schools, and hospitals, through these various forms of examination, the Champions built up a corpus of knowledge about their colleagues, enabling them to determine who was performing well and who badly. This knowledge served to normalise employees, enabling judgements of them, and generating behavioural change to meet the new norm. In turn, as new behaviour occurred, new knowledge was gathered, new judgements could be made, and the norm became a moving, and environmentally improving, target.

The EC initiative thus involved a range of governmental technologies that had the character of a disciplinary dispositive. Through such practices, the Champions sought to 'make up' (Hacking 1986) their colleagues as environmental subjects or, perhaps more accurately, as 'environmental employees', "for whom the environment constitutes a critical domain of thought and action" (Agrawal 2005, p.16). Previous studies that have applied a governmentality framework to pro-environmental behaviour have stopped at this point. After considering the rationalities and technologies developed by programme administrators and managers, they have failed to go further and explore how these have operated on the ground in the context of the many other forms of governmentality that swirl around in everyday life (e.g., Darier 1996a; Slocum 2004; Rutland and Aylett 2008). The next section explores the extent to which the Champions' colleagues accepted the new subject positions being imposed upon them, the extent to which they came to apply the Champions' discipline to themselves, and, crucially, the ways in which they developed forms of counter-conduct that went against the Champions' new programme of government.

### Counter-conduct and the making up of environmental employees

At the end of the initiative, a second audit revealed it had achieved an annual 29% (3.4 tonnes) reduction in waste sent to landfill and a 5.4% reduction (6 tonnes) reduction in $CO_2$ emissions. These levels of savings are roughly average compared to what the EC programme achieves in other organisations (GAP 2006; Hargreaves et al. 2008) and are relatively successful in comparison to other pro-environmental behaviour change initiatives (e.g., Mckenzie-Mohr and Smith 1999; Barr 2008). Following Darier (1996a), however, I would argue that the success or failure of such initiatives should be judged not solely, or even predominantly, in terms of environmental indicators but also 'by the degree of willingness or resistance of the population to internalise environmental values and to self-adopt new environmental conducts' (Darier 1996a, pp.601–2). In this view, the real significance of the EC initiative lies not in its environmental effects, but in the way it sought to open up new spaces for the formation of environmental subjects or environmental employees. Against this criterion the EC initiative achieved mixed results. In some cases, environmental employees appeared to have been successfully made up. In others, however, the initiative faced forms of what Foucault termed 'counter-conduct', that is, the '[active] struggle against the processes implemented for conducted others' (2007, p.201).

The EC initiative was most successful with the Champions themselves who had, in the main, volunteered to take part out of a prior green commitment in their own personal lives. As the initiative progressed, however, several Champions described how it had made them perceive their working environment and working practices in new ways. David, for example, said the initiative had 'attuned' him to environmental 'best practice':

> I [recently] worked in [a different office] for a couple of weeks…and there's certainly huge scope there for a similar scheme…and having sort of become attuned to the best practice here, it was very noticeable working there. (David)

This kind of re-tuning was also exhibited in how the Champions spoke about their colleagues. Here, they began to identify different 'categories of people' according to their environmental credentials:

> We probably had about three categories of people and their response to the campaign. There were those who weren't interested, didn't think they could make a difference. There were those who were willing to come on board, yet there were also those who say 'well I already do this, I already do that.' I think the campaign's helped soften the people who weren't interested to start with. It's definitely brought on board the people who are willing to give it a go. But also its further improved those who did think they really were, erm, you know, doing great environmental things. (Louise)

These and many similar quotations thus suggest that the Champions appeared to have accepted and internalised the new political rationality to the extent that it had changed their perceptions of themselves, their colleagues, and their working practices.

Similar kinds of success, although less thoroughgoing, were found with other employees that the initiative targeted. Some became what David termed 'mini-Champions' and began to assist the Champions by enforcing the new pro-environmental dispositive in their own offices, if not more broadly around the whole head office site. Others, and this appeared true for the majority, saw the EC initiative as 'a good thing' but, when questioned further, saw it as a new set of rules—such as to recycle, switch lights off, or print double-sided—as part of being 'a good Burnetts person' (Lynn, non-Champion). For this group, however, this pro-environmentalism was not extended to other aspects of office practice beyond these rules. In short, for the majority, the new pro-environmental discipline was being followed, but they demonstrated relatively little interest in it and, as such, had not internalised it more broadly into their working or daily lives.

Whilst this relative success was achieved with the majority, the initiative was less successful with many and gave rise to several forms of counter-conduct. Several Champions complained that, despite the whole EC initiative being framed by the senior management team as an environmental-moral good, some very senior figures could simply escape the new disciplinary gaze:

> When we did the electrical audit, there's always one Director, and you couldn't find anything in his office that wasn't left on…The issue with that Tom is then who addresses that issue with that person? Very difficult. For us as Environmental Champions very difficult, because we carry no weight do we, in truth? (Craig)

Similarly, the Facilities Management team regularly rejected the Champions' proposals as contravening health and safety regulations or data protection laws and, as a result, managed to significantly weaken many of the Champions' proposals (Hargreaves 2011). As these examples show, when confronted by pre-existing and more formally established hierarchies and forms of power, the EC initiative could easily be made to look quite powerless.

Less senior figures, however, were forced to generate more creative forms of counter-conduct. In some cases, Champions reported having 'stand-up rows' (Clare) with colleagues who refused to behave pro-environmentally. Some employees invented different excuses for why the Champions' ideas were inappropriate: for example, that double-sided printing was a waste of time because people familiar with single-sided pages might not notice the rear side or, more cleverly, because no one reads more than one side of text anyway (FD:115). Many employees subtly struggled against the new forms of surveillance introduced by the Champions by teasing the Champions for acting as the 'Recycling' or 'Environment Police'. Finally, the least often expressed form of counter-conduct was to argue that pro-environmental behaviour change among individuals in Burnetts's offices was pointless and irrelevant whilst the company's construction sites and broader business model were left unaddressed (FD:79).

It is important to note, however, that none of these forms of counter-conduct rejected the Champions core message—actively reinforced by the senior management team—that action needed to be taken to address environmental problems. As such, they cannot be easily dismissed as ignorance of, confusion about, or apathy over environmental issues, as conventional psychological models of pro-environmental behaviour would suggest (cf. Harrison and Davies 1998). Instead, either they represented expressions of competing and better-established forms of workplace governmentality—such as the need for efficient working practices or healthy and safe offices—that the Champions' pro-environmental dispositive was perceived as challenging, or, in some cases, they represented attempts to challenge existing workplace governmentality more fundamentally by offering a different and more radical understanding of environmental problems as requiring broader structural change rather than small-scale behavioural changes among employees (Maniates 2002; Shove 2010).

In summary, as a governmental project seeking to make up environmental employees, the EC initiative had mixed results. In most cases it was relatively well-received; however, as the initiative progressed, and as different forms of counter-conduct were encountered, the Champions' pro-environmental dispositive was often made to look extremely weak in the face of pre-existing forms of workplace discipline.

## Conclusion: Is discipline a dirty word?

The central aim of this chapter was to explore the workings of power in pro-environmental behaviour change initiatives. To try and achieve this, the chapter applied Michel Foucault's analytic of governmentality to an ethnographic case study of the Environment Champions initiative as it operated in the head offices of a construction company called Burnetts. The chapter focusses on only a single case study and, whilst this has particular value as a rare exploration of a workplace behaviour change programme, any generalisations drawn from it should be made with considerable care. Indeed, it is perhaps preferable to recognise this case study as locally and historically specific and seek instead to develop and explore comparative cases in other settings as a means of learning more about the operation of power in pro-environmental behaviour change initiatives. Nonetheless, the evidence presented here has revealed a number of important and new insights about how this specific behaviour change intervention functioned. First, it showed how the EC initiative introduced a form of pro-environmental political rationality to Burnetts. Through a range of auditing, monitoring, and classificatory techniques the EC initiative served to construct an environmental crisis as emerging in and through working practices. In this way, the case study challenges the realist and rationalist aspects of much work on pro-environmental behaviour by demonstrating how environmental problems must be locally constructed and made sense of. Second, it showed how the EC initiative employed a range of disciplinary techniques or governmental technologies—such as surveillance, normalisation, and examination—in an attempt to spread the environmental rationalities around the offices. In this way, Champions' encouraged their colleagues to internalise a new form of environmental subjectivity—to make themselves up as environmental employees. Thus, the case study questioned the assumed linearity and voluntarism of pro-environmental behaviour change by understanding them as involving mechanisms of power. Third, and finally, the case study provides one of the first examples of attempts to explore the 'messy actualities' of pro-environmental behaviour change by revealing the various forms of counter-conduct the EC initiative generated. Understood using governmentality as an analytic, these active forms of counter-conduct appear not as examples of ignorance, confusion, or apathy—the product of faulty decision-making as conventional psychological understandings would have it. Rather, they were seen to result either from the strength of other, more powerful dispositives already in play at Burnetts, or from cracks in the Champions' pro-environmental dispositive that may enable alternative environmental understandings and forms of pro-environmental change to emerge.

By attending to these mechanisms of governmentality, this chapter has shown that despite the emphasis being placed on their 'non-coercive' (Dolan et al. 2010, p.8) aspects, sustainable and pro-environmental behaviour change initiatives are in fact a long way from being voluntarist measures. Instead, they are perhaps better understood and analysed as attempts at new kinds of social control. As Dryzek and Dunleavy argue, they represent:

> a form of discipline…that deflects attention away from the structural causes of environmental decay…So what looks like a benign and rational individual and community response to environmental crisis is in fact a form of social control. (2009, p.292)

Seen in this light, a range of different questions must be asked of attempts to bring about more sustainable patterns of consumption by changing people's behaviour. At Burnetts, a disciplinary dispositive was introduced—one that, in the main, meshed well with existing disciplinary understandings and techniques around the workplace. In other settings—such as homes or spaces of leisure, for example—one might expect quite different kinds of governmental rationality and technology, or what 'modalities' of power (Foucault 2007, p.5) to circulate and take hold. The key question for the environmental social sciences, therefore, is not merely how to improve such techniques or how to 'work within' (Barr 2008, p.261) the existing system to make it more sustainable, but rather how to generate a wider appreciation of the different kinds of pro-environmental dispositive in circulation, and to open up broader societal debate about their desirability. In short, it should ask whether discipline (or any other modality of power) is a dirty word or if, instead, it may be precisely the kind of restraint required to check the worst excesses of consumer capitalism. (Princen 1997)

These new questions for environmental social science thus open up some potentially promising directions for further research. First, there is a need to re-evaluate forms of pro-environmental behaviour change and other forms of sustainable consumption initiative as attempts to change patterns and distributions of social control and to introduce new governmental rationalities and technologies of power into everyday life. This is precisely the kind of challenge that this collection is attempting to begin, and there are other promising signs of just such an agenda beginning to emerge (e.g., Webb 2012; Jones et al. 2013; Bulkeley et al. 2015; Dilley 2015). Second, and as part of this agenda, a core contribution of this chapter has been to try and go beyond merely analysing governmental plans and programmes to explore how they play out on the ground as well. In doing so, the chapter has drawn attention to the different forms of counter-conduct that they can and will provoke. Taking this seriously suggests that what have previously been understood as the failings and poor results of sustainable consumption or pro-environmental behaviour change initiatives might be productively reconceptualised as sources of counter-conduct. Such a reconceptualisation would open a much broader set of questions about how to bring about sustainable consumption, not least by encouraging researchers to see counter-conduct as having the potential to open up cracks or expose some of the 'tension points' in the dispositives of contemporary capitalism. (Flyvbjerg et al. 2012, p.290)

Finally, for practitioners seeking to bring about more sustainable patterns of consumption, on a rather crude instrumental level, the evidence presented here suggests that practitioners could make use of understandings of governmental rationality and technology in order to develop more effective behaviour change initiatives. Where disciplinary techniques reveal the potential value of surveillance, normalization, and examination, for example, writings on governmentality suggest a vast swath of potential technologies of governance that could be made use of—such as around forms of confession (Foucault 1988) or the use of ideas around freedom and community (Rose 1999). Crucially, however, if practitioners were to make use of such techniques, this must only be done in full recognition that these are attempts to intervene in the workings of power. These approaches must therefore be addressed as attempts at social control that will give rise to forms of counter-conduct. Such a recognition would demand that, prior to their wide circulation, practitioners actively set up and engage in debate about the ends to which such mechanisms might be put. In other words, when recognised as attempts at social control, efforts to bring about pro-environmental behaviour change or to promote sustainable consumption must begin by confronting bigger questions around which trajectories towards sustainability society might wish to pursue and who wins and who loses in the process of getting there. (Flyvbjerg 2001).

## Acknowledgements

This research was conducted as part of my PhD thesis funded by the Economic and Social Research Council (PTA-031-2004-00291). I am also grateful to the ESRC for funding a postdoctoral research fellowship that has enabled me to publish this research more widely (PTA-026-27-2086) and to two anonymous reviewers for helpful comments on an earlier draft.

## Notes

1. To preserve anonymity, the names of the company and of all participants have been changed.
2. All quotations are drawn from members of the Champions team unless otherwise stated.

## References

Agrawal, A. (2005). *Environmentality: Technologies of government and the making of subjects.* Durham and London: Duke University Press.

Barr, S. (2008). *Environment and Society: Sustainability policy and the citizen.* Aldershot: Ashgate.

Bröckling, U., Krasmann, S., & Lemke, T. (2011). 'From Foucault's lectures at the Collège de France to studies of governmentality: An introduction' in Bröckling, U., Krasmann, S., & Lemke, T. (eds.) *Governmentality: Current Issues and Future Challenges.* New York and London: Routledge, pp.1–33.

Bulkeley, H., Powells, G., & Bell, S. (2015). 'Smart grids and the constitution of solar electricity conduct', *Environment and Planning A*, 48(1), pp.7–23.

Charmaz, K. (2006). *Constructing grounded theory: A practical guide through qualitative analysis.* London: SAGE Publications.

Corral-Verdugo, V. (1997). 'Dual 'realities' of conservation behavior: Self-reports vs observations of re-use and recycling behavior', *Journal of Environmental Psychology*, 17, pp.135–145.

Darier, E. (1996a). 'Environmental governmentality: The case of Canada's green plan', *Environmental Politics*, 5, pp.585–606.

Darier, E. (1996b). 'The politics and power effects of garbage recycling in Halifax Canada', *Local Environment*, 1, pp.63–86.

Dean, M. (2010). *Governmentality: Power and rule in modern society.* 2nd edition. London: SAGE Publications.

DEFRA. (2008). *A Framework for pro-environmental behaviours.* London: DEFRA.

DEMOS. (2003). *Carrots sticks and sermons: Influencing public behaviour for environmental goals*. London: DEMOS/Green Alliance report produced for DEFRA.

Dilley, L.T.M. (2015). 'Governing our choices: "Proenvironmental behaviour" as a practice of government', *Environment and Planning C*, 33(2), pp.272–299.

Dolan, P., Halpern, D., Hallsworth, K., King, D., &Vlaev, I. (2010). *MINDSPACE: Influencing behaviour through public policy*. London: The Institute for Government for the Cabinet Office.

Dryzek, J. S., & Dunleavy, P. (2009). *Theories of the democratic state*. Basingstoke: Palgrave Macmillan.

Fadyl, J.K., & Nicholls, D.A. (2013). 'Foucault, the subject and the research interview: A critique of methods' *Nursing Inquiry*, 20(1), pp.23–29.

Flyvbjerg, B. (2001). *Making social science matter: Why social inquiry fails and how it can succeed again*. Cambridge: Cambridge University Press.

Flyvbjerg, B., Landman, T., & Schram, S.F. (2012). 'Important next steps in phronetic social science' in Flyvbjerg, B., Landman, T., & Schram, S.F. (eds.) *Real Social Science: Applied Phronesis*. Cambridge: Cambridge University Press, pp.285–297.

Foucault, M. (1977). *Discipline and punish: The birth of the prison*. London: Penguin.

Foucault, M. (1988). 'Technologies of the Self' in L.H. Martin, H. Gutman & P.H. Hutton (eds.) *Technologies of the Self: A Seminar with Michel Foucault*. The University of Massachusetts Press, pp.16–49.

Foucault, M. (2007). *Security, territory, populations: Lectures at the Collège de France 1977-1978* (Trans. Burchell, G.). Basingstoke: Palgrave Macmillan.

GAP. (2006). *Changing environmental behaviour: A review of the evidence for behaviour change from global action plan*. London: Global Action Plan.

Hacking, I. (1986). 'Making Up People' in Heller, T.C., Sosna, M., & Wellbery, D. (eds.) *Reconstructing Individual-ism: Autonomy, Individuality, and the Self in Western Thought*. Stanford, California: Stanford University Press, pp.222–36.

Hargreaves, T. (2011). 'Practice-ing behaviour change: Applying social practice theory to pro-environmental behaviour change', *Journal of Consumer Culture*, 11(1), pp.79–99.

Hargreaves, T. (2014). 'Smart Meters and the Governance of Energy Use in the Household' in Stripple, J., & Bulkeley, H. (eds.) *Governing the Global Climate: New approaches to rationality, power and politics*. Cambridge: Cambridge University Press, pp.127–143.

Hargreaves, T. (2016). 'Interacting for the Environment: Engaging goffman in pro-environmental action', *Society and Natural Resources*, 29, pp.53–67.

Hargreaves, T., Nye, M., & Burgess, J. (2008). 'Social experiments in sustainable consumption: An evidence based approach with potential for engaging low income communities', *Local Environment*, 13, pp.743–758.

Harrison, C. M., & Davies, G. (1998). *Lifestyles and the environment: Environment and sustainability desk study prepared for the ESRCs environment and sustainability programme*, London: Environment and Society Research Unit, UCL.

Hobson, K. (2002). 'Competing discourses of sustainable consumption: Does the 'rationalisation of lifestyles' make sense?', *Environmental Politics*, 11, pp.95–120.

Jackson, T. (2005). *Motivating sustainable consumption: A report to the sustainable development research network as part of the ESRC sustainable technologies programme*. Guildford: Centre for Environmental Strategy University of Surrey.

Jones, R., Pykett, J., & Whitehead, M. (2013). *Changing behaviours: On the rise of the psychological state*. Cheltenham: Edward Elgar.

Koopman, C., & Matza, T. (2013). 'Putting Foucault to work: Analytic and concept in Foucaultian inquiry', *Critical Inquiry*, 39(4), pp.817–840.

Maniates, M. (2002). 'Individualization: Plant a tree buy a bike save the world?' in Princen, T., Maniates, M., and Conca, K., (eds) *Confronting Consumption Cambridge*. Cambridge, Massachusetts: The MIT Press, pp.43–66.

Maniates, M. (2014). 'Sustainable consumption - Three paradoxes', *Gaia*, 23, pp.201–208.

Mckenzie-Mohr, D., & Smith, W. (1999). *Fostering sustainable behavior: An introduction to community-based social marketing*. 2nd Edition. New Society: Gabriola Island British Columbia.

Miller, P., & Rose, N. (1990). 'Governing Economic Life', *Economy and Society*, 19, pp.1–31.

Miller, P., & Rose, N. (2008). *Governing the present: Administering economic social and personal life*. Cambridge: Polity Press.

Nippert-Eng, C.E. (1996). *Home and work: Negotiating boundaries through everyday life*. Chicago and London: University of Chicago Press.

O'Malley, P., Weir, L., & Shearing, C. (1997). 'Governmentality criticism politics', *Economy and Society*, 26, pp.501–517.

Paterson, M., & Stripple, J. (2010). 'My space: Governing individuals' carbon emissions', *Environment and Planning D*, 28, pp.341–362.

Princen, T. (1997). 'Toward a theory of restraint', *Population and Environment*, 18, pp.233–254.

Raffnsøe, S., Gudmand-Høyer, M., & Thaning, M.S. (2016). 'Foucault's dispositive: The perspicacity of dispositive analytics in organizational research', *Organization*, 23(2), pp.272–298.

Rose, N. (1993). 'Government authority and expertise in advanced liberalism', *Economy and Society*, 22, pp.283–299.

Rose, N. (1999). *Powers of freedom: Re-framing political thought*. Cambridge: Cambridge University Press.

Rose, N., & Miller, P. (1992). 'Political power beyond the state: Problematics of government', *The British Journal of Sociology*, 43, pp.173–205.

Rouse, J. (2005). 'Power/Knowledge' in Gutting, G. (ed.) *The Cambridge Companion to Foucault*. 2nd Edition. Cambridge: Cambridge University Press, pp.95–122.

Rutland, T., & Aylett, A. (2008). 'The work of policy: Actor networks governmentality and local action on climate change in Portland Oregon', *Environment and Planning D*, 26, pp.627–646.

Shove, E. (2010). 'Beyond the ABC: Climate change policy and theories of social change', *Environment and Planning A*, 42, pp.1273–1285.

Shwom, R., & Lorenzen, J.A. (2012). 'Changing household consumption to address climate change: Social scientific insights and challenges', *WIREs Climate Change*, 3, pp.379–395.

Slocum, R. (2004). 'Consumer citizens and the cities for climate protection programme', *Environment and Planning A*, 36, pp.763–782.

Staats, H., Harland, P., & Wilke, H. (2004). 'Effecting durable change: A team approach to improve environmental behavior in the household', *Environment and Behavior*, 36, pp.341–367.

Tamboukou, M., & Ball, S. (2003). 'Introduction. Genealogy and Ethnography: Fruitful Encounters or Dangerous Liaisons?' in Tamboukou, M., & Ball, S. (eds.) *Dangerous Encounters: Genealogy and Ethnography*. New York: Peter Lang, pp.1–36.

Webb, J. (2012). 'Climate change and society: The chimera of behaviour change technologies', *Sociology*, 46(1), pp.109–125.

# 5 Freedom, autonomy, and sustainable behaviours: The politics of designing consumer choice

*Tobias Gumbert*

## Introduction: Designing consumer choice for the environmental challenges ahead

In current governance schemes to "green" societies in Europe and the US, nudging citizens to consume more sustainably is seen as a promising, for some even one of the most crucial undertakings to get there. Nudges refer to policy design that does not restrict individual choice but attempts to point individuals in the "right" direction, as defined by the initiator of a policy, or "choice architect," an individual or collective actor who limits or provides support for particular choice sets.[1] The most prominent examples of nudges that have proven to be more effective than "simple regulation" come from the public health (smoking, alcohol intake, diets, physical activity, organ donation) and public finances sectors (tax compliance, submitting tax declarations) (Rainford and Tinkler 2011).[2] By now, the idea of nudging has been extended to the field of sustainable consumption where it attracted a lot of attention. Discussing nudging as a tool for "greening" consumption and leading to more sustainable lifestyles and necessary behavioral changes, it has been applied to various consumption-relevant domains such as household energy use, personal transport, food consumption, recycling behavior, and household waste production (Mont et al. 2014, Milford et al. 2015).

The utility of choice editing for policy practices in the field of sustainable consumption seems obvious: pure market solutions run the risk of being unsustainable and potentially decrease the wellbeing of present and future generations, while bans and stricter legislative rules might not only constitute a strong interference in individual liberty but also hinder economic growth. Subtle forms of influencing human decision-making could have important consequences for the environment in this respect, and this belief is anchored clearly through the increased focus on the actions of private households and the responsibilities of individual citizens to prevent ecological damage (Ölander and Thogersen 2014, p. 341). This rationale has been labelled the "consumer-citizen" construct, "an individual who simultaneously exercises the choices and freedoms bestowed by a neo-liberal economic model, but does so in a way that is socially, economically, and environmentally responsible" (Barr 2015, p. 93). Thus, nudging represents an attempt to reconcile freedoms associated with liberal democracy with long-term environmental sustainability goals. Put a little differently, the rise of nudging within governing consumption can be ascribed to the firm belief in three overriding principles: that consumers must have freedom of choice, that producers must have freedom from regulation, and that the environment must be preserved in order to preserve those exact freedoms.

For practitioners, this raises first and foremost the question of how to implement such strategies, yet the question is not merely one of choosing an adequate instrument, but rather one of understanding the broader social and political context in which nudge strategies function and the ideas that inform them. The theoretical ideas behind nudging draw from behavioral economics and psychology "to explain why people behave in ways that deviate from rationality as defined by classical economics" (Marteau et al. 2011, p. 228). While marketers and advertisers have used psychological insights for a long time, the same insights are now propagated as being an opportunity to be used by governments to address a host of interrelated issues, including handling environmental problems and increasing consumers' wellbeing. These approaches start from the belief that humans have "bounded rationality," the idea that rational individual decision-making is limited by cognitive, information, and time constraints, which is the reason why individuals are continuously making biased decisions that run counter to their best interests. The politico-philosophical underpinnings have become known as libertarian paternalism: it is legitimate for governments to design the context of individual decision, to practice "choice architecture," to mold the environment of choices in order to help people to maximize their own wellbeing.

What is often overlooked in this regard are the possible political side effects of choice architecture. While established lines of critique either assert that nudging is too paternalistic and restrictive on individual liberty or emphasize the potential for manipulation of citizens' interests and the threat to personal autonomy, the perspective of governmentality taken up in this article extends this literature in important aspects. Governmentality scholars assume that in "contemporary environmental governance, the state is not governing less, but differently through new agent categories and indirect means of regulation and action" (Lövbrand and Stripple 2013, p. 118). It takes a more detailed look at the operating rationality of the state in policy-making and governing consumer conduct, and it looks at the effects of nudging on the level of the subject, how subjectivity is formed and acted upon through political techniques and discourses. This has important implications for the ethics involved in choice editing and the responsibility of so-called choice architects.

This article makes the central argument that in order to design effective nudge strategies in the context of sustainable consumption governance, we need to take these critiques into account. The result is a revised ethics of responsibility that does not reduce consumer-citizens to means fostering sustainable ends, but aims to empower their position in consumption-related everyday matters without condemning choice editing per se. Methodologically, in evaluating choice editing as a tool for governing sustainable consumption, political theory is here understood to contribute in three meaningful ways: first, through conceptualization, it helps to systematize arguments made for and against choice editing, distinguishes between normative and descriptive elements, and reflects upon which idea of the political is implied. Secondly, through the function of critique, internal tensions between norms and practices of choice editing can be problematized in order to question its targets and goals. Lastly, political theory can help to devise principles to inform collectively binding decisions that can be justified on the basis of shared values and political relevance. This has important implications for a political ethics of choice editing.

This article's overall contribution can be summarized as (i) making a theoretical contribution to the debate by using governmentality scholarship to highlight choice editing as a modern exercise of political power; (ii) reflecting on the attempt to improve sustainable consumption through behavioral economics by analyzing the reconstitution of the state-citizen relationship in environmental politics; and, (iii) delineating possible safeguards against misusing nudges by drawing on the ethics involved. First, the paper looks at how choice editing has been discussed in the context of sustainable consumption. Secondly, it refers to broader discussions to identify which notions of the nudge approach have been underrepresented in the debate and introduces the governmentality approach to map the broader political implications of upscaling choice editing. Proceeding from this theoretical overview, the paper exhibits a short illustration of how libertarian paternalism is increasingly informing policy practice on regulating consumer food waste, before it concludes with an assessment of critical issues choice architects need to think about when steering consumption through molding choice environments.

## Choice editing and sustainable consumption

Within the sustainable consumption literature, we find various authors arguing for as well as against choice editing. Proponents of the nudge approach argue that, since "consumers can be greatly affected by apparently modest and inconsequential aspects of the social environment[,] [s]mall changes in that environment may have a large impact on consumer behavior, potentially even larger than that of economic incentives" (Sunstein 2013, p. 2). Small changes are, for example, "green defaults," environmentally friendly settings that apply "when individuals do not take active steps to change them" (Sunstein and Reisch 2013, p. 4). Such defaults may have major impacts on environmental effects similar to mandates and bans (even larger impacts than information, education, or economic incentives), and yet they respect freedom of choice and heterogeneity within society (ibid.: 5). However, encouraging active consumer choices is equally important, especially when public officials lack relevant information (which might result in inadequate default rules), or if groups are relatively diverse (so that single measures might lead to contradictory effects) (Carroll et al. 2009, Sunstein 2013). Combining behavioral tools (such as social norms to stimulate decreases in consumption) with traditional tools (such as economic incentives) promises therefore to be more effective (in motivating long-term changes towards sustainability) than standard environmental policy-making (EC 2016). Even more importantly, by helping consumers to realize their "true preferences" through correcting behavioral biases, the over-all welfare of societies is being maximized.

Critiques most often center around the notion of the "individualization" of consumption and the concealment of business interests. Along this reasoning, policy initiatives designed to nudge consumers mainly target the general population as a set of individual consumers and treat consumption as an economic activity to satisfy basic human needs. By evoking ethical and moral consumption choices through market interactions, responsibility and other forms of voluntary action are individualized and structural constraints are mystified (Goodman 2004, Brooks and Bryant 2014, Maniates 2014). The proposed consumption practices (or "altered choice environments") thus often reflect "the business models and ethos of the mainstream corporate world [...] [and thus] erode support for more radical forms of environmental political action" (Brooks and Bryant 2014, p. 79). It is claimed that there is an unavoidable coercive element to choice editing, since it is an exercise of power (Maniates 2010), for example, in the case of creating the illusion of expanding choice when it is in fact being narrowed. Choice architects are therefore described as being often those whose choice editing is largely oppositional to notions of a good life rooted in sufficiency, product resilience, work-life balance, and simplicity.

From this very short (and necessarily incomplete) sketch of the debate, we see two major points of contention arise: (i) whose interests are reflected and who may legitimately be involved (consumers realizing their true preferences or elites realizing their interests through steering consumer conduct)? And more indirectly: (ii) how does nudging impact the possibility for collective action (does it improve or hinder it, given the tendency to individualize sustainable consumption)? At the heart of these controversies, we find different normative assumptions about the role of the political and how to achieve sustainable transitions (choice editing as a legitimate political or anti-political project), and, equally important, discussions about the exercise of power in society (choice editing as a legitimate democratic or anti-democratic project) (Hall 2016).

The preliminary discussion suggests to either engage in practicing the nudge approach or to avoid it altogether. A middle ground seems hardly possible. A look into how libertarian paternalism has been discussed in political philosophy helps to differentiate the above positions and to get a clearer picture of the possible ramifications.

## The rationality of nudging as a policy practice

According to the original thinkers of the nudge idea, Thaler and Sunstein, a nudge "is any aspect of the choice architecture that alters people's behavior in a predictable way without forbidding any options or significantly changing their economic incentives. To count as a mere nudge, the intervention must be cheap to avoid." (2008, p. 6). The politico-philosophical underpinnings of nudging have been termed by the authors "libertarian paternalism," since the idea embraces first and foremost freedom of choice, hence "libertarian," leaving individuals with the same freedom of choice they would have had without their choice environment being altered. A policy is understood as being paternalistic "if it is selected with the goal of influencing the choices of affected parties in a way that will make those parties better off" (Thaler and Sunstein 2003, p. 175). The form of intervention is therefore also described as "soft paternalism," as giving people soft nudges into the "right" direction (of adopting specific behavioral patterns); a direction that will ultimately benefit them, with or without them realizing it. Such behavioral change is said to be beneficial from a policy-maker's viewpoint as well as from the perspective of individuals, simultaneously enhancing individual wellbeing and social welfare.

Libertarian paternalists argue that this non-coercive force of paternalism is desirable because people tend to make irrational choices that decrease their own wellbeing. If libertarian paternalism is the politico-philosophical program of choice editing, behavioral economics—the application of psychological insights into human behavior to explain economic decision-making—is its modus operandi (see Table 5.1). Using the language of behavioral economics, Thaler and Sunstein distinguish between "Humans"—beings with limited rationality who display self-control problems and altruistic behaviors—and "Econs"—completely rational and egoistic beings, capable of having "complete information, unlimited cognitive abilities, and complete self-control" (Thaler and Sunstein 2008, p. 6). In this line of thought, a number of effects prevent people from making right decisions (e.g., framing effects lead to inconsistent choices, loss aversion leads to very stable, often irrational preferences, etc.) (Thaler and Sunstein 2008). In other words, "Humans" suffer from systemic biases that lead to limited awareness, limited information-processing capacity, and limited self-control. Nudging is described as being a technique that helps to overcome the hiatus between irrational and rational behaviors: "Humans" should be pushed to develop normative desirable behaviors, which will lead in turn to a maximization of their wellbeing, that is, to develop traits of "Econs." Nudging can be employed to either reduce, neutralize, or even use (or "exploit") these systemic biases for policy-making. Thaler and Sunstein describe choice architects as persons who indirectly influence the choices other people make. The authors stress the point that there is "no such thing as a 'neutral' design" (ibid., p. 3), but that many

*Table 5.1* The nudge approach: Overview of connected terms

| | |
|---|---|
| NUDGING | Simplified description of instrumental strategy— Guiding people to alter behavioral biases |
| CHOICE EDITING | Core idea of how nudging works— Editing individual choices |
| CHOICE ARCHITECTURE | Specification of what is being altered— The choice environment is specifically designed |
| LIBERTARIAN (SOFT) PATERNALISM | The politico-philosophical program— Reasoning for applying nudging |
| BEHAVIORAL ECONOMICS | Modus operandi— The method by which nudging is applied |

Source: Own representation

people are nevertheless obligated to design environments in specific ways (such as arranging food in a cafeteria). When faced with a range of design choices, it is best for choice architects to try to conform to the "true preferences" of people, and since they can hardly ever be known, try to make them "best off, all things considered" (ibid.). To that end, choice architecture relies on different instruments to induce desired outcomes: providing feedback (additional information helps "Humans" to make better decisions); providing mappings (structuring information plans); structuring complex choices (to develop simplifying strategies); giving incentives, etc. In short, these policy options stress the importance of information and salience in order to nudge people effectively. Libertarian paternalism's explicit focus is therefore to overcome (or sometimes use) informational deficits to rationalize consumer behavior.

By addressing individual behavior through choice editing on a micro level, policies are aiming to achieve aggregate positive effects on a macro level, in the case of sustainable consumption the 'greening' of societies. However, alleged winwin strategies are not without costs. The nudge approach can be problematized on both micro and macro levels of analysis. The governmentality approach is a useful framework to scrutinize mechanisms at work on both ends, while being able to draw from already established lines of critique within political philosophy and the social sciences.

## Nudging seen through a governmentality lens

The notion of governmentality is useful, especially in its "environmental or green articulations, for addressing political questions about the conduct of conduct by individuals and groups in their interactions with the environment, society, and themselves" (Luke 2016, p. 461). Michel Foucault developed the concept as a modern manifestation of political power in the context of his lectures at the Collège the France in the late-1970s, explicitly deriving it from a genealogy of liberalism and the development of political economy in Western Europe. Foucault's focus was "less on the formal laws and institutions of the modern state than the technologies of power that shaped, directed and regulated individuals' beliefs, desires, lifestyles and actions" (Bevir 2011, p. 461). Governmentality describes essentially a rationality of governing populations, a dominant principle which structures various aspects of actual governance. As a form of meta-governance, Foucault's explanation of the functioning of governmentality as "conducting the conduct" of others (Foucault 2008, p. 186) emphasizes governance as a form of steering conduct and implementing goals and preferences within the common sense of the governed which presents itself as natural and self-evident. The governed are led to believe to share certain hegemonic preferences and desires and are thereby encouraged to act 'voluntarily' on this fabricated common sense. To govern is thus to "shape the field of possible actions of others" (Foucault 1982, p. 221). Through this inscription of dominant rationalities on the level of the subject, alternative possibilities are foreclosed. This 'voluntary acting' is described by Foucault as a technology of the self: individuals are led to govern their own conduct and discipline their own behavior in order to conform to certain norms and desired effects.

Thaler and Sunstein are, just as many other economists, critical of command-and-control regulation. For instance, to improve sustainable mobility, they suggest the use of fuel economy stickers (as introduced by the US Environmental Protection Agency) on the back of cars but opt for the information to be translated from mileage data into dollars to create a standard by which everyone's behavior can be compared and judged (Thaler and Sunstein 2008, p. 203-5). While people are able to signal their green credentials to all around them, this "friendly competition" (ibid., p. 207) removes the steering agent from sight who ipso facto acts at-a-distance. Power is here "not so much a matter of imposing constraints upon citizens as of 'making up' citizens capable of bearing a kind of regulated freedom. Personal autonomy is not the antithesis of political power, but a key term in its exercise" (Rose and Miller 1992, p. 174). The role of freedom and autonomy for the exercise of this modern form of power indicates the centrality of subjectivity and processes of subjectification within Foucauldian research methodologies. A specific question for Foucault was how "conceptions of the human being that are held in particular times (as citizen, schoolchild, customer, worker, manager [, consumer]) […] are problematized and how interventions are devised" (Lövbrand and Stripple 2013, p. 112). Problematizations are a key starting point for investigations into the technologies of government (Dean 1999), as they are a result of particular forms of knowledge and expertise that distinguish between 'right' and 'wrong' forms of conduct at a given time and normalize (or naturalize) them.

Green nudging denotes a certain technique of governing the population in relation to the environment through mobilizing interior processes of the subject towards pre-defined ends. It has therefore also been called "psychological self-governance" (Jones et al. 2013a, 2013b). The politics of nudging establishes behavioral anomalies as a field for intervention that needs to be accessed in order to steer effectively. Rationalization of consumer conduct does not appeal to reason, but instead aims to correct deficiencies, improving the suitability of individuals, and subjects them to the requirements of expert knowledge in the fields of health promotion, retirement planning, or resource-saving behaviors. Let us look in turn at how choice editing can be scrutinized at micro and macro levels of analysis.

## The micro level: Limiting autonomy and deliberation

With regard to autonomy, a governmentality perspective can benefit from already established critiques by libertarian and deliberational (or republican) authors. Since nudges may carry a clear and subjective opinion regarding certain questions (how money should be invested; how much food is to be consumed; etc.), for some authors this kind of influence can be referred to as manipulation, as a technique that "perverts the way [a] person reaches decisions, forms preferences or adopts goals" (Wilkinson 2013, p. 344). A manipulation is seen in this regard as an intervention that involves an intentional actor that causes or encourages an alteration within a person's autonomous decision-making. However, there is such a thing as a "genuine escape clause," "if the nudger sincerely wants the targets not to act in the nudged way if the nudging is unsuitable for them" (ibid., p. 354). This raises the question of nudges interfering with a person's autonomy in a broader sense. For Hausman and Welch, conveying information subliminally and not by rational means qualifies as diminishing autonomy (Hausman and Welch 2010, p. 128). This leads to a state of not fully being in control of one's own actions (Bovens 2009, p. 4). For example, simplifying consumer information is hardly only aiming to rationalize conduct, but plays on emotions and uses social norms strategically, through negative ("smoking hurts those you love") or positive framing ("the probiotics in this yogurt increase your health"). They pre-script and prescribe a reality of moral rights and wrongs, and even if consumers can, in principal, choose to not buy a certain product, choices are made that do not necessarily result from an autonomous decision, but rather conform to implicit external expectations. Ultimately, such non-autonomous preferences may result in an incoherent preference structure or a "fragmented self," leaving people "incapable of taking their lives in their own hands" (ibid., p. 14). Goodwin (2012) is also less positive in his normative evaluation and denies the nudge concept its liberty-preserving character since its conception of liberty is not coupled with individual independence and self-fulfillment and therefore "precludes it from being empowering in any substantive sense" (p. 90).

As for libertarians, other authors also argue that such an environment entails, if taken to its final conclusion, the ruling out of making mistakes (because choices are pre-structured), thus depriving the subject of the possibility to engage in deliberation or developing the capacity for judgment. Deliberative authors therefore reimagine the nudge strategy as a "think strategy" (John et al. 2009, 2011). They assert that given enough time, information, and an appropriate environment, citizens may come to optimal judgments for themselves and others. Citizen assemblies can constitute such a space (among many other formats) to exchange views and experiences that help citizens to reflect on personal needs and their embeddedness in larger social contexts. Empowering citizens is therefore at the heart of the "think strategy," focusing on the process of decision-making and how preferences are shaped therein instead of trying to reveal pre-existent preferences. The core idea is that "democratic deliberation has the capacity to lessen the problem of bounded rationality" (John et al. 2009, p. 13).

These critiques remind us that we should not understand nudging as a technique that would simply reveal "true" consumer preferences when choice architecture has the effect to pre-structure choice sets, thereby creating subjects that fit the desired form of political regulation. In the same vein, there is ample reason to believe that choice editing does not automatically result in citizens acting together to further environmental goals when the larger picture is not available to them. These possible effects on autonomy and the potential for deliberation are deeply connected to political rationalities that enable and legitimate policy interventions on the macro level.

## The macro level: Responsibilization and economization

The political rationality of governmentality as "the condition of possibility and legitimacy of its instruments, the field of normative reason from which governing is forged" (ibid., p. 115) leads subjects to become responsible self-entrepreneurs in line with the morality of the state and the health of the economy, producing green or sustainable citizenship and "civic subjectivities [that] are positioned in dense networks of expert discourse and technical structure such that power and personhood co-evolve" (Luke 2016, p. 462). New forms of governance and their tools and instruments to achieve "green" ends are less concerned with deliberation and justice and more with problem solving and program implementation, benchmarking, and best practices. The contents of governance programs and best practices are increasingly related to consumption, responsible choices, and lifestyle instead of obligations, duties, and solidarity (Soneryd and Uggla 2015, p. 917). From a governmentality perspective, these processes are a slow transformation and normalization of what it means to do politics in the neoliberal age.

Two tendencies of normalization that can be observed in late modernity are especially relevant to understand how the political rationality of governmentality functions: the individualization of societal risks as the growing responsibility of individuals (e.g., for environmental consequences), and the economization of the society as the diffusion of economic criteria into almost every societal sphere. For Wendy Brown, the transformation of liberal governmentality into neoliberal governmentality (the exact features of which Foucault could not have anticipated in the 1980s) is marked by the intensification of the market as a site of "veridiction," as a regime of truth production (the state's legitimacy is linked to the growth of the economy), the replacement of labor through human capital (market actors are rendered as capital rather than workers or consumers), and the replacement of production with entrepreneurship (productivity and enterprise are prioritized over product and consumption) (Brown 2015, p. 65-67). In this context, the state itself is being responsibilized: "The state must support the economy, organizing its conditions and facilitating its growth, and is thereby made responsible for the economy without being able to predict, control, or offset its effects. [...] [E]conomic growth is its raison d'état, and capital appreciation is the presumed engine of growth" (ibid., p. 68).

This means that the state depends on the compliance of individual citizens and has to actively engage in the "building and modeling of a consumer who might have internalized certain social roles and who would adjust his actions according to collective constraints" (Rumpala 2011, p. 671). In the case of choice editing, libertarian paternalism legitimizes interventions that work *though* subjects (i.e., using consumer-citizens as a means), and behavioral economics can be described as its modus operandi, as a political economic apparatus of neoliberal governmentality. The state manages and subjectivizes individuals "by attempting to correct their deviations from rational, self-interested, utility-maximizing cognition and behavior—such that they more effectively and efficiently conform to market logics and processes" (McMahon 2015, p. 137). The failure of individual choice is politically regulated by "preserving, improving and insisting upon individual choice" (ibid., p. 153) through steering rather than restricting individual freedom towards pre-defined ends (i.e., macro sustainability statistics), leading consumers to make "correct choices" and embracing decisions within market interactions over other concerns. These politically desirable traits have to be inscribed on the level of the subject and subsequently "activated" by governments and other choice architects through the design of consumption environments. Food labels, for instance, which are regulated by legislation and promoted via marketing, are in this perspective an instrument to steer sustainable consumption (Mayes 2014, p. 388). The rationale operating through food labels relies on using nutrition science and market logics to normalize subjects as responsible for their own health and thus "securing" the wellbeing of the population through consumption. The same rationality can be applied to "greening" societies through behavioral change: abstract sustainability benchmarks are being defined by external (political and corporate) actors who treat consumer choice as an important variable to achieve such ends. Food labels are but one instrument "to conduct the food-choice of homo œconomicus towards norms of health and responsibility" (Mayes 2014, p. 390), as well as towards sustainability, we might add.

We see that responsibilization and economization can hardly be distinguished other than for analytical purposes. Irrationality poses explicit problems for political and economic agents to minimize future economic risks. It is therefore important that "Humans" realize that they are in fact short-sighted and constantly misjudging beings (homo myopicus), in order for them to truly want to become "Econs" (homo œconomicus). In this way, the problematization of behavioral economics, that health and environmental risks are caused by insufficient cognitive capabilities, preforms its own diagnosis (Bröckling 2017): the consumer-citizen is re-centered at the heart of the economy as an ecologically responsible, rationally economic, and therefore statistically calculable human being.

The next section will introduce a short illustration of how governmental logics are situating the reduction of food waste in Western industrialized countries as a problem of consumption and how they connect sustainable behavior changes to larger economic goals.

## Food waste and the governmentalization of sustainable consumption

The "fight against food waste" is high on political agendas globally, increasingly so in OECD countries, and nudging strategies to regulate consumer behavior are quite readily observable. Using behavioral insights to reduce food waste has been applied, among other European nation states, in Norway, Finland, Italy, Hungary, and Portugal, with the nudge agents ranging from private companies, supermarket chains, and food bank associations to national ministries (EC 2016). If we consider nudging more generally in terms of waste and recycling behavior, the list becomes exceptionally longer and continues to grow. It is believed that the change towards more sustainable consumption patterns has the potential to transform entire food value chains, since specific consumer demand would lead to the production of alternative products and simultaneously to more sustainable production and distribution networks. Thus, the regulation of consumption through information, education, technological solutions, and market approaches is seen as the best way forward, thus broadly legitimating nudges as a policy choice.

If we look at the micro level at how consuming subjects are addressed, one reason for food waste on the consumption stage has been identified as "wrong" shopping behavior. Estimations of the Waste and Resources Action Programme (WRAP) suggest that only two thirds of supermarket customers make a shopping list, and only about half of them stick to it (WRAP 2007, p. 10). Special offers, big package sizes, and specific advertising constitute framings that influence irrational shopping habits which may result in buying more food or food items which end up not being consumed. Other reasons for food waste are described as problems of storage (due to lack of information), cooking and eating habits (people tend to buy fresh food out of good intention, but end up not preparing the food due to self-control problems), or recycling habits (food gets thrown out too early due to lack of information concerning food safety and confusing date labeling) (ibid., pp. 12-15). Policy measures that are undertaken to address these problems include food waste awareness campaigns ("Love Food, Hate Waste") to provide people with information how to best deal with food items (Parfitt et al. 2010), and technological solutions to enhance information on the consumer side (such as fridge cams, smartphone apps, or special scales to measure and track individual food consumption) (Ganglbauer et al. 2013, Kranert et al. 2012). Mappings help to signify the waste of resources, energy, and money that goes along with food waste and also help to make regional products more attractive. The complex choices consumers are faced with in supermarkets today are increasingly being simplified and structured through the redesigning of date labels, more information about food safety, downloadable recipes with ready-to-print shopping lists, etc. Through incentives, such as promotion for perishable food or reduced prices for food approaching the sell-by date, supermarkets can help to steer consumer conduct and prevent food spoilage to a certain degree. One of the most important mechanisms to nudge effectively is the use of social norms that are conveyed through anti-food waste messages that are part of information campaigns and feedback systems (Mont et al. 2014, p. 48). Through the provision of information about others' behavior as well as ideal-type behavior, a sense of appropriateness is construed and made publicly available. "Wasting" is today synonymous with undisciplined and unproductive behavior and therefore a prime example of an unsustainable behavioral trait. Not to waste food becomes an ethical maxim that cannot be contradicted, and self-optimization and rationalization are presented as the self-evident solution: rationalization is a means to an end, while the end is justified on ethical terms. In this respect, we are witnessing what Nicholas Rose (2000) has termed "ethopolitics," the government of behavior which justifies itself on ethical terms. Instead of merely giving consumers information, "ethopower works through the values, beliefs, and sentiments thought to underpin the techniques of responsible self-government and the management of one's obligations to others" (ibid., p. 1399).

Moving to the macro level, within political discourse, this "behavioral work" on the subject has to be legitimized. Although political and scientific discussions to curb food waste are not limited to a particular segment of the food chain, and while various studies reassert the claim, "[that] [f]ood is wasted throughout the entire supply chain, not only during final consumption" (HoL 2014, p. 8), national initiatives in OECD countries predominantly target reductions on the consumption level and thus the wasteful behavior of consumer-citizens (EC 2010). The UK-based Waste and Resources Action Programme (WRAP), a not-for-profit organization charged with the creation of a political agenda for the reduction of food waste, is a case in point. WRAP's work has by and large centered around household food waste, focusing on measures such as educational campaigns and the management of post-consumer discards (Evans et al. 2013, p. 18). Even measures proposed throughout the supply chain, such as packaging and labeling, mirror "the more general tendency to position food waste as a consumer issue" (ibid., p. 19). Evans et al. (2017) label this focus on the consumption level, which attributes the responsibility for the food waste problem clearly to the consumer, as the "initial response" to the problem (from 2007–2013 in the UK) (p. 1402). They assert that during a "second wave" (from 2013–2015), due to supermarkets in the UK increasingly sharing some of the responsibility for the magnitude of wasted food, a sense of "distributed responsibility" emerged along with "'more nuanced ways of thinking about the consumer'" (ibid., p. 1406). The authors show that the notion of singling out and responsibilizing consumers as the sole cause for food waste does not hold true in the UK. However, the social figure of the "consuming subject" is still extensively being mobilized as a "rhetorical device to mediate relationships between strategic and collective actors" (ibid., p. 1407). The consumer is the pivotal point in regulating sustainable practices and serves to "articulate and legitimate a diversity of programmes for rectifying problematic areas of economic and social life" (Miller and Rose 1990, p. 24). Although the involvement of supermarkets in the UK may indicate shared responsibility in reducing food waste, the basic understanding of its drivers, inefficiency, irrationality, and unintentional food losses are reasserted, and retailer engagement does in no way hamper economic growth potentials (action on food waste will even be calculated as an investment in customer loyalty). While the focus is on individual action, and former culprits of unsustainability (such as retailers) materially and discursively engage in moderate forms of "greening" value chains upstream and downstream, the core corporate preferences and the mechanisms through which control over food is maintained are further deferred and steadily removed from democratic legitimation as the space for the exercise of citizenship is slowly narrowed.

Therefore, even when political interventions, such as choice editing, do not responsibilize the consumer-citizen in a strong sense, the figure is used to create direct links between the economic health of the nation and the interests of private individuals. Current governance practices in the EU to regulate food waste behavior can thus be understood to "discipline consumers without disrupting the dynamics of consumption that is supposed to fuel economic growth"

(Rumpala 2011, p. 672). The project of enhancing sustainability depends now right from the beginning on the interest of the citizen and appropriate measures to ensure success. The saturation of the field of sustainable consumption with a "participatory ethos" has wide-reaching political implications. Through the targeting of consumers, the idea of citizenship is enriched, and citizens' attention is drawn to complex issues, to which practical perspectives are offered. Policies promote "small and simple gestures" which should become routine practices (ibid., p. 679). Most importantly, this rationality upholds liberal doctrines, as consumers can continue to do their habitual activities as long as they adopt responsible attitudes. Informing and moralizing individuals marks them as rational yet environmentally responsible actors who freely subject themselves to logics of governance.

## Concluding remarks and insights for practitioners

The paper has argued that a governmentality perspective adds some new arguments to the body of critique on nudging as a policy tool for advancing more sustainable societies, in that Foucault is showing "how a new political and economic subject, a new form of political reason, and above all, a new form of governmental rationality and state legitimacy" (Brown 2015, p. 51) have developed and been extended to sustainable consumption and the regulation of food waste. Behavior change is increasingly central to policy and politics. Libertarian paternalism has been linked to the reconfiguration of the state-citizen relationship, the rise of particular forms of neoliberalism, and new ways of policy-making driven by behavioral-economic and social-psychological discourses and particular forms of governmentality. In this regard, more information, data, and transparency in food consumption are necessary to remove all the different layers of unsustainable behavioral patterns in order to improve the system. The politics of nudging exhibits "governing through freedom," the ways consumers are confronted with ethical and moral choices and called upon to subject themselves willingly, to make the necessary adjustments as "good" citizens. In doing so, such a politics replaces democratic deliberation with expert knowledge, dialogue with behavioral modifications, and persuasive arguments with designed options. Depoliticizing the agency of consumers leaves them less inclined to reflect on the systemic connections of unsustainability and the structural dynamics of competition and economic growth.

The concerns a governmentality perspective voices are real possibilities, and yet I want to echo the call by Cheryl Hall that "completely rejecting these activities is not an option" (Hall 2016, p. 602). Given that behavioral economics as a political-economic apparatus are, for various reasons made explicit in the article, "here to stay," suggestions to inform policy design are all the more necessary. The most practical suggestion that follows from these thoughts is a call to revisit what informs practice: the ethics involved in choice editing (see also Jones et al. 2011). I want to return to the two major points of contention within the sustainable consumption literature that were identified earlier as the question of whose interests are reflected through nudging and the (im)possibility of collective action.

First, if nudges are largely designed to work unconsciously, that is, through dominant norms that are rarely consciously reflected, they have clear effects on individuals' capacity for autonomous decision-making and on how they collectively decide on trajectories for socio-ecological transformation. Consumers like to choose for themselves, and this intrinsic motivation and conscious reflection on personal autonomy and its limits should be strengthened rather than used instrumentally to optimize cost-benefit analyses for policy design. Otherwise, citizens can easily be treated as a means to achieve a certain policy goal rather than seeing the empowerment of citizens as a desired end in itself. Therefore, we are better off asking citizens the relevant questions, to engage in dialogue, and give them the possibility of becoming an environmentally conscious citizen, as opposed to stripping them of their irrational, harmful biases. To that end, nudging could in fact be used to support citizens in "expand[ing] their awareness, experience, and knowledge of the environment in which they live, including their impact on it and its impact on them" (Hall 2016, p. 604).

Secondly, and related to that, an important critique that must be addressed within the design of nudging is the possibility of exploiting consumers' biases. "Softly" charging consumers with making "wrong" decisions and confronting them with their unsustainable behavior might encourage them to pay for either avoiding or correcting bad choices. Products and services are increasingly designed to address self-control problems, altering habits (i.e., snacking), and consumption environments (i.e., the kitchen) in order to lead the individual to self-optimization, turning the external government or corporate nudge into an internal self-nudge. Instead of designing solutions with a price tag and suggesting alternative consumption, it should be about promoting reductions: "every encouragement should be given to the public to rethink the good life and to consume in less damaging ways, even if that comes at the cost of continued rates of growth in some areas of the economy" (Soper 2004, p. 114). For instance, a focus on social practices, the built environment, and the material contexts surrounding us is more apt to promote radical shifts in lifestyles than incremental behavior change (Barr 2015).

And lastly, this "rethinking of the good life" is never an individual process. If we agree that democratic institutions should be strengthened, then it is important to let people reflect on their preferences while deliberating with others, in order to understand how individual choices can harm the welfare of other people, beings, and ecosystems, to weigh moral decisions and cultivate the capacity for political judgment. Presumably, the process is slower and less cost-efficient, the outcome is less conceivable, and people will be resistant or disinterested, especially in the beginning, but doing so will strengthen the citizen-side within the consumer-citizen construct. Doing sustainability without doing democratic politics is simply a bad choice in the long run.

# Notes

1. So-called Behavioral Insights Teams (BIT), or "Nudge Units," are created to apply nudge theory to certain fields to improve government policy and services (and to save the government money). The practice to establish such units is spreading across different administrations rapidly, in most cases under close guidance of the authors of the seminal book *Nudge—Improving Decisions about Health, Wealth and Happiness*, Richard H. Thaler and Cass R. Sunstein.
2. While regulating smoking behavior would entail, for example, increasing the price of cigarettes, a nudge strategy involves reducing the cues for smoking by keeping cigarettes, lighters, and ashtrays out of sight. (Bonell et al. 2011, p. 401).

# References

Barr, S. (2015) "Beyond Behaviour Change: Social Practice Theory and the Search for Sustainable Mobility", in Huddart Kennedy, E., Cohen, M.J. and Krugman, N.T. (eds.) *Putting Sustainability into Practice. Applications and Advances in Research on Sustainable Consumption*. Cheltenham/UK: Edward Elgar, pp. 91–108.

Bevir, M. (2011) "Governance and Governmentality After Neoliberalism", in *Policy & Politics*, 39(4), pp. 457–471.

Bonell, C., McKee M., Fletcher A., Wilkinson P. and Haines, A. (2011) "One Nudge Forward, Two Steps Back", *British Medical Journal*, pp. 342(d401).

Bovens, L. (2009) "The Ethics of Nudge", in Grüne-Yanoff, T. and Hansson, S.O. (eds.) *Preference Change: Approaches from Philosophy, Economics and Psychology*. Netherlands: Springer.

Brooks, A. and Bryant R. (2014) "Consumption", in Death, C. (ed.) *Critical Environmental Politics*. London: Routledge, pp. 72–82.

Bröckling, U. (2017) "Nudging: Gesteigerte Tauglichkeit, vertiefte Unterwerfung" in Bröckling, U. (ed.) *Gute Hirten führen sanft. Über Menschenregierungskünste*. Berlin: Suhrkamp Verlag, pp. 175–196.

Brown, W. (2015) *Undoing the Demos: Neoliberalism's Stealth Revolution*. New York: Zone Books.

Carroll, G.D., Choi, J.J., Laibson, D., Madrian, B.C. and Metrick, A. (2009) "Optimal Defaults and Active Decisions", *The Quarterly Journal of Economics*, 124(4), pp. 1639–1674.

Dean, M. (1999) *Governmentality. Power and Rule in Modern Society*. London: Sage Publications.

European Commission (EC) (2010) "Preparatory Study on Food Waste Across EU 27", Final Report, October 2010. Paris. Available at: http://ec.europa.eu/environment/eussd/pdf/bio_foodwaste_report.pdf (Accessed: 01/09/2018)

European Commission (EC) (2016) "Behavioural Insights Applied to Policy", European Report 2016. Available at: http://publications.jrc.ec.europa.eu/repository/bitstream/JRC100146/kjna27726enn_new.pdf (Accessed: 01/09/2018)

Evans, D., Campbell, H. and Murcott A. (2013) "A Brief Pre-History of Food Waste and the Social Sciences", in Evans, D., Campbell, H. and Murcott, A. (eds.) *Waste Matters. New Perspective on Food and Society*. Malden/Oxford: Wiley-Blackwell, pp. 5–26.

Evans, D. Welch, D. and Swaffield J. (2017) "Constructing and Mobilizing 'the Consumer': Responsibility, Consumption and the Politics of Sustainability", *Environment and Planning A*, 49(6), pp. 1396–1412.

Foucault, M. (1982) "The Subject and Power", in Dreyfus, H. and Rabinow, P. (eds.) *Michel Foucault: Beyond Structuralism and Hermeneutics*. Chicago: The University of Chicago Press, pp. 208–226.

Foucault, M. (2008) *The Birth of Biopolitics. Lectures at the College de France, 1978-79*. New York: Palgrave MacMillan.

Ganglbauer, E., Fitzpatrick, G., and Comber R. (2013) "Negotiating Food Waste: Using a Practice Lens to Inform Design", ACM *Transactions on Computer-Human Interaction*, 20(2), pp. 1–25.

Goodman, M.K. (2004) "Reading Fair Trade: Political Ecological Imaginary and the Moral Economy of Fair Trade Foods", *Political Geography*, 23(7), pp. 891–915.

Goodwin, T. (2012) "Why We Should Reject 'Nudge'", *Politics*, 32(2), pp. 85–92.

Hall, C. (2016) 'Framing and Nudging for a Greener Future' in Gabrielson, T., Hall, C., Meyer, J.M. and Schlosberg, D. (eds.) *The Oxford Handbook of Environmental Political Theory*. Oxford: OUP, pp. 593–607.

Hausman, D.M. and Welch, B. (2010) "Debate: To Nudge or Not to Nudge", *Journal of Political Philosophy*, 8(1), pp. 123–136.

House of Lords European Union Committee (HoL) (2014) "Counting the Cost of Food Waste: EU Food Waste Prevention", 10th Report of Session 2013-14. London: Authority of the House of Lords. Available at: https://publications.parliament.uk/pa/ld201314/ldselect/ldeucom/154/15402.htm (Accessed: 01/09/2018)

John, P., Cotterill, S., Moseley, A., Richardson, L., Smith, G., Stoker, G. and Wales, C. (2011) *Nudge, Nudge, Think, Think. Experimenting with Ways to Change Civic Behaviour*. London: Bloomsbury.

John, P., Smith, G. and Stoker G. (2009) "Nudge Nudge, Think Think. Two Strategies for Changing Civic Behaviour", *Political Quarterly*, 80(3), pp. 361–370.

Jones, R., Pykett, J. and Whitehead, M. (2011) "The Geographies of Soft Paternalism in the UK: The Rise of the Avuncular State and Changing Behaviour after Neoliberalism", *Geography Compass* 5(1), pp. 50–62.

Jones, R., Pykett, J. and Whitehead, M. (2013a) *Changing Behaviours. On the Rise of the Psychological State*. Cheltenham/UK: Edward Elgar.

Jones, R., Pykett, J. and Whitehead, M. (2013b) "Psychological Governance and Behaviour Change", *Policy Press*, 41(2), pp. 159–182.

Kranert, M., Hafner, G., Barabosz, J., Schuller, H., Leverenz, D., Kölbig, A., Schneider, F., Lebersorger, S. and Scherhaufer, S. (2012) "Ermittlung der weggeworfenen Lebensmittelmengen und Vorschläge zur Verminderung der Wegwerfrate bei Lebensmitteln in Deutschland", Stuttgart. Available at: http://www.bmel.de/SharedDocs/Downloads/Ernaehrung/WvL/Studie_Lebensmittelabfaelle_Langfassung.pdf?__blob=publicationFile (Accessed: 01/09/2018)

Luke, T.W. (2016) "Environmental Governmentality", in Gabrielson, T., Hall, C., Meyer, J.M. and Schlosberg, D. (eds.) *The Oxford Handbook of Environmental Political Theory*. Oxford: OUP, pp. 461–474.

Lövbrand, E. and Stripple, J. (2013) "Governmentality", in Death, C. (ed.) *Critical Environmental Politics*. London: Routledge, pp. 111–120.

Maniates, M. (2010) "Editing Out Unsustainable Behavior", in Starke, L. and Mastny, L. (eds.) *State of the World 2010: Transforming Cultures, From Consumerism to Sustainability*. New York: W.W. Norton and Company, pp. 119–126.

Maniates, M. (2014) "Sustainable Consumption – Three Paradoxes", *GAIA*, 23(3), pp. 201–208.

Marteau, T., Ogilvie, D., Roland, M., Suhrcke, M. and Kelly, M.P. (2011) "Judging Nudging: Can Nudging Improve Population Health?", *British Medical Journal*, 342(d228).

Mayes, C. (2014) "Governing Through Choice: Food Labels and the Confluence of Food Industry and Public Health Discourse to Create 'Healthy Consumers'", *Social Theory and Health*, 12(4), pp. 376–395.

McMahon, J. (2015) "Behavioral Economics as Neoliberalism: Producing and Governing Homo Economicus", *Contemporary Political Theory*, 14(2), pp. 137–158.

Milford, A.B., Ovrum, A. and Helgesen, H. (2015) "Nudges to Increase Recycling and Reduce Waste", Discussion Paper No. 2015-01. Norwegian Agricultural Economics Research Institute. Available at: http://hdl.handle.net/11250/2437370 (Accessed: 01/09/2018)

Miller, P. and Rose N. (1990) "Governing Economic Life", *Economy and Society*, 19(1), pp. 1–31.

Mont, O., Lehner, M. and Heiskanen, E. (2014) "Nudging. A Tool for Sustainable Behavior?", Swedish Environmental Protection Agency Report 6643. Available at: http://www.naturvardsverket.se/Documents/publikationer6400/978-91-620-6643-7.pdf?pid=14232 (Accessed: 01/09/2018)

Ölander, F. and Thorgesen, J. (2014) "Informing Versus Nudging in Environmental Policy", *Journal of Consumer Policy*, 37(3), pp. 341–356.

Parfitt, J., Barthel, M. and Macnaughton, S. (2010) "Food Waste Within Food Supply Chains: Quantification and Potential for Change to 2050", *Philosophical Transactions of the Royal Society*, 365(1554), pp. 3065–3081.

Rainford, P. and Tinkler, J. (2011) "Designing for Nudge Effects: How Behaviour Management Can Ease Public Sector Problem", Briefing Paper, LSE Public Policy Group. LSE Research Online: August 2011. Available at: http://eprints.lse.ac.uk/37810 (Accessed: 01/09/2018)

Rose, N. (2000) "Community, Citizenship and the Third Way", *American Behavioural Scientist*, 43(9), pp. 1395–1411.

Rose, N. and Miller, P. (1992) "Political Power Beyond the State: Problematics of Government", *The British Journal of Sociology*, 43(2), pp. 173–2005.

Rumpala, Y. (2011) "'Sustainable Consumption" as a New Phase in a Governmentalization of Consumption', *Theory and Society*, 40(6), pp. 669–699.

Soneryd, L. and Uggla, Y. (2015) 'Green Governmentality and Responsibilization: New Forms of Governance and Responses to, Consumer Responsibility", *Environmental Politics*, 24(6), pp. 913–931.

Soper, K. (2004) "Rethinking the 'Good Life': The Consumer as Citizen", *Capitalism Nature Socialism*, 15(3), pp. 111–116.

Sunstein, C.R. (2013) "Behavioral Economics, Consumption, and Environmental Protection", Regulatory Policy Program Working Paper RPP-2013-19. Cambridge, MA: Mossavar-Rahmani Center for Business and Government, Harvard Kennedy School, Harvard University. Available at: http://citeseerx.ist.psu.edu/viewdoc/download?doi=10.1.1.643.4491&rep=rep1&type=pdf (Accessed: 01/09/2018)

Sunstein, C.R. and Reisch, L. (2013) "Green by Default", *KYKLOS*, 66(3), pp. 398–402.

Thaler, R.H. and Sunstein, C.R. (2003) "Libertarian Paternalism", *The American Economic Review*, 93(2), pp. 175–179.

Thaler, R.H. and Sunstein, C.R. (2008) *Nudge—Improving Decisions about Health, Wealth and Happiness*. New York: Penguin.

Waste and Resources Action Programme (WRAP) (2007) "The Food We Waste", Food waste report v2. Banbury, Oxon. Available at: http://wrap.s3.amazonaws.com/the-food-we-waste-executive-summary.pdf (Accessed: 01/09/2018)

Wilkinson, T.M. (2013) "Nudging and Manipulation", *Political Studies*, 61(2), pp. 341–355.

# 6  The 'double dividend' discourse in sustainable consumption: A critical commentary

*Lucie Middlemiss, David Wingate, and Anna Wesselink*

In a widely cited paper, Jackson asks: 'Is there a "double dividend" in sustainable consumption?' (2005, p.19). Jackson explores the argument that we could 'devise a society in which it is possible to live better (or at least as well as we have done) by consuming less' (*ibid.* p.33). This argument is advanced to varying degrees in a clutch of other works (Jackson, 2006; 2008; Jackson & Michaelis, 2003) and has received significant attention in the sustainable consumption literature (see, for example: Alexander & Ussher, 2012; Berg, 2009; Knight & Rosa, 2011; MacKerron, 2012; Madjar & Ozawa, 2006).

The basic argument is that a) *per capita* consumption—understood as materials passing through the economy—has been increasing in industrialised nations for several decades, b) self-reported happiness has not been increasing at the same rate and therefore c) we can safely reduce environmentally damaging consumption (materials throughput) without causing any loss of happiness. The double dividend then takes this one step further by arguing that d) consumption—specifically consumption carried out as part of a consumer culture (Slater, 1997)—is antithetical to happiness, therefore a reduction in consumption would not only benefit the environment, but would also make us happier: hence the *double* dividend.

The arguments made in support of the double dividend stand in direct opposition to the received view that consumption is a way in which people pursue happiness. According to the received view, consumption is the result of revealed preference in the marketplace; the cumulative effect of the rational decisions of informed actors seeking the greatest utility at the lowest cost (Mankiw, 2007). Within this paradigm, a higher income provides greater purchasing power, which in turn enables the pursuit of happiness. The received view is not just a micro-economic theory, it also has a macro-economic and political dimension in its assumption that economic growth is a necessary and beneficial social goal and that such growth produces 'trickle-down' effects through the increase and distribution of wealth. The double dividend mainly challenges the micro-scale logic of the received view, using empirical research to contest the link between income and happiness (such as Inglehart *et al.*, 2008) and in doing so aligning itself with critiques of consumer culture (such as Kasser, 2002; Schor, 1999). While in this chapter we mainly focus on this micro-logic, we should note that the supremacy of economic growth is challenged by the macro-level critique to which the double dividend belongs (Jackson, 2009; Kallis, 2011).

The double dividend has become part of the lexicon of sustainable consumption. For this reason alone the concept deserves scrutiny. While authors cite the double dividend with varying levels of enthusiasm, they rarely take a critical eye to the concept and to the body of work it draws on. In this paper, therefore, we set out to critically examine the double dividend: dismantling it, identifying the components from which it is formed, analysing the coherence and limits of these components, and revealing the tensions between them. We find that despite its attempt to position itself in opposition to the received view, at this micro-level the double dividend is built on a logic of incentivisation, individualisation, self-interest, and rational choice, all of which are hallmarks of the received view of consumption. In espousing this logic, the double dividend risks distracting attention from the core goals of sustainable consumption: to end environmental degradation and material inequality.

The paper proceeds as follows: we begin by characterising the double dividend in more detail. Next, we show how the evidence on happiness, and a distinct ontological position espousing a universalist notion of human nature and needs, are mobilised in support of the double dividend argument. In providing a critical analysis of the double dividend, we focus on unpicking the logic of the foundational ideas of the double dividend, and on considering how this logic, evidence, and ontology might be contested. We finish by following Ahmed (2010) in asking 'what does the double dividend *do*?' or how do these ideas play out in practice?

## Characterising the double dividend

Here we characterise the double dividend: establishing its key premises and showing how it positions itself in relation to other perspectives. First, we explain how the double dividend is set up as a counter-narrative to the received view of consumption. Second, we look at how the double dividend draws on research on happiness and well-being to evidence its claims and how this relies on a universalist understanding of human nature and needs. Third, we show how the anti-consumerist movement known as voluntary simplicity adopts these ideas in practice. This exposition of the double dividend on its own terms will allow us to take a more critical stance in the rest of the chapter.

### The double dividend versus the received view

Although the double dividend's arguments are widely used, few scholars have been as instrumental in its impact as Tim Jackson, whose work is cited throughout the sustainable consumption literature. With this in mind, we will use Jackson's exposition of the double dividend as a starting point for our analysis and discussion.

Jackson's (2005) conception of the double dividend is rooted in what he calls the 'eco-humanist' view of consumption, largely drawing on ideas from the psychology of consumer behaviour. For Jackson, the eco-humanist view arises as 'a dialectical response to the conventional economic insatiability of wants' (*ibid.* p.32), which is embedded in the received view of consumption. Jackson makes reference to the economic tropes of 'self-interest' and 'rational choice' (2005), as well as the 'individualism' encouraged under a consumption-based economy (2008), implying that these concepts are at best over-simplistic, and at worst profoundly damaging to society and the environment. The double dividend—and the eco-humanist view in general—is intended as an antidote to the values of individualisation, self-interest, and rational choice that underpin the received view of consumption.

Indeed, Jackson (2006) situates the double dividend within a dichotomy, arguing that sustainable consumption definitions and prescriptions vary between those which advocate consuming *differently* and those which advocate consuming *less*. 'Consuming differently' involves ecological modernisation, resource efficiency, market mechanisms, techno-fixes, and decoupling of economic growth from pollution; whereas 'consuming less' functions as a critique of consumer culture, looking to a more radical reorganisation of social and economic structures and practices in order to minimise the primacy of production and consumption. For the purposes of our understanding of the double dividend: consuming differently aligns with the received view, while consuming less aligns with the double dividend. Note that this is where the micro-economic ideas associated with both double dividend and the received view tie into macro-economic and political ideas about how society should be organised: in pursuit of degrowth (consume less, double dividend) or economic growth (consume differently, received view).

The reality is obviously more complex—as indeed is pointed out by Jackson (2008). More recent writing in this field has tended to see these ideas as sitting on a spectrum rather than as a dichotomy, in connection with a trend towards a systemic approach to tackling this problem (O'Rourke and Lollo, 2015), and the role of the circular economy in addressing sustainable consumption advances (Mont and Heiskanen, 2015). Elsewhere, however, the dichotomy persists, and is also linked with broader macro-social arguments in this field, such as the contrast between degrowth and green consumerist objectives (Akenji, 2014; Lorek and Fuchs, 2013). In any case, even as an ideal type distinction this perspective has value in unpicking the logic and implications of the double dividend. Certainly the 'dialectic response'that the double dividend represents is intended to challenge the received view and offer an alternative story about the relationship between consumption and well-being.

### The use of evidence and ontological premises

The concept of happiness is central to the double dividend argument, which draws on a body of evidence on the relationship between income and happiness. According to Inglehart *et al.* (2008), drawing on survey data averaged across countries and income—or GDP *per capita*—contributes to happiness up to a point, but thereafter exhibits rapidly diminishing returns. The implication is that earning more—and by implication consuming more—does not make you happier. Note that the connections between income and consumption are not as clear cut as they might seem, as income can be used for a range of purposes such as saving, spending, or investment. However there is evidence, for instance, that people consume more—and pollute more—the more that they earn (Hubacek et al., 2017).

This forms the basis of what we might call a *single* dividend—where a reduction in consumption could conceivably deliver environmental benefits without necessarily reducing happiness. However, in order to achieve a *double* dividend the reduction must have a further positive effect—living better rather than not living worse. The double dividend draws on other evidence from the happiness studies literature, such as a rise in reported depression and anxiety in income-rich countries, high levels of reported happiness in some income-poor countries, and studies correlating 'materialistic values' with low levels of psychological well-being (Jackson, 2005; 2008).

The work of Schor (1999) and Kasser (2002), who make similar points as to the possible detrimental effect of consumption, are important in the construction of this argument. Schor's (1999) sociological study of the 'life/work balance' explores a growing discontent with the culture of working longer hours to consume more, which has prompted some people to 'downshift'—to work fewer hours or choose a less stressful job—for the sake of their happiness. Schor argues that the unhappiness caused by working longer hours or in stressful occupations outweighs any benefits brought about by greater purchasing power. Kasser's (2002) empirical work is based on quantitative social psychology and suggests a strong correlation between 'materialistic values' and unhappiness. Kasser believes that this link is causal: that a less materialistic lifestyle would satisfy what he refers to as 'intrinsic' human motivations, resulting in greater psychological well-being.

For clarity: the double dividend argument, built on evidence from happiness studies, sociology, and psychology, is that increasing consumption reduces well-being; therefore, reducing consumption will increase well-being. In other words, there is a causal relationship between consumption and well-being. To make this argument, the double dividend relies on a particular ontological understanding of human nature and needs. In particular, such claims belie a universalist understanding: a belief that all people essentially need the same things to maintain well-being. This also links with a willingness within the environmental movement to categorise some forms of consumption as 'necessary' and some as merely 'desire'.

Indeed, Jackson draws attention to 'an essential distinction, present in the writings of all those concerned with human well-being' (*ibid*. p.24): the notion that there are *subjective* desires which are distinct from *objective* needs. In the case of the double dividend, Jackson reasons, our subjective desires override our objective needs to the detriment of our well-being. The particular theory of needs to which Jackson defers is that of Max-Neef (1991), who presents a list of fundamental human needs that must be satisfied in order to meet the conditions of well-being.

For Jackson (2005), not only can these needs be met with fairly low levels of consumption, but some forms of consumption are in fact violating those needs and therefore obstructing the conditions required for well-being. The crucial component of such an argument is universality; a belief in a universal human nature and associated set of needs is necessary when attempting to define what is universally 'good for us'.

### The double dividend and voluntary simplicity

The ideas associated with the double dividend are already being pursued by the anti-consumerist movement known as 'voluntary simplicity', which advocates reducing consumption for the benefit of personal well-being. This amounts to a practical manifestation of the argument that reducing consumption can increase well-being, also demonstrating the performative power of these ideas.

Much of the literature on voluntary simplicity is written by and for its proponents (Alexander & Ussher, 2012; Elgin, 1993; Schor, 1999), which results in a rather evangelical tone. For instance, Elgin, an influential author within the movement, describes voluntary simplicity as:

> …a manner of living that is outwardly more simple and inwardly more rich, a way of being in which our most authentic and alive self is brought into direct and conscious contact with living…
>
> (Elgin, 1993, p.25)

Elgin's language—'inwardly rich', 'authentic', 'alive self'—implies that 'we' are currently disconnected from our proper state of being, which can only be remedied through practicing voluntary simplicity. This language implies the same universalist ontology: that there is such a thing as an 'authentic alive self'—a natural state of being or shared human nature—and that 'inward richness' only exists in tandem with 'outward simplicity'—a reference to reduced consumption.

Jackson's writing on the double dividend mirrors this closely. We can see this in his assertion that:

> …we could collectively devise a society in which it is possible to live better (or at least as well as we have done) by consuming less, and become more human in the process…
>
> (Jackson, 2005, p.33)

'Live better' takes the place of 'inwardly rich', 'consume less' replaces 'outwardly simple', and 'become more human' follows the 'authentic alive self'. The same ontological standpoints are implied: that there is a shared human nature, that it is possible to become 'more human', and that 'living better' is a direct result of 'consuming less'.

## In summary

The double dividend offers an alternative narrative to the received view of consumption, which claims that increased consumption results in greater happiness. The double dividend draws on a range of evidence on the causes of happiness—although principally evidence from happiness studies—to argue against the received view: claiming that increased consumption does not result in greater happiness. In doing so it espouses a universalist view of human nature and human needs. The voluntary simplicity movement represents a practical manifestation of these ideas, which also looks to find happiness away from consumption.

So far we have attempted to understand the double dividend on its own terms: to understand what components it is made of. The next step is to approach the concept more critically, analysing how these components cohere, and if tensions exist between them. To do this we need first to delve more deeply into the key body of evidence that the double dividend relies on: happiness studies.

## Happiness studies: Their uses and implications

The term 'happiness studies' has become a catchall for the various strands of research investigating happiness and well-being. Although traditionally a philosophical pursuit, the study of happiness and well-being is now more readily associated with psychology, through numerous studies associated with the concept of subjective well-being (SWB). The resultant body of literature has found its way into a range of other disciplines, permeating discussion across the social sciences and humanities, capturing the attention of the wider public, and influencing government policy.

Since the double dividend uses SWB as a knowledge base, understanding the nature of that knowledge and its use is important. To that end, we start by problematising how the work on SWB is used to evidence the double dividend. We continue by applying critiques of happiness studies in the context of the double dividend. The concern of critics encompasses the *production* of knowledge, as well as the *use* of such knowledge in shaping discourse, policy, and behaviour. We draw on this work to ask the question 'what does happiness do?' in relation to the double dividend—following Ahmed (2010). We find that when happiness becomes a duty, it detracts and distracts from other potential duties, such as addressing inequality or reducing environmental degradation.

### The science of subjective well-being and the double dividend

Subjective well-being (SWB) is a dominant concept in happiness studies and is founded on the principle that psychological well-being is best determined by the individual experiencing it. Often presented as the 'science of happiness' (see Diener et al., 1999 for an overview), its methodologies are mostly quantitative, relying on numerical data gathered from experimentation, observation, and surveys—a typical survey question being: 'on a scale of one to ten, how satisfied are you with your life as a whole?' (Inglehart *et al.*, 2008). Large national or cross-national studies compile survey data from huge datasets such as the World Values Survey (2013), the Gallup World Poll (2013), and the World Database of Happiness (2013), aggregating results to represent large groups of people. Of course, SWB data averaged across entire countries do not represent the diverse range of experiences within those countries, nor does a single SWB score take into account the range of factors that constitute happiness or well-being; rather, these large studies can be thought of as an 'economics of happiness'.

The double dividend uses the science of SWB as part of its argument that a reduction in consumption would result in an increase in well-being. However, a careful review of the SWB literature reveals that this is not supported by the data. This can be observed in the three SWB topics most relevant to consumption: income, discrepancy, and adaptation. Those studying the relationship between SWB and income argue that rising incomes—and by implication, rising consumption—go hand in hand with rising SWB, but beyond a modest point offer greatly diminishing returns or at worst simply plateau. None, however, claims that rising incomes actually reduce SWB, and many point out that high earners within countries are much more likely to report higher SWB than their low earning compatriots (Diener & Seligman, 2004; Diener *et al.*, 1999; Easterlin, 1995; Frank, 2012; Hagerty & Veenhoven, 2003; Inglehart *et al.*, 2008; Stevenson & Wolfers, 2008; Zuzanek, 2012). Similarly, SWB studies that look into the effects of discrepancy and adaptation—commonly known as 'keeping up with the Joneses' and 'the hedonic treadmill' respectively—do not support Jackson's (2005; 2008), Kasser's (2002), or Schor's (1999) assertions that consumption leads to unhappiness, either through the discrepancy revealed by social comparison or the insatiable desire for more consumption borne of adaptation. Rather, the SWB literature suggests that different personalities react in different ways to their own diverse circumstances (Brown & Dutton, 1995; Diener & Fujita, 1997; Diener *et al.*, 2006; Diener *et al.*, 1999; McFarland & Miller, 1994). This is not to say that the findings of SWB studies disprove the double dividend, merely that the double dividend's claims are not supported by those findings. Instead, the evidence seems to suggest that a reduction in consumption would result in a reduction in SWB in the short term—due to the discrepancy with our previous state—followed by a return to a baseline of SWB in the long run—due to adaptation—but that it would not make us any more or less happy overall (see Veenhoven, 2004, who speaks directly about sustainable consumption from the perspective of a SWB researcher).

### Beyond subjective well-being: 'What does happiness do?'

Beyond the field of psychology, there is a broader debate about how happiness and well-being are situated in relation to wider issues of society, culture, and politics. This is far removed from the 'scale of one to ten' measurements that underpin the science of SWB. For our purposes, Sara Ahmed's cultural study of happiness is productive here, asking 'not so much "what is happiness?" but rather "what does happiness do?" (2010, p.2). With this line of enquiry Ahmed is focussing not on the description or measurement of happiness itself but rather on the influence, effects, and consequences of its use in academia, government, and everyday life.

Happiness is so embedded in the language of success and aspiration that its correlates—as measured by the science of SWB—easily slip into the role of causation. The SWB literature contains many examples of correlations implied to be causal, but the evidence showing the direction or even the existence of causation is thin on the ground (Diener & Fujita, 1997; Diener et al., 1999). As the same correlations are reiterated time and again, the message that filters through into everyday understanding is that 'scientists know what makes us happy'.

The notion that sustainable consumption will cause happiness is built in to the double dividend. This claim not only reproduces the causation myth, but also feeds into what Ahmed refers to as 'the happiness duty'. Ahmed writes, 'by finding happiness in certain places, [SWB] generates those places as being good, as being what should be promoted as goods... if we have a duty to promote what causes happiness, then happiness itself becomes a duty' (ibid. 6–7). When viewed through this lens, the happiness generated by the double dividend is used to characterise sustainable consumption as 'good'; the duty to consume sustainably is linked to a duty to pursue happiness. This risks eclipsing a reading of sustainable consumption as a duty to end environmental degradation or material inequality.

For Ahmed, the happiness duty forms part of a social obligation: 'so much happiness is premised on, and promised by, the concealment of suffering, the freedom to look away from what compromises one's happiness'(ibid. p.196). This analysis is also applicable to the double dividend's use of happiness. The underlying arguments for sustainable consumption are fundamentally 'unhappy'—ecological ruin, global inequality—to conceal them is ethically problematic, to reveal them is to be a 'kill joy', as Ahmed would put it, to draw attention to these unhappy starting points. When Jackson states that we will require 'more than wishful utopian thinking or angry ecologism' (2005, p.21), he alludes to the failure of environmentalists to win the 'moral' argument, precisely because of their gloomy message. The double dividend is using happiness to incentivise sustainable consumption rather than to moralise, and in doing so it diverts attention from its unhappy origins.

In the context of sustainable consumption, the desire to look away from what compromises one's happiness alludes to a tacit knowledge of the environmental degradation and global inequality that marks current patterns of production and consumption. Ahmed argues that 'we recognize how much the promise of happiness depends upon the localisation of suffering; others suffer so that a certain 'we' can hold on to the good life" (2010, 195). Consumption-based happiness depends on both the suffering of others and the concealment of that suffering. For Ahmed this phenomenon is not new: happiness was used as a justification for imperial colonialism—happiness for both the empire that gains resources and for the colonial subject who would be 'civilised'—as well as for the subjugation of women. The received view of consumption, which the double dividend is intended to refute, also uses happiness to rationalise the expansion of production and consumption. There are useful parallels here with Anantharaman's critique of the sustainable consumption literature, which outlines how much activity on sustainable consumption relies on a system of privilege, inequality, and resulting injustice (2018).

The double dividend discourse explicitly seeks to overturn the belief that consumption leads to happiness. It does so by aligning itself with a distinct epistemological position in relation to happiness (in line with the 'science of happiness'). By positioning happiness as an incentive for sustainable consumption, it reproduces and legitimises happiness as a noble reason for action—past and present. By foregrounding happiness as a reason for action, the double dividend risks marginalising its own aim of reducing consumption. To be blunt there is the risk that by focussing on happiness we lose sight of more fundamental goals of sustainable consumption (reducing material throughput, reducing inequality of access to materials), and in doing so inadvertently reproduce the conditions that led to the environmental destruction and global inequality it seeks to redress.

## Human nature, needs, and universalism

Alongside this body of evidence on happiness, the double dividend asserts a number of ontological beliefs about human nature and needs: namely, that there is such a thing as universal human needs, which can be known, and which in itself implies a universal human nature. The basic premise of the double dividend—that high levels of consumption are not 'good for us'—positions 'us', the human race, as a single entity. It also implies that this universal 'good' is a fixed condition or an essential set of needs to which all human beings are predisposed. The double dividend's ontology is therefore rooted in universalist understandings of human nature and needs. Debates on universality are long established, and the literature is vast, so we do not intend to reproduce them here. Our focus is on how universalist understandings are used to argue that the double dividend is an outcome of reduced consumption and in turn that reducing consumption is the most desirable end for society. We will address human nature and human needs in turn.

### Human nature

Notions of human nature are universalist: the concept implies that humans share an agreed list of 'essential' features which make them human. The implication of such universalism is that if people do not share these features, they must be somehow 'less human'. Jackson's assertion that we could 'live better... by consuming less, and become more human in the process' (2005, p.33)—perhaps inadvertently—positions the high consuming subject as being 'less human', for instance.

Questions of whether or not there is a universal human nature and what that human nature consists of are somewhat beside the point. To a great extent this is an unresolved/unresolvable conflict, borne of divergent ontological and epistemological assumptions. More significant is how the idea of human nature is *used*. Ashcroft *et al.*'s post-colonial interpretation of universalism is helpful here: 'The assumption of universalism is a fundamental feature of the construction of colonial power because the "universal" features of humanity are the characteristics of those who occupy positions of political dominance' (1995, p.55). Those who dominate use the idea of human nature to justify and legitimise their dominance, and those who *wish* to dominate use the idea of human nature to justify and legitimise their ascension.

We can see the double dividend participating in such a bid for power in competition with the dominant view of consumption—the received view. The latter has its own discursive truths about human nature and needs rooted in economics: consumption as rational choice or revealed preference, and *Homo-economicus* acting out of self-interest to maximise utility. The double dividend is set up in opposition to these dominant truths. Persistent discourses challenging the ills of consumerism—going 'back' to a more 'natural' state, becoming 'more human'—are adapted into the double dividend, and these alternative truths of human nature serve to legitimise its construction. The double dividend then uses these alternative truths about human nature, rooted in the 'science of happiness', to justify a particular political position—reducing consumption—as if it were the only rational position to take.

## Needs

Theories of human needs can attract similar challenges to theories of human nature: claims to universality are falsifiable, and theories of needs can be revealed to be justifying and legitimising particular political positions. Again, where you stand on this issue is somewhat beside the point; instead, we are concerned with how universal ideas of needs and desires are used in arguing for the double dividend.

Jackson (2005) rejects the conventional economic doctrine—that there are no 'needs' as such, only desires, preferences, and demands—and instead shows support for a theory of needs set out by Max-Neef (1991). Max-Neef's work belongs to a family of theories that propose a list of universal needs, common to everyone (see also Doyal & Gough, 1991; Nussbaum, 2001), as opposed to theories in which individual, geographical, or cultural factors generate relative needs depending on context (*cf.* Sen, 1999). In making the case for the double dividend, Jackson (2005) endorses an essential distinction between *objective* 'needs' and *subjective* 'desires' familiar to scholars of sustainable consumption. The assumption is that consumption borne out of subjective desires can be curtailed without causing any 'real' harm, leaving greater resources to provide for objective needs.

If we were to start from the opposing perspective—that all needs are subjective—then the objective/subjective split could be read as a normative distinction, the authentic/inauthentic needs of worthy/unworthy consumers. Which precise needs end up on each side of these distinctions becomes a matter of normative judgement, and by extension of politics: what counts as 'good' or 'bad'. The use of needs in this way evokes what Ahmed describes as a 'moral economy' (2010, p.34), where judgements of taste translate into value judgements; if our 'needs' have been deemed mere 'desires', then they are less 'worthy', because they are 'inauthentic'.

So, while the double dividend attempts to distance itself from a moralistic environmentalism, in differentiating needs and wants it clearly exercises moral judgements about people's consumption habits. Further, by embracing a universal understanding of needs it risks applying such moral judgements regardless of social difference. Note that even judgements about delineating so-called basic or survival needs are political: witness the gradual degrading of a perceived need for a regular income, heat in the home, or even food under austerity in the UK in recent years (Middlemiss, 2017).

In summary, the double dividend advocates a universal understanding of human nature and needs, which amounts to an alternative set of truth claims to those in the dominant, economics-inspired discourse. In doing so it is challenging the received view of consumption on its own terms: by constructing an alternative vision of reality—describing what people are like and what they need—that holds strongly to universalist principles. While its use of universal understandings of human nature and needs are held up as good sense—'live better by consuming less'—the double dividend is actually exercised in making moral judgement about people's consumption habits and failing to account for the complexities of people's consumption needs.

## What does the double dividend do?

In the spirit of Ahmed (2010), we here consider the influence, effects, and consequences of the double dividend's use. We have shown above how the discourse is constructed, how it is informed by and informs the voluntary simplicity movement, and how it has been recognised as a potential policy objective. Here we consider how the use of the double dividend shapes discourse, policy and behaviour around sustainable consumption. Much of this discussion revolves around the kind of subject that is created by the double dividend, inspired work on subjectivity, for instance, by Nikolas Rose (1999). We characterise this subject as a rational, self-interested individual responding to incentives of happiness instead of price—strongly reminiscent of *Homo Economicus*.

One of the key functions of the double dividend discourse is to reframe sustainable consumption in a positive light. This stems from a recognition that the 'doom and gloom' of messages about, for instance, catastrophic climate change, do not motivate widespread engagement with environmental issues. The perceived association between moralistic environmentalism and imagined subjects such as 'tree huggers' can act as a barrier to involvement for people who do not see themselves as political activists (Hobson, 2011). Popular rhetoric valorising a return to 'old fashioned' values and consumption practices, or 'giving stuff up' in sacrifice to the common good, constitutes further attempts to make a moral case for 'environmental citizenship'—which have also failed to gain significant support.

In its attempt to put a positive spin on environmentalism, the double dividend turns from a *moral* case to *incentivisation*. Its basic argument—that a reduction in consumption not only would benefit the environment, but also would also make us happier—is a way of selling the practice of sustainable consumption. The message of 'choose to consume less and you will be happier' is indeed a variation on 'choose to consume *this* and you will be happier'. To this end, the double dividend discourse inverts the received view that 'consumption makes us happy'. It deploys knowledge from the psychological and social sciences in an attempt to legitimise this counter-intuitive 'truth'. The consuming subject—the individual—is then faced with a rational choice: consume more and lose, or consume less and gain. The ideal subject of the double dividend, therefore, risks being positioned as a *self-interested, rational actor*.

As noted, this echoes the received view of the consumer, to which the double dividend is set in opposition. In the received view, the subject is self-interested, rational, and fully agentive. In the alternative narrative of the double dividend, 'consume less and you will be happy' implies a similar subject. Such a close relation between two subject positions could prove counter-productive: by assuming people behave as self-interested, rational actors, the double dividend may reproduce a culture of self-interest (Middlemiss, 2014). Promoting happiness as the result of self-interest and rational choice could also result in these being reified as a means of performing one's 'happiness duty' (as per Ahmed, 2010). Happiness becomes an instrument as well as a consequence here. It functions to uphold market interactions, or the lack of them, as the primary means of organising society—what Couldry (2010) describes as 'neo-liberal doctrine', or what Binkley (2011) aligns with a 'programme of neo-liberal governmentality': happiness-seeking as a personal identity project, regulating the self-governing individual.

The idea that lifestyle change, particularly through voluntary simplicity, will lead to greater happiness is a familiar trope throughout the sustainable consumption literature. Its effect is *individualising*: it situates the problem as belonging to the individual, with happiness measured as a property of the individual. It also positions the subject as responsible for the solution, for finding happiness—in this case through reduced consumption—and the 'solution' to consumerism and its ostensible ills is the pursuit of individual development, as opposed to societal development (Middlemiss, 2014).

The expectation that the agency of the individual will create both a happier and greener society reproduces the notion that social change is equivalent to the sum of individual actions. This is rather an 'article of faith' as Humphery (2010) puts it, given both that voluntary simplicity is a minority interest and that sustainability is often argued as requiring action at more than the individual level. There are tensions in such an individualised approach to sustainable consumption that have been recognised more broadly, not least that the individual is unlikely to possess sufficient agency and resources to effect substantive change (Maniates, 2001). Further, the promotion of individual happiness as a goal could be seen to be at odds with attempts at collective responses to the challenges of sustainable consumption (Middlemiss, 2014). The consuming subject brought about by the double dividend discourse looks less like the environmental subject acting for the common good and increasingly like a self-interested hedonist, rationally seeking out a better life for themselves—unlikely to be what the double dividend's proponents had in mind.

## Concluding remarks

The idea of the double dividend discourse has garnered significant attention and has noticeably influenced sustainable consumption debates in academia, in policy circles, and in relation to everyday life. In the absence of a robust critical analysis, its assumptions and arguments have passed largely unchallenged in the sustainable consumption literature, allowing the idea to take root and flourish.

Over the course of this analysis, we have dismantled the double dividend discourse to reveal its ontological and epistemological basis—along with some inherent tensions. We have shown the similarity between the double dividend and voluntary simplicity discourses and how they rely on particular conceptions of happiness and human nature to build a rational argument for reduced consumption. Further, we have identified two important points about what the double dividend discourse *does*:

First, the double dividend uses knowledge to occupy spaces of power in academic and public discourse. The psychological and social sciences are deployed to lend a particular type of legitimacy to the double dividend discourse, feeding on the popular conception that scientists *know* what *makes* us happy. This legitimacy risks being used to justify sustainable consumption on the basis that it will *cause* happiness and the promise of happiness to *incentivise* individuals to reduce their consumption, where *moralising* doomsayers have failed in the past. We showed how the received view of consumption has its own discursive truths about happiness and human nature and how this knowledge has been used to legitimise current patterns of production and consumption. In response, the double dividend uses alternative truths to legitimise its own view of consumption.

Secondly, whereas the struggles over legitimacy take the form of an ontological and epistemological dispute within the space of academia, the double dividend discourse also has the more explicit aim of shaping policy and behaviour across consumer culture. To this end, particularly in a context in which economic explanations dominate, the double dividend is likely to be deployed as a means of incentivising individuals to act out of self-interest and make a rational choice to consume less. Paradoxically, this characterisation of the double dividend reproduces the economic doctrine of *incentivisation, individualisation, self-interest,* and *rational choice*—at odds with the explicit values of the double dividend's proponents. In reproducing this economic orthodoxy, the double dividend risks reproducing the conditions that enable the environmental destruction and global inequality it seeks to redress.

# References

Ahmed, S. 2010. *The promise of happiness*. Durham: Duke University Press.

Akenji, L. 2014. 'Consumer scapegoatism and limits to green consumerism'. *Journal of Cleaner Production*, 63, 13–23.

Alexander, S. & Ussher, S. 2012. 'The voluntary simplicity movement: A multi-national survey analysis in theoretical context'. *Jurnal of Consumer Culture*, 12(1), 66–86.

Anantharaman, M. 2018. 'Critical sustainable consumption: A research agenda'. *Journal of Environmental Studies and Sciences*, 1–9.

Ashcroft, B., Griffiths, G., & Tiffin, H. 1995. 'Universality and difference: Introduction', in Ashcroft, B., Griffiths, G., & Tiffin, H. (eds). *The post-colonial studies reader*. London: Routledge.

Berg, A. 2009. 'Down-to-earth economy: The discursive contribution of sustainable consumption and production debate', in Koskela, M. & Vinnari, M. (eds). *Future of the consumer society*. Proceedings of the conference 'Future of the consumer society', 28–29 May 2009, Tampere, Finland. Helsinki: Finland Futures Research Centre.

Binkley, S. 2011. 'Happiness, positive psychology and the program of neoliberal governmentality'. *Subjectivity*, 4(4), 371–394.

Brown, J. D. & Dutton, K. A. 1995. 'Truth and consequences: The costs and benefits of accurate self-knowledge'. *Personality and Social Psychology Bulletin*, 21(12), 1288–1296.

Couldry, N. 2010. *Why voice matters: Culture and politics after neoliberalism*. London: Sage.

Diener, E. & Fujita, F. 1997. 'Social comparisons and subjective well-being', in Buunk, B. P., Gibbons, F. X., & Buunk, A. (eds). *Health, coping, and well-being: Perspectives from social comparison theory*. London: Lawrence Erlbaum.

Diener, E., Lucas, R. E., & Scollon, C. N. 2006. 'Beyond the hedonic treadmill: Revising the adaptation theory of well-being', *American Psychologist*, 61(4), 305–314.

Diener, E. & Seligman, M. E. P. 2004. 'Beyond money: Toward an economy of well-being', *Psychological Science in the Public Interest*, 5(1), 1–31.

Diener, E., Suh, E. M., Lucas, R. E., & Smith, H. L. 1999. 'Subjective well-being: Three decades of progress'. *Psychological Bulletin*, 125(2), 276–302.

Doyal, L. & Gough, I. 1991. *A theory of human need*. Basingstoke: Macmillan Education.

Easterlin, R. A. 1995. 'Will raising the incomes of all increase the happiness of all?' *Journal of Economic Behavior & Organization*, 27(1), 35–47.

Elgin, D. 1993. *Voluntary simplicity: Toward a way of life that is outwardly simple, inwardly rich*, 2nd ed. New York: Harper.

Frank, R. H. 2012. 'The Easterlin Paradox Revisited'. *Emotion*, 12(6), 1188–1191.

Gallup. 2013. *Gallup World Poll Knowledge Center*. Published online. Retrieved: 29th May 2013 (URL: http://www.gallup.com/strategicconsulting/en-us/worldpoll.aspx?ref=f)

Hagerty, M. R. & Veenhoven, R. 2003. 'Wealth and happiness revisited—growing national income does go with greater happiness.' *Social Indicators Research*, 64(1), 1–27.

Hobson, K. 2011. 'Environmental politics, green governmentality and the possibility of a "creative grammar" for domestic sustainable consumption', in Lane, R. & Gorman-Murray, A. (eds). *Material geographies of household sustainability*. Farnham: Ashgate.

Hubacek, K., Baiocchi, G., Feng, K., & Patwardhan, A. 2017. 'Poverty eradication in a carbon constrained world', *Nature Communications*, 8, 1–9.

Humphery, K. 2010. *Excess: Anti-consumerism in the west*. Cambridge, UK: Polity.

Inglehart, R., Foa, R., Peterson, C., & Welzel, C. 2008. 'Development, freedom, and rising happiness: A global perspective (1981–2007)'. *Perspectives on Psychological Science*, 3(4), 264–285.

Jackson, T. 2005. 'Live better by consuming less? Is there a "double dividend" in sustainable consumption?', *Journal of Industrial Ecology*. 9(1–2), 19–36.

Jackson, T. 2006. 'Beyond the "wellbeing paradox": Wellbeing, consumption growth and sustainability', *Centre for Environmental Strategy*, Working Paper 06/06. Published online: June 2006. Retrieved: 9th December 2012 (URL: http://www.surrey.ac.uk/ces/files/pdf/0606_WP_Wellbeing_and_SD.pdf)

Jackson, T. 2008. 'Where is the" wellbeing dividend"? Nature, structure and consumption inequalities', *Local Environment*, 13(8), 703–723.

Jackson, T. 2009. *Prosperity without growth*. London: Earthscan.

Jackson, T. & Michaelis, L. 2003. *Policies for sustainable consumption: A report to the Sustainable Development Commission*. Published online: 20th May 2003. Retrieved: 16th December 2012 (URL: http://www.sd-commission.org.uk/data/files/publications/Policies_sust_consumption.pdf)

Kallis, G. 2011. 'In defence of degrowth', *Ecological Economics*, 70, 873–880.

Kasser, T. 2002. *The high price of materialism*. Cambridge MA: MIT Press.

Knight, K. W. & Rosa, E. A. 2011. 'The environmental efficiency of well-being: A cross-national analysis', *Social Science Research*, 40(3), 931–949.

Lorek, S. & Fuchs, D. 2013. 'Strong sustainable consumption governance–precondition for a degrowth path?', *Journal of cleaner production*, 38, 36–43.

MacKerron, G. 2012. 'Happiness economics from 35 000 feet', *Journal of Economic Surveys*, 26(4), 705–735.

Madjar, M. & Ozawa, T. 2006. 'Happiness and sustainable consumption: Psychological and physical rebound effects at work in a tool for sustainable design', *The International Journal of Life Cycle Assessment*, 11(1), 105–115.

Maniates, M. F. 2001. 'Individualization: Plant a tree, buy a bike, save the world?', *Global Environmental Politics*, 1(3), 31–52.

Mankiw, N. G. 2007. *Principles of microeconomics*, 5th ed. Mason: South-Western

Max-Neef, M. A. 1991. *Human scale development: Conception, application and further reflections*. New York: Apex Press.

McFarland, C. & Miller, D. T. 1994. 'The framing of relative performance feedback: Seeing the glass as half empty or half full', *Journal of Personality and Social Psychology*, 66(6), 1061–1073.

Middlemiss, L. 2014. 'Individualised or participatory? Exploring late-modern identity and sustainable development', *Environmental Politics*, 23(6), 929–946.

Middlemiss, L. 2017. 'A critical analysis of the new politics of fuel poverty in England', *Critical Social Policy*, 37, 425–443.

Mont, O. & Heiskanen, E. 2015. 'Breaking the stalemate of sustainable consumption with industrial ecology and a circular economy', in Reisch, L. & Thogersen, J. (eds). *Handbook of Research on Sustainable Consumption*. Cheltenham, UK: Edward Elgar.

Nussbaum, M. C. 2001. *Women and human development: The capabilities approach*. Cambridge: Cambridge University Press.

O'Rourke, D. & Lollo, N. 2015. 'Transforming consumption: From decoupling, to behavior change, to system changes for sustainable consumption', *Annual Review of Environment and Resources*, 40, 233–259.

Rose, N. 1999. *Governing the soul: The shaping of the private self*. London: Free Association Books.

Schor, J. B. 1999. *The overspent American: Why we want what we don't need*. New York: HarperCollins.

Sen, A. 1999. *Development as freedom*. New York: Alfred & Knopf.

Slater, D. 1997. *Consumer culture and modernity.* Cambridge: Polity.

Stevenson, B. & Wolfers, J. 2008. 'Economic growth and subjective well-being: Reassessing the Easterlin paradox', *Brookings Papers on Economic Activity*, (Spring Issue) 1–102.

Veenhoven, R. 2004. *Sustainable consumption and happiness.* Published online (http://www2.eur.nl/fsw/research/veenhoven/Pub2000s/2004d-full.pdf) Retrieved: 30th November 2012.

World Database of Happiness. 2013. *World Database of Happiness.* Published online. Retrieved: 29th May 2013 (URL: http://www1.eur.nl/fsw/happiness/).

World Values Survey. 2013. *World Values Survey.* Published online. Retrieved: 29th May 2013 (URL: http://www.worldvaluessurvey.org).

Zuzanek, J. 2012. 'Does being well-off make us happier? Problems of measurement', *Journal of Happiness Studies.* Published online: 23rd June 2012 (DOI: 10.1007/s10902-012-9356-0)

# Section III
# On the politics of identity and difference in sustainable consumption

# 7 Housing as a function of consumption and production in the United Kingdom

*Mari Martiskainen*

## Introduction: The challenge of providing sustainable homes

Homes are causes and places of consumption, through the use of materials in the construction of buildings and household's use of energy, water, food, and consumer goods to meet everyday needs. Homes are fundamental when considering sustainable consumption. Most activities taken in the home are likely to consume resources, be it for maintaining a comfortable temperature, preparing meals, or undertaking leisure activities. Globally, all buildings (including homes and non-domestic buildings) consume the largest chunk of energy, approximately 32%, while the construction industry is responsible for over 30% of global resource consumption (Rode, Burdett, and Soares, 2011). Consumption and related emissions from homes come from a two-fold angle: the way homes are built and the way they are used. The development of suburbs and the growth in home ownership have gone 'hand-in-hand with developments in consumer goods' (Madigan and Munro, 1996, p. 42). In other words, homes cannot be separated from consumption but they are intertwined, having direct consequences on sustainable, or in many cases non-sustainable, consumption and contributing, among other things, to how climate change impacts are mitigated. Furthermore, poor housing conditions, such as the use of low-quality building materials, can increase emissions and be detrimental to wellbeing, as uncomfortable living conditions can have negative health impacts. Fuel poverty or 'energy poverty' (e.g., the inability to have an adequate level of energy services due to a combination of high energy bills and poor housing conditions), often adds another unwanted dimension to homes and remains an issue in many countries.

This chapter examines housing sustainability in the United Kingdom (UK), focusing on analysing why sustainable homes have not become the norm. The UK can, to some extent, be considered one of the front runners in climate change politics, given that in 2008 it became the first country in the world to set a legally binding target to reduce greenhouse gas (GHG) emissions, by 80% by 2050[1]. However, despite a long history, interest, and expertise in sustainable homes (e.g., homes that minimise resource use) (Pickerill, 2016), the actual number of such homes built in the UK remains limited. The Low Energy Building Database, for example, lists only 350 projects (LEBD, 2018), a drop in the ocean compared to the 28 million total housing stock.

Most people in the UK aspire to homeownership at some point in their lives, and this focus on homeownership has been the aim of several successive UK governments, underpinning much of the country's housing policy. Approximately 63% of all homes in England[2] are owned (34% being owned outright and 29% with a mortgage) (DCLG, 2017). There is a strong link in the UK between the housing market and personal wealth creation, but due to large differences in income distribution and equality, many people in the UK cannot afford to buy a home. House prices have increased considerably in recent years, with the capital, London, leading this trend as a centre for jobs, international investors, and high-income middle classes (Martin, 2011). There has also been an increase in homeowners who live outside the UK but invest in the London housing market to '*use its property market as a safe deposit for their wealth, in the expectation of continuing capital gains*' (Johnston et al. 2016, p. 358). The UK media and political discourse around homes thus regularly refers to the country having a 'housing crisis' (e.g., there not being enough affordable and decent homes for everyone). Headlines such as '*Britain's housing crisis is so serious that it must be tackled now*' (The Guardian, 2016) and '*The housing crisis has spread to everybody*' (Fraser, 2017) regularly appear in the British press.

In 2006, the UK Labour government announced that from 2016 onwards, all new homes would be zero carbon. This was a key announcement, as it recognised, at the highest policy level, the impact that homes have on the environment and climate. The policy, nevertheless, did not materialise, as it was removed by a Conservative government in 2015. After preparing for almost ten years for a new, zero carbon housing stock, the UK was faced with a situation where little policy support existed for sustainable homes, both in the new-built and existing homes sectors. Much of the UK's policies related to improving the sustainability of existing homes are now based on voluntary measures. This chapter highlights the complexities and also the conflicts underlying sustainable homes in the UK. It first discusses the meaning of a sustainable home before outlining the UK's housing profile. It then discusses, through pioneering cases of sustainable homes and policy development, how especially the Conservative government's austerity politics have been key reasons why sustainable homes in the UK remain a niche.

## Exploring a 'sustainable home'

Before moving on to discussing sustainable homes in the UK, it is important to note what is meant by a 'home' and how to define a 'sustainable home'. Homes are different from houses or buildings – in fact buildings house homes. A home can be considered to be a place where one feels comfortable, as indicated by the saying 'home is where the heart is'. Homes provide shelter and a place of comfort and safety. People unwind, rest, and act their needs and desires at home. A home offers a place for the creation and expression of identity—our beliefs and values are often stated through the physical and material aspects of our homes (Madigan and Munro, 1996; Easthope, 2004). Homes are ever changing and dynamic spaces with '*a complex range of symbolic meaning*' (Steward, 2000, p. 105). They are also spaces for personal and social interactions between household members, as well as visitors, neighbours, and the immediate local community. While most of these interactions are confined by the bricks and mortar of homes, they also have implications that go beyond the physical boundaries of a home. Following technological developments and widening digitalisation of society, homes have increasingly become places of work, and of different types of work relative to traditionally gendered housework (Madigan and Munro, 1996). People increasingly work from home in professional roles (Hampton, 2017) and also as carers looking after others (Steward, 2000). Thus, homes have interlinking cultural, economic, historical, political, and psychological meanings, uses, and connotations (for a detailed discussion, see Pickerill, 2016). Nowicki (2018) argues that the two main UK political parties (Labour and The Conservatives) have both used 'homeliness' and 'homemaking' as central concepts in regard to citizenship construction and nation building. In other words, they see homemakers as 'good' citizens, though this is contested, as not everyone is able to become a homemaker due to lack of access to the housing market.

Given that the term 'home' is open to subjective, contextual, and cultural interpretation, the term 'sustainable home' can be fluid too. In this chapter, a sustainable home is understood to mean a home which minimises resource use, energy, and water, and maximises the use of renewable energy and renewable materials throughout the lifecycle of the home (Pickerill, 2016). Such homes include 'eco-homes', 'passivhauses', or existing homes that have gone through extensive 'retrofits'[3]. As Pickerill states, '*the main purpose of an eco-house is to reduce waste—in its construction, occupation and demolition*" (Pickerill, 2016, p. 17). Once a home has been built, it will be used for several decades, locked into the materials used to build it. Sustainable homes are not just homes that have gone through technical energy efficiency fixes (see Chapter 1); they have also taken on a more holistic view that includes the whole lifecycle of building materials and uses.

## State of many UK homes: Old and cold

In terms of addressing sustainable consumption through housing, the UK has a challenging context: of the country's 28 million existing homes, almost a third were built before 1918 and do not adhere to current day building regulations[4]. Despite many older homes being expensive to heat and maintain, they are nevertheless sought after and often protected by planning laws for their heritage value (Pickerill, 2016). People in the UK generally prefer homes that come with 'period features', such as Victorian fireplaces and sash windows, and also often solid walls with no insulation. Such older homes often have poor energy efficiency and large heat loss—UK homes are responsible for approximately 23% of the country's carbon dioxide ($CO_2$) emissions (Bonfield, 2016). Furthermore, a survey of the

British public found that four in ten British homes are not considered to be up to standards in terms of decent conditions, affordability, space, stability, and neighbourhood (Shelter, 2016). Fuel poverty (i.e., not being able to have access to basic energy services such as light, heat, and hot water (Bouzarovski and Petrova, 2015)), was initially brought to the attention of UK policy makers by Dr Brenda Boardman in 1991 (Boardman, 1991, 2010), and has been an ongoing problem since. The plight of those living in poor housing and struggling to pay fuel bills is widely documented in the UK (e.g., Walker, Thomson, and Liddell, 2013), and this complex problem has been shown to have adverse health consequences (Marmot Review Team, 2011) and social policy implications (Baker, Mould, and Restrick, 2018). In England, approximately 11% of households live in fuel poverty (BEIS, 2018), but, for example, in Scotland this rises to 26.5% (Scottish Government, 2018). Not only does the UK's inefficient housing stock have negative climate impacts, but poor-quality homes can also affect householders in detrimental ways.

Delivering the required level of housing improvements to meet climate targets and reduce fuel poverty is an urgent, and complex task. The UK Green Building Council (UK-GBC) has estimated that to meet current emissions targets, 25 million UK homes will require retrofitting to the highest standards by 2050 (UK-GBC, 2017). Retrofitting existing homes can be costly (Jones, Lannon, and Patterson, 2013) and requires specific technical skills to avoid poor installations (Dowson et al., 2012). While ideally a whole home would be addressed in retrofitting, in reality retrofitting is often a long-term process involving several stages (Fawcett and Killip, 2014), requiring the acknowledgment that each home, and the use of each home, is unique, involving different householder practices (Gram-Hanssen, 2014).

New homes, which usually have better sustainability objectives than existing homes due to better building standards, are much debated in the UK. Generally, the rate of building new homes is slow—the UK is building fewer new homes today than it did in 1980 (ONS, 2016). An important factor in relation to new homes is cultural preference. New built homes are less popular; 47% of UK adults would prefer to buy an older home compared to 21% preferring a new build (HomeOwners Alliance, 2017). The new-built sector is not helped by media stories of housebuilders cutting corners by building low quality homes and then requiring non-disclosure agreements that prevent homeowners from speaking about potential problems (Ruddick, 2017). This suggests a sector partly tarred by profiteering and malpractice. Following reports that new homes 'are quite simply uninhabitable' (APPGEBE, 2016, p. 4), the government's All Party Parliamentary Group for Excellence in the Built Environment (APPGEBE) reported that, while the majority (86%) of new home owners reported being satisfied with their homes, 'housebuilders should be upping their game and putting consumers at the heart of the business model' (APPGEBE, 2016, p. 7). Many of the required sustainable housing solutions already exist, having been championed by dedicated eco-pioneers and champions, but these have never made it to the mainstream largely due to lack of policy support.

# The failure of UK politics to deliver sustainable homes

## 1970–1989: Early pioneers of sustainable homes and housing privatisation

The driving ideologies behind sustainable homes in the UK are often traced back to the 1970s oil crisis, which had a profound impact on early pioneers and also to some extent on government policy. While the 1970s eco-pioneers and governments had a common objective (i.e., to reduce reliance on oil), they did it for differing motives. Early eco-pioneers of sustainable homes often had 'deep-green' environmental values, aiming towards self-sufficiency, and alternatives to fossil fuels[5]. The 1970s Labour and Conservative governments, meanwhile, were driven by markets and efficiency. Early pioneers advocating alternative homes and sustainable living (Smith, 2005; Lovell, 2009) included, for example, architects Brenda and Robert Vale, who published a ground-breaking book 'The Autonomous House' in 1975 and advocated off-grid living (Vale and Vale, 1975). [The Vales went on to build their autonomous house in 1993 and designed another pioneering sustainable housing development, the Hockerton Housing Project, in 1998 (Lovell, 2007).] The Centre for Alternative Technology (CAT), meanwhile, was established in 1973 as a co-operative in an old quarry site in Wales, also championing autonomous living and sustainable building materials, such as straw bale houses and renewable energy installations (Seyfang, 2010). Some of the onsite housing designs at CAT were developed by architect Walter Segal (Pickerill, 2016), who was influenced by an anarchist housing movement that 'often requires unconventional societal structures, such as sharing homes through multi-family occupation, communes and co-operatives' (Pickerill, 2016, p. 73). CAT went on to host a cohousing community, based on the idea of shared facilities (for more on cohousing, see Lietaert, 2010), as well as a visitor centre and educational courses (CAT, 2017). CAT was an early pioneer of cohousing, which still today in the UK is an unconventional way of living (UK Cohousing lists 21 completed projects and 41 in development (UK CoHousing, 2018). While CAT has inspired others to build sustainable homes over the years (Martiskainen and Kivimaa, 2018), it has also questioned the UK's individualistic (e.g. Middlemiss, 2014) homeowner norms of everyone owning their own home. In effect CAT represents some of the early ideas for the degrowth housing movement, that of low impact living through shared and collective action that also considers social and environmental justice (Schneider and Nelson, 2018).

Early government action for making homes more sustainable followed 'energy conservation' becoming a government objective for successive Labour and Conservative governments in the early 1970s (Mallaburn and Eyre, 2014). From 1979 until 1997 the UK had a Conservative government, which took a neoliberal, market-based approach to housing and energy consumption, with reduced state interference (Mallaburn and Eyre, 2014). Some government funding was allocated, for example, for testing new technologies such as the Bradville Solar House, the first experimental solar house built in Milton Keynes in 1973 (McVeigh 1983).

Milton Keynes was one of 28 new towns established in the 1960s, many of which were inspired by the principles of Sir Ebenezer Howard's 'garden cities' movement first initiated in 1898 (Cook & Branson 2012). Garden cities were envisaged as places that would create towns outside major metropoles like London, avoid the need for commuting, and combine both town and country living. They had plenty of green space, community landownership, job opportunities (Cook & Branson 2012), and opportunities to develop new housing concepts at a larger scale (Horton 1987). However, these new cities were also criticised for market-led economic expansion, reliance on the use of personal cars, and lack of social and gender equality (Aldridge, 1996)—a very different approach from the more inclusive developments such as CAT.

The most important policy development of the 1970s was the introduction of Part L1A of Building Regulations—Conservation of Fuel and Power in New Dwellings in 1976. This addressed energy consumption of new buildings for the first time, and even to date has been the key policy for addressing the energy use of new homes. Building regulations have been tightened several times, most recently in 2006, 2010, and 2014—though their enforcement has often lacked (Fischer and Guy, 2009). It is not uncommon to buy a new home in the UK just to find out that building regulations were not properly followed during construction, often due to lack of local authority enforcements (Pan and Garmston, 2012).

In the 1980s, government focus shifted from conservation to 'energy efficiency', with year 1986 announced as an 'energy efficiency year' (Mallaburn and Eyre, 2014). By this time, Milton Keynes had become a research hub for new homes and showcased 53 new energy efficient homes that incorporated the latest innovations and designs, going beyond building regulations at the time (Horton, 1987), which even today is a rare occurrence. But this was still a very efficiency-focused approach to housing. Key government housing policy of the 1980s was the 'Right To Buy' scheme, announced by the Conservative government in 1980 and which enabled people to buy their local authority-provided houses at heavily discounted prices (Disney and Luo, 2017). This also started a government-backed discourse on homes as both the building blocks of a nation and as personal equity (Nowicki, 2018). As Nowicki argues, 'homeownership has been politically promoted and publicly understood as the ultimate attainment goal for hard-working citizens' (2018, p. 650). Right To Buy was the single largest privatisation during 1980–2005 in the UK, 'raising considerable sums for central government and increasing the share of owner occupation in the UK by almost 15%' (Disney and Luo, 2017, p. 65). Some three million homes were sold from the public sector to the private sector, either bought by those tenants with sufficient incomes or by non-profit housing associations (Valença, 2015). Reduced government funding for maintaining local authority housing at the time meant that remaining local authority housing tended to be very poor quality and occupied by those in the lowest incomes (Valença, 2015), causing further inequalities and marking remaining social tenants as 'unengaged with individualism and wealth creation, the bastions of neoliberal ideology' (Nowicki, 2018, p. 655). The sale of local authority-owned housing also meant a trend towards more homes being rented in the private sector (over time these increased from 2.06 million in 1984 to 5.3 million in 2014). Karakusevic has argued that these market ideologies replacing state provision caused a 'chronic crisis in supply' of decent local authority provided housing (Karakusevic, 2018, p. 51), a debate which continues to date. This has had direct implications on housing sustainability, as private landlords have been much less willing to improve the sustainability of their properties.

### 1990–2009: Fuel poverty and climate change emerge with aspirations towards zero carbon homes

In the late 1980s, concerns over global warming had started to emerge also in the UK, influenced by green European movements (Mallaburn and Eyre, 2014). The Conservative government published the UK's first environmental White Paper, 'This Common Inheritance', in 1990, which saw the government commit to its first emissions reduction targets and positioned energy efficiency as a key measure in getting to those targets (Mallaburn and Eyre, 2014). However, the government considered households as rational economic actors in relation to their housing-related consumption (e.g., Mallaburn and Eyre, 2014), an approach which was later shown to be too simplistic and dismissed the influence of habits, for example (e.g., Jackson, 2005). In addition to global warming concerns, fuel poverty became a policy driver for improving the energy efficiency of homes. The Warm Homes and Energy Conservation Act became law in 2000, and the subsequent Fuel Poverty Strategy of 2001 pledged to end fuel poverty in vulnerable households in England first by 2010, and then by 2016 (Marmot Review Team, 2011), officially recognising fuel poverty as a social problem instead of as a subset of poverty (Stockton and Campbell, 2011). Even though progress was made with reducing the number of fuel poor households between 1996 and 2004 (Stockton and Campbell, 2011), a combination of poor housing stock, rising energy bills, and stagnating wages meant that the target of eradicating fuel poverty was not met.

During the early 2000s, climate change concerns deepened following international summits and EU directives addressing energy performance of housing. In 2002, environmental NGO WWF-UK launched a 'One Million Sustainable Homes' (OMSH) campaign at the Johannesburg World Summit on Sustainable Development (Pickvance, 2009), calling on the UK government to commit to building one million sustainable homes (WWF-UK, 2006). WWF-UK became a key voice campaigning for sustainable homes (Pickvance, 2009), linking their importance to combating climate change. WWF had published the first of its bi-annual Living Planet reports in 1998, highlighting that we only have the resources of one planet to live on (WWF, 2016). One high-profile sustainable housing development of the time included BedZED, completed in 2002 by environmental charity Bioregional, architect Bill Dunster, and housing provider Peabody (Bioregional, 2018). BedZED consisted of 100 homes, office space, and community facilities. It was promoted by both government and policy actors as a best-practice case study, feeding into the UK's policy process on energy, climate, and housing policy (Lovell, 2009, p. 502). The learning from BedZED and inspiration from the WWF Living Planet report also motivated Bioregional to develop a 'One Planet Living' housing concept in 2003, centring around ten sustainability objectives: zero carbon; zero waste; sustainable transport; sustainable materials; local and sustainable food; sustainable water; land use and wildlife; culture and community; equity and local economy; and health and happiness. This was a holistic take on construction, including the importance of lifestyles in developing sustainable homes. BedZED had been, for example, a pioneer in car-free housing development. It achieved a large part of its emissions reductions through reduced car use, and at the same time highlighted UK households' heavy reliance on personal car-ownership and its implications on sustainability.

WWF's campaign efforts culminated in the Labour government announcing a journey towards sustainable homes in 2006, with an objective that, from 2016 onwards, all new homes would be 'zero carbon', and a voluntary Code for Sustainable Homes was announced to work towards that ambition. The government policy rhetoric changed from energy efficiency and emissions reduction to zero carbon emissions. There was a realisation, at the highest policy level, that significant changes were needed in the way UK homes were constructed and what their role was in combating climate change (Kivimaa and Martiskainen, 2018). This was an exciting time for sustainable home proponents in the UK, with the first long-term policy objective created for the sector. Further Labour government commitment to climate action was shown by the 2008 Climate Change Act, committing the UK to 80% GHG emissions reduction by 80% 2050. While the zero carbon homes announcement focused on new homes, a joint government and social housing sector action was set for existing homes through the 'Retrofit for the Future' programme. The £17 million programme was funded by the government during 2009–2013 to retrofit social housing. Its objective was to achieve an 80% emissions reduction in 100 projects (Gupta et al., 2015). However, only three projects met the emissions reduction targets, showing the complexities related to retrofits, for example, in terms of costs, technical viability of solutions, and the disruption that retrofit works can cause to tenants (Gupta et al., 2015).

Following the zero carbon announcement, the Zero Carbon Hub was set up as a government and industry initiative in 2008 to define what a zero carbon home would mean in practice (Greenwood, 2012). This involved organisations such as UK-GBC and Good Homes Alliance, building industry, NGOs, and policy makers, who started work towards developing the zero carbon homes concept. Zero Carbon Hub started at a turbulent time in the UK, as the country had been hit by a recession following the global financial crisis of 2008. The recession impacted the rate of new build properties and also meant stricter mortgage availability (ONS, 2016), causing a drop in housing supply. Nevertheless, some housing developers were also keen to test how they could achieve zero carbon in practice. For example, a large developer, Crest Nicholson, who had partnered with Bioregional before the recession, built One Brighton between 2007–2010. One Brighton became the first large-scale One Planet Living, zero carbon development in the UK (Kivimaa and Martiskainen, 2017). It aimed to be a truly sustainable housing development, from construction process to use, including also an objective to provide affordable housing. It is a mixed-use development, consisting of 172 flats, of which 54 are affordable social housing homes, and it has rental space for community organisations. One Brighton had ambitious objectives and faced several challenges in reaching zero carbon status, but its innovative solutions included car-free development, on-site renewables, roof top gardens, and a construction process that considered sustainability from the start (Kivimaa and Martiskainen, 2017). The focus on affordable and sustainable homes was welcome, as far too often sustainable homes in the UK have been portrayed as expensive and only available to a certain 'green elite' (Pickerill, 2016).

### 2010–2017: Austerity politics override focus on climate politics

A Conservative-Liberal Democrat coalition government came into power in 2010 and following the recession, implemented austerity politics. Austerity measures lead to government funding cuts in the public sector (Poinasamy, 2013) and also overriding the previous two Labour governments' concerns over climate change (e.g. Gillard, 2016). In a bid to reduce 'red tape', government intervention, and costs, a number of green policies were removed in 2015. These included the zero carbon homes objective and the Code for Sustainable Homes. Also, the Green Deal, a programme which had offered loans for home energy efficiency improvements, was removed. The Green Deal was terminated after only 2.5 years of operation, becoming an infamous policy failure (e.g. Rosenow and Eyre, 2016) that many stakeholders had predicted would fail due to its market-based, complicated, and expensive nature. The removal of the zero carbon homes objective was met with resistance from over 200 companies involved in the housing and construction industry (Murray, 2015). Other stakeholders, however, argued that the zero carbon target was too ambitious to begin with and that the UK's conservative building industry was not ready for the costs associated with zero carbon homes—even when there were clear indications that those costs would come down (Kivimaa and Martiskainen, 2018). The Zero Carbon Hub, for example, had ended up watering down initial zero carbon requirements, due to concerns over what was realistically achievable in the industry (Osmani and O'Reilly, 2009). The removal of the Green Deal, meanwhile, meant that the UK was left without any government policies in place that would encourage those able to pay to improve the sustainability of their homes. In effect, improving the sustainability of homes was left for the individuals to decide.

Around the time of the removal of green policies, the government's rhetoric on fuel poverty also changed drastically. Instead of eradicating fuel poverty, as had been the objective since the 2000s, the government's 2015 Fuel Poverty Strategy (DECC, 2015) (published for the first time in 14 years) set out that the new target was *'to ensure that as many fuel poor homes as is reasonably practicable achieve a minimum energy efficiency rating of Band C, by 2030'* (A being best, G worst rated) (DECC, 2015, p. 12). The problem was that government measures relating to fuel poverty had largely focused on incremental monetary and technical measures, such as helping with winter fuel bills or installing energy efficiency measures through energy suppliers, rather than taking a more holistic approach. An issue which evidently goes beyond energy had been addressed through incumbent energy companies (Rosenow, Platt, and Flanagan 2013), which are not experts in social or health policy but are in the business of making profits from their customers. Fuel poverty thus persists in the UK and in many instances has been left for various voluntary and third-sector organisations to combat. For example, community groups such as South East London Community Energy (SELCE) have worked tirelessly organising 'energy cafes', which provide energy advice sessions in libraries and community centres to help people vulnerable to fuel poverty (Martiskainen et al., 2018).

The government austerity cuts also affected those providing social housing (Hopkin et al., 2016). Compared to the private rented and owner-occupied homes, social and local authority provided homes had generally been at the forefront of providing new housing improvements despite their poor reputation in the 1980s. Sustainable homes usually cost less to run, providing a win-win situation for both landlords and tenants, with landlords having more secure rental income revenue as tenants have to pay less for energy bills (Green Alliance, 2013). In 2015, 24%, of owner-occupied homes had an energy efficiency rating of A–C (with A being the best and G the worst), compared to 48% of homes in the social housing sector and 26% in the private rented sector (DCLG, 2017). However, the heavy impact of austerity politics and government cuts was tragically evidenced in 2017, when 71 people were killed in a fire of a high-rise residential building, Grenfell Tower, in London. The intense and fast-spreading fire was caused by a combination of retrofitted insulation and flammable cladding that did not meet fire safety standards (Monaghan, 2017). Subsequent government enquiry showed that similar unsafe materials, which are cheaper than their non-flammable counterparts, were used in at least 82 other residential high-rise buildings (Walker, 2017). Fire safety was compromised over cost savings. Grenfell Tower started a public and political debate on the Conservative government's austerity politics (The Economist, 2018), and the way in which social housing tenants are treated not only by the government but by their landlords, and society as a whole. For a long time, those not aspiring to homeownership or being unable to afford a home were seen as not contributing to nation building (Nowicki, 2018, p. 655) and were therefore neglected in cases like Grenfell.

## Concluding remarks: The future of sustainable homes in the UK

Sustainable homes in the UK have not made it to the mainstream despite a long history and legacy of developments such as CAT and BedZED, which have also questioned the UK's individualistic home ownership model. These eco-pioneers went on to develop such homes without much policy support. While the UK was on par to have strong policies on the sustainability of future homes—with the government announcing in 2006 that all new homes would be zero carbon from 2016—that housing transformation never took place. Driven by the ideals of austerity and a reduced role for the state, the Conservative government not only removed the zero carbon homes objective but also many other green policies. This has left the UK in a situation where building regulations remain the only tool for providing decent new homes, and even they are not always followed through. For existing homes, and those homeowners who are able to pay for housing improvements, there are very few incentives to do so. This has meant that housing policy in the UK still follows the rhetoric of homeownership as the ability to gain personal wealth, rather than homeownership as the ability to mitigate the impacts that homes have on climate and the environment. Homes for many have become capital assets either as pensions or as second incomes through either the rental market (Martin, 2011) or initiatives such as Airbnb. People often talk about 'getting on to the housing ladder', which they are then expected to 'climb', meaning starting by buying their first home and later upgrading, or buying larger or multiple homes, and generating wealth in the process. However, the slow rate of house building has resulted in high house prices and rents, with, for example, young people now living longer with their parents, and social housing having long waiting lists (Jefferys and Lloyd, 2015). A 'generation rent' has emerged (Hoolachan et al., 2017) with more people renting homes today (Jefferys and Lloyd, 2015). At the same time, social housing, which has often had better sustainability credentials than owner-occupied or private rented homes, has been diminishing largely due to reduced local authority budgets following austerity measures. This limited role of the state in providing sustainable homes has meant that such homes still remain in the niche in the UK, and are driven by modern-day eco-pioneers, those individuals with strong environmental values and the financial means to do so. This approach of leaving the provision of sustainable housing to individuals and basing measures such as retrofits on choice leaves many people unable to participate, creating further inequalities. Those on low incomes, facing fuel poverty and living in rented homes may not be able to choose to improve the sustainability of their homes due to other pressing economic and social concerns. Given the UK's climate targets and ongoing problem of fuel poverty, housing policies need a radical rethink to avoid the country's homes being locked into polluting and harmful solutions for decades to come.

## Notes

1. The Climate Change Act, which became law in 2008, requires that the UK reduces GHG emissions by 80% by 2050 (compared to 1990 levels).
2. While the chapter's focus is on the whole of the UK, some of the housing figures are given for England only to illustrate points and are based on the English Housing Survey (see DCLG, 2017). Scotland (http://www.gov.scot/Topics/Statistics/SHCS), Wales (http://gov.wales/statistics-and-research/welsh-housing-conditions-survey/?lang=en) and Northern Ireland (https://www.nihe.gov.uk/index/corporate/housing_research/house_condition_survey.htm) have their own separate housing condition surveys.
3. Retrofitting, i.e. the 'construction approach involving the action of introducing [retrofitting] new materials, products and equipment into an existing building with the aim of reducing the use of energy of the building' (Baeli, 2013, p. 17), is different from renovating or refurbishing, which usually refer to work undertaken to repair homes so that they are made 'better' or aesthetically more pleasing (Baeli, 2013).

4. Approximately 27% of UK housing was built before 1918, 19% between 1919–1945, and 32% between 1946–1970, and only 22% of UK homes have been built since 1970 (Pickerill, 2016; DCLG, 2017).
5. However, Pickerill argues that the history of eco-homes in fact goes much further than this, highlighting, for example, 17–18th century vernacular traditional buildings in Wales that used ecological construction materials (Pickerill, 2016).

## References

Aldridge, M. (1996) 'Only demi-paradise? Women in garden cities and new towns', *Planning Perspectives*, 11(1), pp. 23–39.

APPGEBE (2016) 'More homes, fewer complaints. Report from the Commission of Inquiry into the quality and workmanship of new housing in England', All Party Parliamentary Group for Excellence in the Built Environment (APPGEBE). Available at: http://cic.org.uk/admin/resources/more-homes.-fewer-complaints.pdf (Accessed: 11 September 2018).

Baeli, M. (2013) *Residential retrofit: 20 case studies*. London: RIBA Publishing.

Baker, K., Mould, R. and Restrick, S. (2018) 'Rethink fuel poverty as a complex problem', *Nature Energy*, 3, pp. 610-612.

BEIS (2018) 'Annual fuel poverty statistics report, 2018 (2016 Data: England)', Department for Business, Energy & Industrial Strategy. Available at: https://www.gov.uk/government/statistics/annual-fuel-poverty-statistics-report-2018 (Accessed: 11 September 2018).

Bioregional (2018) *BedZED* [online]. Available at: http://www.bioregional.com/bedzed/ (Accessed: 11 September 2018).

Boardman, B. (1991) *Fixing fuel poverty: Challenges and solutions*. London: Belhaven Press.

Boardman, B. (2010) *Fixing fuel poverty, challenges and solutions*. London: Earthscan.

Bonfield, P. (2016) 'Each home counts. An independent review of consumer advice, protection, standards and enforcement for energy efficiency and renewable energy'. Available at: https://www.gov.uk/government/uploads/system/uploads/attachment_data/file/578749/Each_Home_Counts__December_2016_.pdf. (Accessed: 11 September 2018).

Bouzarovski, S. and Petrova, S. (2015) 'A global perspective on domestic energy deprivation: Overcoming the energy poverty-fuel poverty binary', *Energy Research and Social Science*, 10, pp. 31–40.

CAT (2017) 'Zero carbon britain, making it happen', Centre for Alternative Technology. Available at: http://zerocarbonbritain.com/images/pdfs/ZeroCarbonBritain-MakingIt Happen.pdf. (Accessed: 11 September 2018).

Cook, B. and Branson, A. (2012) 'Suburban renaissance', *Planning*, 1936, pp. 19–21.

DCLG (2017) *English Housing Survey. Headline report, 2015-16* [online]. Available at: https://www.gov.uk/government/collections/english-housing-survey (Accessed: 11 September 2018).

DECC (2015) 'Cutting the cost of keeping warm - A fuel poverty strategy for England, March 2015'. HM Government. Available at: https://www.gov.uk/government/uploads/system/uploads/attachment_data/file/408644/cutting_the_cost_of_keeping_warm.pdf (Accessed: 11 September 2018).

Disney, R. and Luo, G. (2017) 'The Right to Buy public housing in Britain: A welfare analysis', *Journal of Housing Economics*, 35, pp. 51–68.

Dowson, M., Poole, A., Harrison, D. and Susman, G. (2012) 'Domestic UK retrofit challenge: Barriers, incentives and current performance leading into the Green Deal', *Energy Policy*, 50, pp. 294–305.

Easthope, H. (2004) 'A place called home', *Housing, Theory and Society*, 21(3), pp. 128–138.

Economist, The (2018) 'The aftershocks of Grenfell Tower and the future of austerity', *The Economist*, 24 June [online]. Available online: https://www.economist.com/leaders/2017/06/24/the-aftershocks-of-grenfell-tower-and-the-future-of-austerity (Accessed 7 September 2018).

Fawcett, T. and Killip, G. (2014) 'Anatomy of low carbon retrofits: Evidence from owner-occupied Superhomes', *Building Research & Information*, 42(4), pp. 434–445.

Fischer, J. and Guy, S. (2009) 'Re-interpreting regulations: Architects as intermediaries for low-carbon buildings', *Urban Studies*, 46, pp. 2577–2594.

Fraser, I. (2017) '"The housing crisis has spread to everybody", says former boss of Shelter', *The Telegraph*, 8 January [online]. Available at: https://www.telegraph.co.uk/property/house-prices/robbthe-housing-crisis-has-spread-everybody/ (Accessed 7 September 2018).

Gillard, R. (2016) 'Unravelling the United Kingdom's climate policy consensus: The power of ideas, discourse and institutions', *Global Environmental Change*, 40, pp. 26–36.

Gram-Hanssen, K. (2014) 'Retrofitting owner-occupied housing: Remember the people', *Building Research & Information*. 42(4), pp. 393–397.

Green Alliance (2013) 'Seven steps to reducing energy bills. How greater ambition on home energy efficiency can bring down the cost of living', Green Alliance. Available at: http://www.green-alliance.org.uk/resources/Seven steps to reducing energy bills.pdf (Accessed 7 September 2018).

Greenwood, D. (2012) 'The challenge of policy coordination for sustainable sociotechnical transitions: The case of the zero-carbon homes agenda in England', *Environment and Planning C: Government and Policy*, 30(1), pp. 162–179.

Guardian, The (2016) 'Britain's housing crisis is so serious that it must be tackled now', *The Guardian*, 20 November [online]. Available at: https://www.theguardian.com/business/2016/nov/20/britains-housing-crisis-must-be-tackled-now (Accessed 7 September 2018).

Gupta, R., Gregg, M., Passmore, S. and Stevens, G. (2015). 'Intent and outcomes from the Retrofit for the Future programme: Key lessons', *Building Research & Information*, 43(4), pp. 435–451.

Hampton, S. (2017) 'An ethnography of energy demand and working from home: Exploring the affective dimensions of social practice in the United Kingdom', *Energy Research and Social Science*, 28, pp. 1–10.

HomeOwners Alliance (2017) 'The HomeOwner Survey 2017. Issues, trends and how we feel about our homes', HomeOwners Alliance. Available at: https://hoa.org.uk/catalogues/homeowners-survey-2017/files/assets/common/downloads/publication.pdf (Accessed 7 September 2018).

Hopkin, T., Lu, S., Hopkin, T., Lu, S., Rogers, P. and Sexton, M. (2016) 'Detecting defects in the UK new-build housing sector: A learning perspective', *Construction Management and Economics*, 34, pp. 35–45.

Horton, A. (1987). 'Energy Iniatitives in Milton Keynes', *Property Management*, 5(2), pp. 122–130.

Hoolachan, J., McKee, K., Moore, T. and Soaita, A. M. (2017) '"Generation rent" and the ability to "settle down": Economic and geographical variation in young people's housing transitions', *Journal of Youth Studies*, 20(1), pp. 63–78.

Jackson, T. (2005) 'Motivating Sustainable Consumption, a review of evidence on consumer behaviour and behavioural change', Sustainable Development Research Network. Available at: http://sustainablelifestyles.ac.uk/sites/default/files/motivating_sc_final.pdf (Accessed 7 September 2018).

Jefferys, P. and Lloyd, T. (2015) 'Why Don't We Build Enough New Homes in England?', *Built Environment*, 41, pp. 166–182.

Johnston, R., Owen, D., Manley, D. and Harris, R. (2016) 'House price increases and higher density housing occupation: The response of non-white households in London, 2001–2011', *International Journal of Housing Policy*, 16(3), pp. 357–375.

Jones, P., Lannon, S. and Patterson, J. (2013) 'Retrofitting existing housing: How far, how much?', *Building Research & Information*, 41(5), pp. 532–550.

Karakusevic, P. (2018) 'A new era of social housing, architecture as the basis for change', *Architectural Design*, 88(4), pp. 48–55.

Kivimaa, P. and Martiskainen, M. (2017) 'Intermediation in a low energy building project: A case of One Brighton housing development', in *Proceedings of eceee 2017 Summer Study on energy efficiency Consumption, efficiency and limits*, pp. 575–584.

Kivimaa, P., and Martiskainen, M. (2018) 'Dynamics of policy change and intermediation: The arduous transition towards low-energy homes in the United Kingdom', *Energy Research & Social Science*, 44, pp. 83–99.

LEBD (2018) *Low Energy Building Database* [online]. Available at: http://www.lowenergybuildings.org.uk/projectbrowser.php (Accessed: 31 July 2018).

Lietaert, M. (2010) 'Cohousing's relevance to degrowth theories', *Journal of Cleaner Production*, 18(6), pp. 576–580.

Lovell, H. (2007) 'The governance of innovation in socio-technical systems: The difficulties of strategic niche management in practice', *Science and Public Policy*, 34(1), pp. 35–44.

Lovell, H. (2009) 'The role of individuals in policy change: The case of UK low-energy housing', *Environment and Planning C: Government and Policy*, 27(3), pp. 491–511.

Madigan, R. and Munro, M. (1996) '"House Beautiful": Style and consumption in the home', *Sociology*, 30(1), pp. 41–57.

Mallaburn, P. S. and Eyre, N. (2014) 'Lessons from energy efficiency policy and programmes in the UK from 1973 to 2013', *Energy Efficiency*, 7(1), pp. 23–41.

Marmot Review Team (2011) 'The health impacts of cold homes and fuel poverty', Written by the Marmot Review Team for Friends of the Earth. Available at: https://doi.org/10.1136/bmj.d2807 (Accessed: 31 July 2018).

Martin, R. (2011) 'The local geographies of the financial crisis: From the housing bubble to economic recession and beyond', *Journal of Economic Geography*, 11(4), pp. 587–618.

Martiskainen, M., Heiskanen, E. and Speciale, G. (2018) 'Community energy initiatives to alleviate fuel poverty: The material politics of Energy Cafés', *Local Environment*, 23(1), pp. 20–35.

Martiskainen, M. and Kivimaa, P. (2018) 'Creating innovative zero carbon homes in the United Kingdom — Intermediaries and champions in building projects', *Environmental Innovation and Societal Transitions*, 26, pp. 15–31.

McVeigh, J.C. (1983). *Sun Power. An Introduction to the Applications of Solar Energy*. Second edition. Oxford: Pergamon Press.

Middlemiss, L. (2014) 'Individualised or participatory? Exploring late-modern identity and sustainable development', *Environmental Politics*, 23(6), pp. 929–946.

Monaghan, A. (2017) 'Improving fire safety in high-rises after Grenfell blaze "could take years"', *The Guardian*, 24 September [online]. Available at: https://www.theguardian.com/business/2017/sep/24/grenfell-tower-work-to-upgrade-fire-safety-in-high-rises-could-take-years (Accessed 7 September 2018).

Murray, J. (2015) 'Over 200 businesses call on Chancellor to save zero carbon homes standard', *BusinessGreen*, 20 July [online]. Available at: https://www.businessgreen.com/

bg/news/2418362/over-200-businesses-call-on-chancellor-to-save-zero-carbon-homes-standard (Accessed 7 September 2018).

Nowicki, M. (2018) 'A Britain that everyone is proud to call home? The bedroom tax, political rhetoric and home unmaking in U.K. housing policy', *Social and Cultural Geography*, 19(5), pp. 647–667.

ONS (2016) 'UK perspectives 2016: Housing and home ownership in the UK', Office for National Statistics. Available at: http://visual.ons.gov.uk/uk-perspectives-2016-housing-and-home-ownership-in-the-uk/ (Accessed 7 September 2018).

Osmani, M. and O'Reilly, A. (2009) 'Feasibility of zero carbon homes in England by 2016: A house builder's perspective', *Building and Environment*, 44(9), pp. 1917–1924.

Pan, W. and Garmston, H. (2012) 'Building regulations in energy efficiency: Compliance in England and Wales', *Energy Policy*, 45, pp. 594–605.

Pickerill, J. (2016) *ECO-Homes: People, place and politics*. London: Zed Books.

Pickvance, C. (2009) 'The construction of UK sustainable housing policy and the role of pressure groups', *Local Environment*, 14(4), pp. 329–345.

Poinasamy, K. (2013) 'The true cost of austerity and inequality, UK Case Study', Oxfam Oxfam International. Available at: https://www.oxfam.org/sites/www.oxfam.org/files/cs-true-cost-austerity-inequality-uk-120913-en.pdf (Accessed 7 September 2018).

Rode, P., Burdett, R. and Soares, J. C. (2011) 'Buildings: investing in energy and resource efficiency', *Towards a green economy: Pathways to sustainable development and poverty eradication*, pp. 331–373. United Nations Environment Programme. Available online: https://sustainabledevelopment.un.org/index.php?page=view&type=400&nr=126&menu=35 p (Accessed 7 September 2018).

Rosenow, J. and Eyre, N. (2016) 'A post mortem of the Green Deal: Austerity, energy efficiency, and failure in British energy policy', *Energy Research & Social Science*, 21, pp. 141–144.

Rosenow, J., Platt, R. and Flanagan, B. (2013) 'Fuel poverty and energy efficiency obligations – A critical assessment of the supplier obligation in the UK', *Energy Policy*, 62, pp. 1194–1203.

Ruddick, G. (2017) 'New home owners gagged over poor build and compensation claims', *The Guardian*, 16 February [online]. Available at: https://www.theguardian.com/business/2017/feb/16/new-home-owners-gagged-over-poor-build-and-compensation-claims (Accessed 7 September 2018).

Schneider, F. and Nelson, A. (2018) 'Housing for degrowth', in Institutionalisation of Degrowth and Post-Growth: The European Level Seminar, pp. 1–10.

Scottish Government (2018) 'High quality sustainable homes', Scottish Government. Available at: http://www.gov.scot/About/Performance/scotPerforms/partnerstories/HARO/Indicators/High-quality-sustainable#A1 (Accessed 7 September 2018).

Seyfang, G. (2010) 'Community action for sustainable housing: Building a low-carbon future', *Energy Policy*, 38(12), pp. 7624–7633.

Shelter (2016) 'Living home standard. Developed by the British public to define what everyone needs from a home in order to live rather than just get by', Shelter. Available at: http://www.shelter.org.uk/livinghomestandard?utm_source=google&utm_medium=cpc&utm_campaign=LHS&utm_content=Text_ad_7&gclid=CKT_y8DBqNECFQmeGwodkMAC1Q (Accessed 7 September 2018).

Smith, A. (2005) 'The Alternative Technology Movement: An Analysis of its Framing and Negotiation of Technology Development', *Human Ecology Review*, 12(2), pp. 106–119.

Steward, B. (2000) 'Living space: The changing meaning of home', *British Journal of Occupational Therapy*, 63(3), pp. 105–110.

Stockton, H. and Campbell, R. (2011). 'Time to reconsider UK energy and fuel poverty policies?', Joseph Rowntree Foundation. Available at http://www.jrf.org.uk/publications/time-reconsider-uk-energy-and-fuel-policies (Accessed 8 September 2018).

UK CoHousing (2018) *Cohousing in the UK* [online]. Available at: https://cohousing.org.uk/information/uk-cohousing-directory/ (Accessed 7 September 2018).

UK-GBC (2017) 'Building places that work for everyone. Industry insights into key Government priorities', UK Green Building Council. Available at: https://www.ukgbc.org/sites/default/files/08488%20Places%20for%20Everyone%20WEB.pdf (Accessed 7 September 2018).

Vale, B. and Vale, R. (1975) *Autonomous House: Planning for Self-sufficiency in Energy*. London: Thames & Hudson Ltd.

Valença, M.M. (2015) 'Social rental housing in HK and the UK: Neoliberal policy divergence or the market in the making?', *Habitat International*, 49, pp. 107–114.

Walker, R., Thomson, H. and Liddell, C. (2013) 'Fuel poverty 1991 – 2012. Commemorating 21 years of action, policy and research', University of Ulster and University of York. Available at: https://www.precarite-energie.org/IMG/pdf/Fuel-poverty-anniversary-booklet.pdf Accessed 7 September 2018).

Walker, P. (2017) 'Building regulations to be reviewed after safety tests following Grenfell', *The Guardian*, 28 July [online]. Available at: https://www.theguardian.com/uk-news/2017/jul/28/government-announces-independent-review-building-regulations-grenfell-tower-fire (Accessed 7 September 2018)

WWF (2016) 'Living Planet Report 2016', WWF. Available at: http://wwf.panda.org/about_our_earth/all_publications/lpr_2016/ (Accessed 7 September 2018).

WWF-UK (2006) 'One Million Sustainable Homes, moving sustainable homes from the fringes to the mainstream of UK housing. Project number 2236/December 2006.' WWF-UK. Available at: http://assets.wwf.org.uk/downloads/omsh_report.pdf (Accessed 7 September 2018)

# 8 Power and politics in the (work–life) balance: A mixed methods evaluation of the risks and rewards of downshifting

*Jacobs Hammond and Emily Huddart Kennedy*

## Can we live well while consuming less?

Among the panoply of individual-level solutions to reducing societal environmental impact, downshifting (voluntarily reducing income) stands out as particularly promising given the "double-dividend hypothesis" (Jackson, 2005, p. 19; see Chapter 7). In a discursive landscape in which calls to reduce impact are associated with sacrifice and threat to life satisfaction (Princen, 2006, p. 1), reducing income and consumption by decreasing work hours promises two "dividends": advancing life satisfaction and reducing environmental impact. Given evidence that at the national level, work hours are positively associated with carbon dioxide emissions (Knight et al., 2013, p. 691), and that roughly 25% of people in advanced industrialized nations have downshifted (Schor, 1998, p. 114; Hamilton, 2003, p. vii; Hamilton and Mail 2003, p. 14; Chhetri et al., 2009b, p. 350; Kennedy et al., 2013, p. 773), investigating this process is a valuable and timely endeavor.

Existing literature on downshifting has examined methods for reducing income, evaluated the environmental rewards of downshifting, and assessed impact on quality of life. Through this body of work, we know people often downshift by switching to a less demanding job, retaining their current job but reducing work hours, or quitting work altogether (Schor, 1998, p. 115; Hamilton, 2003, p. viii; Hamilton and Mail, 2003, p. 18; Chhetri et al., 2009b, p. 354). Research on those who downshift notes reduced environmental impacts (Warren Brown and Kasser, 2005, p. 349; Alexander and Ussher, 2012, p. 74; Kennedy et al., 2013, p. 764). Of the limited research examining life satisfaction, we see mixed conclusions, with downshifting having either nonsignificant (Kennedy et al., 2013, p. 764) or negative impacts (Chhetri et al., 2009a, p. 64) on satisfaction. Yet, studies on voluntary simplifiers—a group of self-identified downshifters who actively restrain their personal consumption—find increases in satisfaction (Warren Brown and Kasser, 2005, p. 349; Alexander and Ussher, 2012, p. 76). Some argue the satisfaction benefits experienced by voluntary simplifiers are partly due to gratification associated with demonstrating to others the possibility of an enjoyable life with restricted consumption (Levy, 2005, p. 180; Warren-Brown, 2005, p. 361; Kennedy, 2011, p. 857).

In this chapter, we focus on the subjective perceptions of life satisfaction, asking: what factors explain variation in the life satisfaction of downshifters? We have two related aims: the first is to determine whether demonstrating restricted consumption to others positively affects satisfaction, controlling for income. The second aim is to provide a rich description of the process of downshifting as experienced by people from a range of socio-economic statuses, focusing on impacts on satisfaction. Using survey data (Study 1) we confirm that, controlling for income, the perception of serving as a model to others positively impacts satisfaction. Drawing on semi-structured interviews (Study 2), we find that social location stratifies the experience of downshifting and the satisfaction it affords. High socio-economic status (SES) downshifters can deploy their resources to achieve increased work-life balance and life satisfaction, while low-SES individuals face significant constraints and experience poor satisfaction outcomes.

Our results have methodological and theoretical implications. Methodologically, our results suggest that common filter questions used to identify downshifters in survey research may be problematic. A standard filter question to identify downshifters is *have you voluntarily reduced income in the last X number of years?* In our survey (Study 1), we utilized a similar method to categorize downshifters, with little apparent problem. However, it was immediately apparent during our interviews with downshifters (Study 2) that this categorization process is actually quite complex. While the common filter question focuses on change in income, when confronted with the ambiguity described above, we found greater value in employing a more conceptual definition of downshifting as an attempt to *slow the pace of life* or to *achieve greater work-life balance*. Theoretically, our work sheds light on why surveys of downshifting report mixed and non-positive relationships between downshifting and life satisfaction. Past qualitative research explains satisfaction outcomes based on relatively socioeconomically privileged groups (e.g., see the model developed by Tan (2000, p. 176–177) and adapted by Hamilton and Mail (2003, p. 12) in Figure 8.1). Considering the various stages illustrated in Tan's model, our objective for Study 2 was to provide a rich description of the process of downshifting, focusing on impacts on life satisfaction, as experienced by people from a range of social locations. We find Tan's model does not accurately describe the process of downshifting for low-SES participants.

Today, sustainable consumption researchers call for solutions to reduce global resource use and to more fairly distribute resources. Yet, rather than mitigating the effects of power and inequality on satisfaction, the results of our two studies indicate these effects are reproduced and made increasingly salient throughout the downshifting process. Our findings demonstrate that while downshifting may offer an environmental dividend, in the current social, political, and economic context, it delivers the life satisfaction dividend only to those with considerable resources.

## Study 1: Surveying downshifters in Canada

Empirical survey research has operationalized downshifting by defining it as a *voluntary, long-term change which results in making less money—aside from taking a planned retirement* (Schor, 1998, p. 206; Hamilton, 2003, p. 6; Hamilton and Mail,

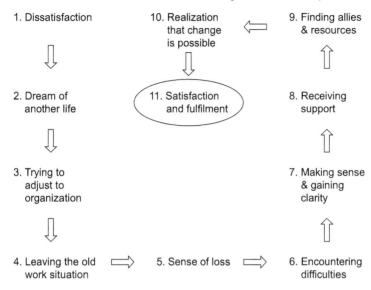

*Figure 8.1* The downshifting process.

Source: Hamilton and Mail (2003, p. 12), adapted from Tan (2000, p. 176–177)

2003, p. 6; Chhetri et al., 2009a, p. 62). For the sake of continuity, we also utilized the italicized operational definition in both our studies. However, in Study 2, we discuss the apparent ambiguity of this question for our interview participants.

## Methods

The data for Study 1 were collected via surveys distributed door-to-door in a western Canadian city in 2010. In total, 712 households were surveyed, and 491 surveys were returned (RR=69%). Our analysis here examines only those 124 respondents categorized as downshifters, who constituted 26% of the sample. We identified downshifters by examining responses to two items. The first item asked, "In the past 5 years, has anyone in your household voluntarily made changes in their life that resulted in your household making less money?" The second item asked, "In the past 5 years, has anyone in your household voluntarily made changes in their life that resulted in your household having more leisure time?" Downshifters were defined as those respondents who answered affirmatively to both items. Respondents were asked to reference the downshifting behavior of any member of the household, rather than solely that of the respondent, due to the study's focus on household-level environmentally sustainable practices and life satisfaction, which can be seen as either individual or household characteristics. After removing cases with missing observations, we have an analytic sample size of 110.

The goal of this study is not to find whether downshifters have higher satisfaction than non-downshifters, but rather to *identify factors that lead to variability in* satisfaction among downshifters. More specifically, *this study asks whether demon-strating restricted consumption to others positively affects satisfaction, controlling for income.* We use ordinary least squares (OLS) regression models to estimate the effects of income and modeling restrained consumption on downshifter satisfaction, controlling for socio-demographic factors.

## Variables

For the dependent variable *satisfaction*, we constructed a scale from items asking respondents to self-report their satisfaction with their health, job, finances, time use, and life in general (Alpha = .781). Our independent variables are *household income* and modeling reduced consumption for others (*modeling*). *Household income* is measured as an ordinal variable with six categories. *Modeling* is derived from a question that asks, "In 2009, how often did your household behave in ways that show others how they could reduce their consumption?" (never, rarely, sometimes, often or always). We also included several control variables: gender, home ownership, relationship status (married/not married), residential location (urban/suburban), and education (measured as a seven-category ordinal variable). We expect that both income and modeling reduced consumption for others will have positive effects on satisfaction, controlling for these socio-demographic factors.

## Results & discussion

Our models confirm our expectations (though due to the exploratory nature of this study we raised the level of significance to consider variables that have a p-value that slightly exceeds .05). Specifically, household income and modeling reduced consumption to others were found to be significant, positive predictors of satisfaction (Table 8.1). Although it is not surprising that higher income is associated with higher self-reported satisfaction, given that income has been found to predict

*Table 8.1* Satisfaction among downshifters: OLS regression models (standardized slopes)

|  | Model 1 | Model 2 | Model 3 |
| --- | --- | --- | --- |
| Gender (female = 1) | −.006 | −.006 | −.017 |
| Spouse (yes = 1) | .084 | .043 | .108 |
| Owns home or rents (owns = 1) | .048 | .019 | .048 |
| Age (years) | −.019 | .002 | −.004 |
| Neighborhood (urban = 1) | −.062 | −.041 | −.060 |
| Education | .210* | .154 | .149 |
| Household Income | – | .197* | .197* |
| Modeling | – | – | .208** |
| Adjusted R2 | .022 | .044 | .079 |
| N | 110 | 110 | 110 |

*p < .10; **p < .05[1]

satisfaction in the general population (Khaneman and Deaton, 2010, p. 16489), this is still a result worth discussing. Considering the analysis examines only downshifters, or those who voluntarily reduced income to secure greater leisure time, we had considered that these respondents might be less susceptible to this effect given our assumption that they downshifted because they valued time more than money. However, downshifters appear to be better off with higher levels of income. Thus, high-income downshifters seem to get the best of both worlds; they potentially gain leisure time and work-life balance, yet still have the financial means to avoid the stresses accompanying tight budgets. Finally, the effect of income remained significant, even when controlling for home-ownership and education, two additional measures of SES.

Households that regularly modeled reduced consumption to others reported higher satisfaction, controlling for other factors such as education, income, and marital status. We suggest three possible explanations for this relationship. First, it is possible that by demonstrating an environmentally friendly lifestyle, people are perceived as having higher status. This interpretation is in keeping with Horton's (2003, p. 74) argument that for individuals with high cultural capital and low economic capital, *green capital* can offset the diminished standing that might otherwise accompany low economic capital. A second explanation is that people interpret the act of demonstrating to others as a conduit to positively impacting sustainability. While scholars have noted that green consumers often doubt the material impact of their lifestyles (Lorenzen, 2012, p. 104), they credit their capacity to serve as exemplars as culturally significant (Kennedy, 2011, p. 857). This would support Levy's (2005, p. 176) argument that life satisfaction is enhanced when people feel they are contributing to socially valued goals. Finally, modeling environmentally friendly behaviors may be positively associated with satisfaction because it serves to clarify to a downshifter's social network that their diminished income is in fact their *choice*, rather than a result of economic uncertainty or tenuousness (Anantharaman, 2016, p. 864).

## Conclusions

Findings from this study are limited and conditional due to the small sample size and nonrandom sampling. Nonetheless, it is interesting to note the persistent relevance of income in the satisfaction of downshifters and the positive impact of modeling reduced consumption to others. Further, this study makes clear that downshifting is not experienced uniformly. Resources and values matter: wealthier downshifters tended to have a more positive experience than poorer downshifters, and downshifters who actively demonstrated the possibility of living well with less had better satisfaction outcomes than those who did not. Study 1 suggests that individuals who align non-material attitudes with a lifestyle that deemphasizes the centrality of financial gain tended to be relatively satisfied with their lives and that wealthier people are more likely to benefit from downshifting.

Study 1 left us with several questions: Why does having more income lead to better life satisfaction outcomes among downshifters? How do people negotiate the impact of work on other spheres of their lives, whether downshifting or not? Is downshifting universally sought after? And crucially, we wanted to know how low-SES individuals experience downshifting, as existing research focuses on relatively well-off populations (e.g., Iwata, 1997, p. 233; Iwata, 1999, p. 380; Grigsby, 2004, p. 17; Sandlin and Walther, 2009, p. 303; Walther and Sandlin, 2013, p. 38).

## Study 2: Interviewing downshifters in Washington State, U.S.A.

Prior research on downshifting has illuminated *how* individuals downshift, but we know less about *why* they do it, the circumstances under which they make this decision, the degree of agency they experience throughout the lifestyle change, and how the experience and rewards of downshifting vary for people across social strata. Empirical studies of downshifting and life satisfaction often use survey data (e.g., Schor, 1998, p. 206; Hamilton, 2003, p. vii; Hamilton and Mail, 2003, p. 13; Chhetri et al., 2009a, p. 60; Chhetri et al., 2009b, p. 349; Kennedy et al., 2013, p. 764). These studies illustrate overall patterns, such as a tendency for downshifters to be relatively educated, white, and middle-SES. Yet, these surveys are relatively silent on how downshifting is experienced. For example, Study 1 showed us that income and modeling reduced consumption to others are positively associated with life satisfaction, but revealed nothing about how these factors operate, what additional elements may matter, nor how individual and structural variables can influence the downshifting process and its impact on satisfaction. Much of the existing popular and scholarly literature on downshifting has operated under the assumption that downshifting is a relatively standardized process (Tan, 2000, p. 176–177). We argue, based on results from Study 2, that downshifting is a highly variable experience shaped by resources that map onto SES.

## Data and methods

During the summer of 2016, we conducted 44 semi-structured interviews that included questions about downshifting and life satisfaction. We identified three communities in Washington State, U.S.A., representing urban, urban cluster, and rural categories. In each community, we used census tract data and data on home values to select a high-income and a low-income neighborhood to obtain a sample of respondents from a range of social locations. To select respondents, the research team went door-to-door in each selected neighborhood, knocking at every third house. Interviews ranged from 45 minutes to over three hours and were conducted in respondents' homes, workplaces, and in public meeting spaces. In total our sample includes 8 low-SES respondents, 23 middle-SES respondents, and 13 high-SES respondents.[2]

When conducting the interviews, we identified downshifters by adapting a standard filter question taken from prior surveys of downshifters (Schor, 1998, p. 206; Hamilton, 2003, p. 6; Hamilton and Mail, 2003, p. 6; Chhetri et al., 2009a, p. 62; Kennedy et al., 2013, p. 771). The item asked, "In the last 5 years, has someone in your household made a long-term change which resulted in a significant change in income—other than taking a regularly scheduled retirement?" If the interviewee responded affirmatively, we asked them to describe the change, and then followed up with a series of questions regarding particular aspects of their lives (e.g., eating, travel/commuting, interaction with community, time-use), their satisfaction with various life domains (finances, employment, health, time-use, life in general), and questions pertaining to their life goals. When informants responded that no one in the household had downshifted, they were asked to imagine how their life might change if they experienced a significant increase or decrease in income, and how this might affect their satisfaction. These informants were also asked questions regarding their satisfaction with life domains (e.g., finances, employment, health, time-use, life in general) and life goals. All participants filled out a follow-up questionnaire to collect data on socioeconomic status.

## Analysis

During the research process, we utilized the constant comparative data analysis method where data collection and data analysis proceed simultaneously (Glaser and Strauss, 1967, p. 102). Analysis began with post-interview memos, in which we reflected upon questions pertaining to sections of the interview guide. Each transcript was coded, line-by-line, in NVivo to identify salient categories and themes as described in Rubin and Rubin (2005, p. 201). We created "nodes" for events, topical markers, themes, examples, and concepts based on our reading of the transcripts. Within each node, we looked for agreement and disagreement and used matrix queries to note socio-demographic patterns.

## Results

While popular literature on downshifting has described relatively privileged individuals who aspired to downshift and achieved greater satisfaction when they did (Elgin, 2010, p. 5; Robin et al. 2008, p. xvii), our interviews with socioeconomically diverse individuals demonstrated that the experience of downshifting is shaped by social location. We found high-SES individuals downshifted due to their aspiration for greater work-life balance and were able to draw on their resources at critical stages during the downshifting process (e.g., after leaving a job) to circumvent potential negative impacts of downshifting on life satisfaction. Downshifting thus resulted in greater autonomy and meaning, and enjoyable challenges. These individuals described a high degree of life satisfaction, and a lifestyle transition in keeping with optimistic portrayals of downshifting emanating from popular literature. Conversely, low- (and some middle-)

SES individuals started downshifting due to an inability to continue, or obtain, their desired work situation. Lacking in credentials and resources, these individuals encountered significant obstacles throughout the downshifting process, and tended to end up with unsatisfactory work arrangements that contributed to lower levels of life satisfaction. This suggests that instead of marginalizing the effects of power and inequality on satisfaction, inequality is reproduced and made increasingly salient throughout the downshifting process. These findings lead us to question whether environmental solutions predicated on downshifting can function democratically, or provide equality of access, in the absence of social policies.

## Ambiguous categorization

Downshifting has been previously defined in the literature as reducing income through one's own volition (Schor, 1998, p. 206; Hamilton, 2003, p. 6; Hamilton and Mail, 2003, p. 6; Chhetri et al., 2009a, p. 62; Kennedy et al., 2013, p. 771). Therefore, if someone was fired, laid off, demoted against their will, or opted for a regularly scheduled retirement, they did not qualify as a downshifter. What members of the research team quickly came to understand is that categorizing people in an interview setting is complicated, suggesting it may be similarly complicated for survey participants to choose between "yes" and "no" response options. The theme of ambiguity is not intended to shed light on the relationship between downshifting and satisfaction, but to provide a behind-the-scenes look at how a standard operationalizing question is interpreted. We noted ambiguity in three ways: first, when respondents struggled to answer "yes" and "no"; second, by respondents answering clearly but then adding details that suggested their experience was at odds with existing definitions in the literature; and finally, when reducing income was one, relatively unimportant, piece of a broader lifestyle move intended to support a higher quality of life.

Often, even when informants were laid off or demoted, they still responded affirmatively to the question asking whether they had voluntarily reduced income. That is, they experienced that event as reflecting free will though their description of events suggested otherwise. For example, Don, a 66-year-old taxi driver, had made more money in a previous position as a chef. He was eventually fired from that position, an event that he was reluctant to elaborate on but which clearly soured him to the occupation. In reaction, he decided not to look for another chef position and now makes much less income driving a taxi. Don stated he had voluntarily made a long-term change that resulted in making less income. This hesitancy to admit a transition was not voluntary reflects existing evidence that the working poor in America prefer to see their situation as voluntary, temporary, and positive (Sherman, 2009, p. 98). In a society where involuntary poverty is stigmatized and often attributed to personal failure, it is possible individuals who portray an involuntary reduction in income as voluntary may do so to avoid being perceived as a "failure," and accruing the stigma associated with this designation.

At times, individuals' work-related decisions were nested in broader lifestyle choices. The rural site in our sample is an amenity-rich, island community known for its scenic beauty and slow pace of life. Due to a tourism-based economy, it is also an area with relatively high rates of unemployment during the offseason (US Bureau of Labor Statistics, 2017). Thus, for many, living on the island requires reducing their pay and increasing their work hours. Even those who held full-time positions were still sometimes in keeping with the "spirit" of downshifting. Some had left higher paying jobs off-island to live in a valued place. Others, like Caitlyn, a 38-year-old full-time bartender who relished her job because of the flexibility it provided, emphasized work-life balance through their choice of occupation.

In summary, while filter questions commonly used on surveys focus on change in income, when confronted with the ambiguity described above, we found greater value in employing a more conceptual definition of downshifting as an attempt to slow the pace of life or achieve greater work-life balance. Next, we describe themes that helped us to understand the relationship between downshifting and satisfaction, drawing on evidence from a range of socioeconomic groups.

## The pushed/pulled continuum

Descriptions of downshifting emanating from popular literature paint a picture of a downshifted lifestyle that is preferable to full-time work (Robin et al. 2008, p. xvii; Elgin, 2010, p. 5). Yet, in our interviews this was not consistently the case, a fact which seems related to the nuance surrounding the word "voluntary." A straightforward interpretation of "voluntary" leads to a definition of downshifting as any instance in which the individual initiates the action of reducing work hours, reducing income, quitting a job, retiring early, or shifting jobs. Yet, simply because one initiates a career change does not necessarily mean they *aspire* to such a change. Rather, some informants explained that they had entered into downshifting as a compromise, brought on by factors largely outside their control. We describe these distinct experiences as opposite ends of a *pushed/pulled continuum*. Some downshifters viewed their achieved lifestyle as an ideal to which they had long aspired, or been *"pulled"* to fulfill, while others reported their downshifting resulted from compromises made due to personal and external constraints, which had *"pushed"* them to alter their work arrangements.

Another way to make this distinction between subgroups of downshifters is by applying Tan's (2000, p. 176–177) downshifting framework to our sample of downshifters from across social strata. Upon doing so, it is apparent that our downshifters enter Tan's framework at different stages. Many of our "pulled" downshifters began with Step 1 (see Figure 8.1). These individuals tended to be high-SES and often engaged in a period of planning prior to downshifting. They experienced dissatisfaction at work, which led them to consider alternative work arrangements. These individuals engaged in considerable deliberation of alternatives, and eventually decided to initiate downshifting by transitioning away from their previous jobs. However, many low- and some middle-SES downshifters entered Tan's process model at Step 4 (leaving the old work situation) and had not considered downshifting prior to doing it. Something happened to these downshifters that pushed them to leave work (e.g., injury, ill relative, childcare responsibilities). Subsequently, these individuals reacted by making work-related decisions in keeping with the downshifting "spirit," such as retiring early, pursuing less demanding jobs, or quitting work entirely. Yet, these "pushed" downshifters *did not aspire to downshift*. Instead they downshifted out of necessity and limited alternatives.

## Stratified resources

The downshifters we describe here as "pulled" tend to be middle- and high-SES, while "pushed" downshifters are often middle- and low-SES. We argue SES influences downshifting through the *capacities* individuals have to draw upon. We understand capacities to include the *resources* individuals possess. Key resources identified included access to supplementary income, personal health, and level of educational attainment. Satisfied downshifters were often able to draw on supplementary income sources, such as financial support from a close relation (partner, parents, extended family) or accumulated savings. In addition, these happy downshifters often possessed educational credentials that widened their employment options upon re-entering the labor market. They were generally healthy, and thus were not hampered by physical or mental disabilities. Unhappy downshifters, on the other hand, typically lacked supplementary income, possessed lower educational attainment, and often suffered from health conditions.

### Supplementary income

While high-SES downshifters benefited from supplementary income from partners, family inheritances, or accrued savings, low- (and sometimes middle-) SES downshifters lacked this financial security, creating barriers to their pursuit of desired work arrangements. Don, described above, had been a chef, but was fired from this position. This experience left him disillusioned to the point that, upon reentering the job market, he chose not to pursue other chef positions, and instead made significantly less money driving taxi. Yet, even at the age of 66, Don aspired to a different life. Though he drove taxi for a living, Don identified primarily as an artist. He had experienced some success with his art, and he had hoped to grow his art from a hobby to a career, which had not yet materialized due in part to financial restrictions. As a renter, and without the finances to rent a workspace, he was unable to practice his art, a fact that bothered him. Don wanted to go back to school to become qualified to teach art history at the college level. However, his "subsistence level" income and lack of supplementary income and savings were thwarting these aspirations. Charles, 66 and low-SES, retired early from a career as a truck driver because he had accumulated injuries which made it unbearable to perform the physical labor demanded by the position, yet he soon discovered social security was not enough to live on. Therefore, Charles had to take whatever temporary work he could obtain (and which his body could handle), regardless of its appeal. Had financial concerns not been so central, Charles might have focused more of his energies on his passion, which was acting.

Middle-SES individuals did not report these same accounts of being limited by income, but nonetheless reported being pushed to downshifting because of a shortage of financial resources. For instance, Addy, 40, had alternated between staying home with her two young children and working part-time jobs. Prior to becoming a parent, Addy worked in management for a non-profit organization, but she had chosen to stay home once her children were born. When asked if staying home with the kids was her ideal arrangement, Addy said: "Uh, no, because I like working. I like doing things...I would like to only work part-time, for myself and make plenty of money to not have financial stress...I would like to have plenty of time with my family and plenty of money at the same time." Addy had alternated between staying home full-time and working part-time because she missed work when she was away from it. Yet, each time she went back to work she found the part-time work she was able to obtain was neither satisfying nor provided sufficient income to cover childcare costs. This *pushed* her toward downshifting, though it was not an optimal situation. Despite Addy's middle-SES position, her status as a mother with small children, combined with a less-than-ideal part-time job market and the expense of privately run childcare, left her unsatisfied with her downshifted life.

Others who downshifted with greater financial security described a much more positive experience, more in keeping with the optimistic portrayals characteristic of popular literature on downshifting (Robin et al. 2008, p. xvii; Elgin, 2010, p. 5). For example, Annie, 59 and high-SES, is a former IT specialist who became exhausted by long hours and lack of flexibility, and decided to shift to a career as a real estate agent. She loved being her own boss and voiced a high degree of satisfaction with her new career. As a real estate agent, Annie worked on commission, so she had no income until she started making sales. Annie was still making significantly less as a real estate agent than she made at her previous job, but her satisfaction was much higher. This was, at least in part, because her husband had a steady job and had been supporting her financially, alleviating the financial strain she might otherwise have experienced with such a career transition.

Myra, 45, is another happy, middle-SES downshifter. She used to work at a bank, but now stays home and writes. She credits her ability to downshift successfully to her husband's salary:

> ...he does like half-time ministry and half-time small business. But he kind of got to the point where the small business was making enough that I didn't need to work at the bank...I do the bookkeeping stuff for him. We do a lot of hospitality and having people in. So really for us it works a lot better to have someone (at home).

The financial support Annie and Myra had from their partners allowed them to choose vocations they were drawn to. Unlike Addy, they were not restricted to choosing occupations for their salary. Annie was able to live comfortably during her transition to real estate. Myra was able to focus on her passion (writing). In both cases, being supported financially allowed them to pursue meaningful work that aligned with their life goals. As a whole, this allowed both of them a high degree of autonomy and provided motivating challenges without financial stress.

Another example of a happy, high-SES downshifter was Ben, 77, who reflected on his downshifting experience, which began in his 40s. Ben had been working full-time but decided to quit and go back to school.

> ... I was always interested in financial planning. In college I took classes in financial planning and I had read a lot of books about it. I thought about how much freedom that would give me to be my own boss and do my own thing. And so I went back to school and became a certified financial planner. And then we did drop out and go sailing for two and half years...[T]hen I did the financial planning business and I did that for about 20 years ...

Like Annie and Myra, Ben did not experience financial insecurity from downshifting. While Ben does not directly speak to this fact, the story lends itself to that interpretation. After quitting his job, Ben went back to school. Upon completing school, Ben and his wife immediately took two-and-a-half years off from work to go sailing. When Ben was asked if he had missed the income as a result of taking this time off, he noted: "When we went sailing we were on a budget of $2000 a month and that was in the late 80's so that was (a) pretty skinny budget...we could go to marinas we had to anchor off... we did it really on the cheap." We do not have detailed information regarding Ben's financial situation at the time of his travels. However, Ben and his wife were secure enough financially to take two-and-a-half years off from work while spending approximately $25,000 per year.

The financial security Myra, Annie, and Ben experienced during their downshifting process is starkly different from what our low-SES downshifters described. The lack of financial strain allowed each to be selective in their career path. If they needed to go back to school for additional training, they could afford to do so. Yet, lacking financial resources was deleterious to downshifters' satisfaction and to people's ability to *imagine* downshifting as an attractive alternative. When low-SES respondents who were working full-time were asked to imagine what it would be like to downshift, they tended to have negative reactions. Jim, 29 and a chef, was not only averse to the idea of downshifting, but felt guilty he was not working *more* than 40 hours per week. For Caitlyn, 38 and a bartender, the mere thought of downshifting triggered anxiety. "I would hate to have that thing, like being worried about, am I going to be able to make my power bill this month, am I going to be able to afford my phone, you know what I mean?...It worries me even thinking about having to worry about that." Financial resources appear to stratify both the experience of downshifting and the anticipated experience of it.

### Health

Health was a critical resource that varied among the downshifters we interviewed and either enabled or thwarted their pursuit of desired work arrangements. Some downshifters experienced significant impairment due to conditions that made continuing in their previous occupation untenable. For example, Charles, noted above, ended up working limited hours at odd jobs to accommodate his physical limitations. Yet he desired to work more and explained that his life tended to lose structure when he was not working. "I waste a lot more than I did. I love being productive...there's the money thing, but also I'm working because I need some kind of work going on to set up the rest of my day around."

William, 65 and low-SES, is another individual whose life satisfaction was not improved by downshifting. William initially told us he retired early. However, we eventually learned that he had been laid off from his previous job. Due to a history of struggles with mental health, William rejected the possibility of pursuing alternate employment in favor of early retirement. However, his experience of retirement was not positive. His dwindling savings left him worried he would outlive his financial resources. "I'm in a state of unknown," explained William. "I've got longevity in my genes...It's been on my mind." Longevity, in this instance, was not an asset but a liability.

For downshifters with good health, their ability to use their physical and mental abilities widened the range of available opportunities for work. Like Charles, Denny, 44 and middle-SES, had quit his former job due to health issues. Denny had previously worked on fire crews, and the hazardous conditions had taken a toll. Yet, unlike Charles, upon quitting, Denny remained healthy enough to support himself by working carpentry while he returned to school. Because he was able to do this physical work, he was close to completing a Bachelor's degree in preparation for his desired job as a youth counselor.

High-SES downshifters frequently mentioned past health issues voluntarily, crediting their decision to reduce work hours as the reason for health improvement. However, low-SES downshifters were more reticent about their health; when probed, they tended to describe ongoing conditions that had not significantly improved in the downshifting process. High-SES downshifters did not necessarily enjoy perfect health, but they did not experience conditions that significantly restricted their ability to perform their choice of work. Thus, health functioned as a critical resource when navigating the downshifting process and one that interacted with income. Low-SES downshifters with poor health found their options significantly constrained, while unencumbered downshifters had a far greater range of possibilities to explore. This finding maps onto a voluminous body of research which finds health outcomes are often stratified by SES (Semyonov et al., 2013, p. 10; Denney et al., 2014), and demonstrates how inequality contributes to a vicious cycle for those at the bottom by diminishing health, and therefore hindering one's ability to climb out of poverty.

### Educational attainment

Those with less education tended to experience more barriers in the downshifting process. Charles, quoted earlier, had not finished high school. Due to numerous ailments, he had left a physically demanding job but due to his limited education, was still limited to manual labor work. This work was unsatisfying, inconsistent, and low-wage. Don tells a similar story. While he aspired to work as an art history professor, he did not have the qualifications to pursue his goal. This left Don dissatisfied with his current work arrangement, but with limited means to address the situation.

Downshifters with more education had an easier time finding desirable work. Annie, quoted above, had an MA degree and had left a position working as an IT specialist for the state government. Annie did not mention any obstacles when making the change to a career in real estate, typical of other high-SES downshifters. Similarly, Carissa, 37 and middle-SES, had a PhD and had previously held a high-status position working for the federal government. When Carissa realized she wanted to go back to school to make a career change, she was able to use her salary and savings to cover tuition, and she had the educational qualifications necessary to get into graduate school. While Carissa had not yet achieved her desired position, she was confident in her ability to do so.

Low-SES downshifters with little education and low-status former careers found their future employment options restricted. Because of their limited savings, paying for additional training was a significant obstacle to finding more meaningful work. Conversely, middle- and high-SES downshifters with more education were able to afford additional training and possessed the professional skills to succeed in these efforts.

## Implications

Our analyses complicate a widely held assumption that downshifters are making an ideological, voluntary decision to reduce income and live a simpler life (Robin et al., 2008, p. xxi; Elgin, 2010, p. 4). The empirical basis for this assumption often relies on purposive samples of relatively well-educated and privileged individuals. In our socioeconomically diverse sample, we find low-SES downshifters felt little capacity to customize their working arrangements to foster satisfaction. However, high-SES downshifters experienced much more agency (and satisfaction) during the downshifting process because they had access to considerable resources. While Tan's model (Figure 8.1) captures the high-SES process, it does not reflect the experiences of low-SES participants. We depict the low-SES downshifting model in Figure 8.2. Comparing these models, we see the downshifting experience varies significantly across SES. Contrasting these two figures provides

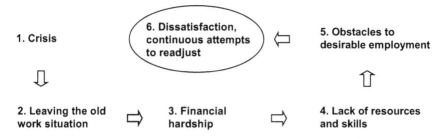

*Figure 8.2* The low-SES downshifting process.

Note: This model builds off research by Tan (2000)

a visual representation of the *pushed/pulled continuum*. Figure 8.2 represents the experience of (largely low-SES) individuals who felt "pushed" to downshift by personal or external forces, while Tan's model (Figure 8.1) reflects those (largely high-SES) individuals who felt "pulled" to this lifestyle.

In Figure 8.2, readers should note that low-SES downshifters did not aspire, or plan, to downshift. Rather, they reacted to a crisis compelling them to leave their old work situation. Having downshifted, they experienced financial hardship because of a lack of supplementary income. Low-SES downshifters often had less education, which limited their opportunities to obtain ideal employment. In short, low-SES downshifters resorted to undesirable work out of financial need, contributing to their dissatisfaction.

## Conclusions

In Study 1, we identified *income* and *modeling* reduced consumption to others as significant in explaining life satisfaction. Our survey data demonstrate the effects of variables of interest (modeling, income) on satisfaction, while statistically controlling for others. Our interviews (Study 2) illuminate the process through which variables such as income influence satisfaction while also shedding light on how informants perceived the act of downshifting itself. We note that income is significant because it allowed downshifters to buffer financial pressures, be selective in choosing a new career, and obtain additional training. Downshifters with financial security were more likely to achieve desirable and relatively high-status work that aligned with their life goals and provided them with a significant degree of autonomy, desirable challenges, and which contributed to positive life satisfaction outcomes. Satisfied downshifters were better educated, providing them with marketable skills when re-entering the job market, and they were less likely to experience debilitating health conditions (and more likely to report improvements in health through the downshifting process). Financially insecure downshifters experienced limited autonomy throughout the downshifting process. These downshifters felt forced to take whatever work was readily available due to immediate financial need. When they lacked supplementary income, these participants were limited in pursuing the additional training that would enhance their ability to be choosy in the job market. Finally, the tendency for some low-SES individuals to view their situation as voluntary, even when the research team felt otherwise, demonstrated the difficulty of defining downshifting as "voluntary" and pointed to the necessity of recognizing a continuum of agency experienced by individuals throughout the downshifting process.

In opposition to the common framing of downshifters as individuals making an ideological, voluntary decision to reduce income and live a simpler life (Robin et al., 2008, p. xxi; Elgin, 2010, p. 5), low-SES downshifters often entered into the lifestyle change as a compromise in the face of limited alternatives. For example, some downshifters quit work to care for an ill family member; others downshifted to accommodate physical limitations; while still others downshifted when faced with the expense of childcare. In many cases, these downshifters had enjoyed their previous work and did not wish to change paths but were *pushed* toward this option by the inflexibility of their workplaces.

We conceptualize low-SES downshifters as being "pushed" toward downshifting by personal and external constraints. Conversely, high-SES were "pulled" by their aspirations for a downshifted lifestyle. This discrepancy was evident in high- and low-SES downshifters' comments about their new lifestyle. High-SES downshifters highlighted the benefits (i.e., greater leisure time, ability to pursue their passions, alleviation of health problems), while low-SES described downshifting as a compromise necessitated by circumstances beyond their control. This suggests we cannot presume downshifting will have either uniformly positive *or* negative impacts on life satisfaction, but that its effects will vary depending on the resources of the downshifting individual and the sociopolitical context in which they act. Our findings cast doubt on suggestions that downshifting presents a viable individual-level solution to mitigate environmental degradation based on a double-dividend model (Jackson, 2005, p. 19). While downshifters have been found to have a lower environmental impact than non-downshifters (Warren Brown and Kasser, 2005, p. 349; Alexander and Ussher, 2012, p. 74; Kennedy et al., 2013, p. 764), findings from our studies lead us to believe that the satisfaction payout of the double-dividend is really only available to a privileged group. For low-SES downshifters, the picture is much less positive.

As countries transition to a governance model that places the responsibility to advance sustainable consumption on individuals (Soneryd and Uggla, 2015, p. 87), it is tempting to embrace policy solutions based on individual-level actions (Maniates, 2001, p. 32). However, our findings suggest that, far from side-stepping political entanglements, downshifting is imbued with politics and power dynamics. While policy solutions like taxing carbon may meet with resistance in the political arena, such solutions target the key drivers of environmental problems more effectively and therefore possess the potential to make a greater impact. Further, our findings suggest a need for environmental policy makers to think more broadly about the guidelines and legislation governing work hours, medical and leave benefits, guaranteed annual income thresholds, and the costs of postsecondary education and childcare. We suggest that downshifters cannot evade the structural parameters shaping the labor force, the home, and care work. For downshifting to offer a truly transformative contribution to the pursuit of sustainability, scholars and policy makers must address and redress the social structures currently stratifying opportunity and fulfillment in the downshifting context.

## Notes

1. Coefficients have been converted to standardized beta coefficients, indicating how many standard deviations the dependent variable (Satisfaction) changes with an increase of one standard deviation in the independent variables (listed in the left-hand column). This allows us to determine the relative magnitude of the effect of different independent variables on the satisfaction of downshifters. OLS regression analysis allows us to test the relationship between independent variables and Satisfaction, while holding other (control) variables constant. The results are displayed across several models to illustrate relationships between variables. If a coefficient decreases when new independent variables are introduced, that tells us the new variable(s) mediate(s) the effect of $x$ on $y$. For example, part of the effect of the control variable 'Education' on Satisfaction is attributable to Income, as the coefficient falls in Model 2 and the relationship moves from significant to non-significant.
2. We operationalized socio-economic status (SES) by combining responses to three items: education, income, occupational status. These variables are categorical, with education broken into three categories and income and occupation into four categories. We ranked categories from low (1) to high (3 or 4). Based on these scores, informants were categorized as low (3–5), middle (6–8), or high (9–11) SES. When values were missing on a variable, the research team considered other indicators of SES from the interview data to make a final decision on placement.

## References

Alexander, S., and Ussher, S. (2012) "The Voluntary Simplicity Movement: A multinational survey analysis in theoretical context", *Journal of Consumer Culture*, 12(1), pp. 66–86.

Anantharaman, M. (2016) "Elite and ethical: The defensive distinctions of middle-class bicycling in Bangalore, India", *Journal of Consumer Culture*, 0(0), pp. 1–23.

Bureau of Labor Statistics, U.S. Department of Labor. (2017) *Local area unemployment statistics map* [Online] Available at: https://data.bls.gov/map/MapToolServlet?survey=la&map=county&seasonal=u&datatype=unemployment&year=2015&period=M03&state=53/(Accessed: 24 February 2018)

Chhetri, P., Khan, A., Stimson, R., and Western, J. (2009a) "Why bother to 'downshift'? The characteristics and satisfaction of downshifters in the Brisbane-South East Queensland region, Australia", *Journal of Population Research*, 26(1), pp. 51–72.

Chhetri, P., Stimson, R., and Western, J. (2009b) "Understanding the downshifting phenomenon: A case of southeast Queensland, Australia", *Australian Journal of Social Issues*, 44(4), pp. 345–362.

Denney, J., Krueger P., and Pampel, F. (2014) "Socioeconomic status and health behaviors", *The Wiley Blackwell Encyclopedia of Health, Illness, Behavior, and Society*, [online]. Available at: https://onlinelibrary.wiley.com/doi/abs/10.1002/9781118410868.wbehibs54 (Accessed 1 February 2018)

Elgin, D. (2010) *Voluntary simplicity: Toward a way of life that is outwardly simple, inwardly rich.* 2nd ed. New York: Harper Collins.

Glaser, B. and Strauss, A. (1967) *The discovery of Grounded Theory: Strategies for qualitative research.* New York: Aldine.

Grigsby, M. (2004) *Buying time and getting by: The Voluntary Simplicity Movement.* Albany, NY: SUNY Press.

Hamilton, C. (2003) *Downshifting in Britain: A sea-change in the pursuit of happiness.* Discussion paper 50. Canberra: Australia Institute.

Hamilton, C. and Mail, E. (2003) *Downshifting in Australia: A sea-change in the pursuit of happiness.* Discussion paper 50. Canberra: Australia Institute.

Horton, D. (2003) "Green distinctions: The performance of identity among environmental activists", *The Sociological Review*, 51(2), pp. 63–77.

Iwata, O. (1997) "Attitudinal and behavioural correlates of Voluntary Simplicity lifestyles", *Social Behaviour and Personality*, 25, pp. 233–240.

Iwata, O. (1999) "Perceptual and behavioural correlates of Voluntary Simplicity lifestyles", *Social Behaviour and Personality*, 27(4), pp. 379–383.

Jackson, T. (2005) "Live better by consuming less? Is there a 'double dividend' in sustainable consumption?", *Journal of Industrial Ecology*, 9(1–2), pp. 19–36.

Kahneman, D. and Deaton, A. (2010) "High income improves evaluation of life but not emotional wellbeing", *Proceedings of the National Academy of Sciences*, 107(38), pp. 16489–16493.

Kennedy, E.H. (2011) "Rethinking ecological citizenship: The role of neighbourhood networks in cultural change", *Environmental Politics*, 20(6), pp. 843–860.

Kennedy, E.H., Krahn, H., and Krogman, N. (2013) "Downshifting: An exploration of motivations, quality of life, and environmental practices", *Sociological Forum*, 28(4), pp. 764–783.

Knight, K., Rosa, E., and Schor, J. (2013) "Could working less reduce pressures on the environment? A cross-national panel analysis of OECD countries, 1970-2007", *Global Environmental Change*, 23, pp. 691–700.

Lorenzen, J. (2012) "Going green: The process of lifestyle change", *Sociological Forum*, 27(1), pp. 94–116.

Levy, N. (2005) "Downshifting and meaning in life", *Ratio* 18(2), pp. 176–189.

Maniates, M. (2001). "Individualization: Plant a tree, buy a bike, save the world?", *Global Environmental Politics*, 1(3), pp. 31–52.

Princen, T. (2006) "Consumer sovereignty and sacrifice: Two insidious concepts in the expansionist consumer economy", Prepared for the conference "*Sustainable Consumption*", Madison, WI, June 1–3, 2006.

Robin, V., Dominguez, J., and Tilford, M. (2008) *Your money or your life: 9 steps to transforming your relationship with money and achieving financial independence.* New York: Penguin.

Rubin, H. and Rubin, I. (2005) *Qualitative interviewing: The art of hearing data.* 2nd ed. Thousand Oaks, CA: Sage.

Sandlin, J. and Walther, C. (2009) "Complicated simplicity: Moral identity formation and social movement learning in the Voluntary Simplicity Movement", *Adult Education Quarterly*, 59(4), pp. 298–317.

Schor, J. (1998) *The overspent American: Why we buy what we don't need.* New York: Basic Books.

Semyonov, M., Lewin-Epstein, N., and Maskileyson, D. (2013) "Where wealth matters more for health: The wealth–health gradient in 16 countries", *Social Science & Medicine*, 81, pp. 10–17.

Sherman, J. (2009) *Those who work, those who don't: Poverty, morality, and family in rural America*. Minneapolis: University of Minnesota Press.

Soneryd, L. and Uggla, Y. (2015) "Green governmentality and responsibilization: New forms of governance and responses to 'consumer responsibility'", *Environmental Politics*, 24(6), pp. 913–931.

Tan, P. (2000) *Leaving the rat race to get a life: A study of midlife career downshifting*. Doctoral thesis. Melbourne: Swinburne University of Technology.

Walther, C. and Sandlin, J. (2013) "Green capital and social reproduction within families practising voluntary simplicity in the US", *International Journal of Consumer Studies*, 37(1), pp. 36–45.

Warren Brown, K. and Kasser, T. 2005. "Are psychological and ecological wellbeing compatible? The role of values, mindfulness, and lifestyle", *Social Indicators Research*, 74(2), pp. 349–368.

# 9 Who participates in community-based sustainable consumption projects and why does it matter? A constructively critical approach

*Manisha Anantharaman, Emily Huddart Kennedy, Lucie Middlemiss, and Sarah Bradbury*

## Introduction

For scholars who doubt the tenability of individualizing the responsibility to protect the environment through, for example, recycling and bicycling, the prospect of community-led sustainability initiatives holds much promise. Indeed, since the 2000s, there has been growing interest in community as a site of collective action that can support and promote sustainable consumption. This interest has been documented by academics, who initially characterized community as a site of social transformation that seemed to counteract the trend towards the individualization of sustainable consumption policy (Middlemiss, 2011; Seyfang, 2009). As political will to address environmental problems has dissipated, governments' have increasingly shifted responsibility for environmental management to individuals, communities, and corporations, in keeping with the broader project of privatizing environmental governance (Kennedy and Bateman, 2015; Middlemiss, 2014). We use the term "community-based sustainable consumption projects" to refer to "civil–society-based social innovation" that seeks to improve environmental outcomes (Seyfang and Haxeltine, 2012, p.381).

Today, community-based sustainable consumption projects appear in both top-down and bottom-up forms, the former evolving in response to formal participatory mechanisms (e.g., citizens' fora convened by municipal governments) and the latter commonly initiated by well-resourced, middle-class members of the community (e.g., neighborhood-led tool lending libraries).[1] A growing critical literature on community-based sustainable consumption (e.g., Bulkeley and Fuller, 2012; Grossmann and Creamer, 2016; Taylor Aiken et al., 2017; Anantharaman 2018) argues that neither top-down nor bottom-up community-based projects can be assumed to advance inclusion and democracy and equitably represent all stakeholders. Process-related questions, such as who gets to take part and whom these projects represent are rarely raised; in many cases this silence exacerbates a democratic deficit and inadvertently reproduces existing distributions of power and privilege (Lee, McQuarrie, and Walker 2015). Building on such observations, we draw on case studies of community-based sustainable consumption projects in the UK, Canada, and India to address three questions: *Who participates in community-based sustainable consumption projects and in what ways? What are the mechanisms of exclusion and inclusion operating in these projects? And, how do these mechanisms relate to the goals, processes, and outcomes of sustainable consumption projects?*

We contribute to emergent scholarship that critically evaluates the impact of community-based sustainable consumption projects on equity and democracy by identifying specific mechanisms through which community-based projects become exclusive and apolitical. Our case studies illustrate that as these projects are frequently initiated and designed by middle-class members, they exude identities and sensibilities that appeal to middle-class prospective members. Middle-class-led community initiatives tend to privilege apolitical tactics and behavioral solutions to environmental problems, subjugating the democratizing promise of community-based sustainability initiatives. Further, an issue of representation arises when political participation is "professionalized" and subject to middle-class tastes and etiquette. Through a feedback cycle, these themes (individualization, apolitical engagement) then influence who becomes involved in community-based projects (i.e., mostly middle class) and what is achieved. Thus, even when projects do not start with the explicit intention of being exclusive or apolitical, they become so through this feedback cycle, normalizing and legitimizing existing inequities in access to resources and access to participation in decision-making, and cloaking exclusion under the veneer of community action.

## What is participation in community-based sustainable consumption?

The term "community-based sustainable consumption projects" has been used in the literature to describe a range of initiatives, and in this paper we refer to projects that operate outside governmental oversight and depend largely on the unpaid, voluntary work of individuals who are motivated either by environmental or civic concerns. These projects appear in both top-down and bottom-up forms. While some projects might involve participation by government actors or be anchored in "formal" organizations like NGOs, others are more informal in their composition and governance. Projects might be geographically focused in specific neighborhoods or localities, or span larger geographies but are united by shared ideologies and practices. We thus use the term in a pluralist sense to capture a range of projects that go beyond the individual but largely function outside of the state or market.

In early writing on community-based sustainable consumption projects, scholars and policy-makers expressed hope that these citizen-led efforts might increase participation in environmental governance, whether by increasing action or increasing voice (Defra, 2005; Seyfang, 2009). More recently, scholarship has evolved to develop a more critical approach to evaluating such initiatives. A review of this emerging body of critical research on community-based environmental projects (Aiken et al., 2017) highlights concerns with issues of representation and, by extension, of democracy and legitimacy. The new critical work on community notes that participation in community-based sustainable consumption projects is rarely inclusive (Bulkeley and Fuller, 2012; Grossmann and Creamer, 2016). It documents mounting evidence that such projects have mostly attracted middle-class, educated, and relatively well-off members of the public, and that this narrow representation may winnow the transformative impact these projects have for justice and sustainability.

Before we unpack who participates in community-based sustainable consumption projects, we need to understand the range of projects undertaken *and* the various forms of participation at play. Scholars have evaluated a range of projects, from radical and political action (Schlembach, 2011); to community action tied into local concerns (Eliasoph, 1998; Perrin, 2006; Bennett et al., 2013); to action funded by government to meet environmental targets (Hauxwell-Baldwin, 2013; Creamer, 2014; Lee et al., 2015). We argue that the form of participation influences who participates and who does not, and what goals are pursued and achieved, and which are not.

Participants in community-based sustainable consumption projects come from two subgroups: environmental advocates and proponents of community development. In North America, Western Europe, and India, both subgroups tend to be more white (or upper-caste in India), middle class, and/or educated than the general population (Horton, 2003; Baviskar, 2011; Evans, 2011; Isenhour, 2012; Anantharaman, 2016). Whereas once environmentalists were radical outsiders, ecologically oriented identities have become mainstream (Shirani et al., 2015), in particular those that reflect the logics of middle-class and non-activist groups. People involved in community development also tend to come from middle-class backgrounds. In the UK and Canada, community actors are known to be more educated, female, white, and middle-aged than the average population (Kitchen et al., 2006; Cabinet Office, 2007; Fong and Shen, 2016). In India, community actors involved in issues that are explicitly identified as civic or environmental are often exclusively middle class (Mawdsley, 2004), though working-class groups are more involved in civic issues that have justice or equity goals. This means that community activists on sustainable consumption issues are doubly likely to be relatively privileged (Aiken, 2012).

As well as community-based sustainable consumption projects drawing largely on middle-class participants, the practices of such projects are shown in ethnographic research to tend towards a rejection of typically "activist" forms of politics. In this body of research, the move away from the political is justified by people in community-based projects as a more effective way of making social change (Bennett et al., 2013; Kennedy, Johnston, and Parkins, 2017). This rejection of confrontational engagement represents an avoidance of the dominant trope of the left-wing, radical environmentalist. A more contextual factor influencing the move away from traditional politics may be the trend, within the broader neoliberal project, for environmentalism to increasingly prescribe individualized and behavioral responses to environmental problems (Maniates, 2001; Szas, 2007; Middlemiss, 2014). Relatedly, there is evidence that within such "apolitical" engagement, it is more palatable to demand that individuals take actions to achieve desired goals than for state or corporate actors to bear responsibility. For instance, in Newell's (2005) account of well-resourced climate groups, communities take on the task of meeting government targets on household carbon reduction. Such projects can turn into attempts to change individual behavior, losing a sense of collective endeavor (Hauxwell-Baldwin, 2013).

The perceived need to create distance from the political may impact the nature and goals of community-based projects. In trying to "do" environment apolitically, community projects tend to focus on consensus and collaboration (Kenis and Mathijs, 2014). This focus can have unintended consequences for participation—and by extension—for representation. For instance, the transition network, which promotes a hugely successful model of community action on environment (Transition Towns), and represents one of the commonly cited project types in this field, places a substantial emphasis on being apolitical. Analyzing Transition Towns in Belgium, Kenis and Mathijs (2014, p.180) articulate how this conciliatory tone impacts its framing of participation: "Inclusiveness, in Transition Towns' discourse, primarily seems to mean being non-oppositional, strongly collaborative, and pursuing harmony through complementarity amongst individuals and their interests." In Belgium and elsewhere, Transition Towns conceives of their community as sharing common goals, with participation taking the form of a dialogue leading to agreement rather than any kind of contestation (see Chatterton and Cutler, 2008; Connors and McDonald, 2011; Aiken, 2012; Grossman and Creamer, 2016; Kenis, 2016).

Recognizing diverse understandings of participation in the context of community-based sustainable consumption, we distill this diversity into a simplified framework that distinguishes three forms of participation observed in community-based sustainable consumption projects (Table 9.1). The categories we identify—activist, communitarian, and low-impact self-discipline—relate to the overall goals of the project and to the nature and structure of participation. In our view, the activist form is less commonly adopted in community-based sustainable consumption projects although the categories in Table 9.1 are more fluid than they appear; a group or project may move through these forms depending on event and context. We fully expect there to be tensions within groups as to the best way to frame participation in their activities, as well as some projects that use elements of several of these categories. Below, we draw on our case studies to understand how projects frame participatory action, so that we can move on to our next focus: understanding who participates. This is important since, as we will show, patterns of inclusion and exclusion are reciprocally related to the goals and outcomes of community-based groups (see Figure 9.1).

*Table 9.1* Three forms of participation in community-based sustainable consumption projects

| Forms of participation | Overall goals of project | Who participates | Nature and structure of participation |
|---|---|---|---|
| **Activist** | Radically reforming the economic and social system to produce substantial reduction of environmental damage. | People who have strong green and social values, and who believe radical reform is necessary. | Members should resist the status-quo and act to transform it; should aspire to produce systemic change. |
| **Communitarian** | Taking "apolitical" action at a local level as a result of a conviction that government is failing on environmental governance. | People who believe the community is best suited to resolving issues of importance. | Consciously apolitical action, focused on local change, members should work together in consensus to create local, low-impact alternatives that align with shared values. |
| **Low-impact self-discipline** | To encourage people in the community to change their behavior and reduce their impacts on the environment. | People who believe that everyone is responsible for, and capable of, addressing environmental problems; people who believe change starts with the individual. | Members should unobtrusively and "apolitically" demonstrate to others that being green is straightforward, enjoyable, and morally correct. |

## Who participates in community-based sustainable consumption: Lessons from the UK, Canada, and India

We now turn to case studies from the UK, Canada, and India to explore representation in community-based sustainable consumption. For each case we note who participates and in what ways, or stages of the project, and use the framework in Table 9.1 to characterize how participation is framed. We consider the mechanisms of exclusion and inclusion active in each case, and the impacts of these mechanisms on the goals, processes, and outcomes of the projects. Following detailed elaboration of the cases below, we discuss how these insights contribute to understanding how community-based sustainable consumption projects can intentionally avoid framing participation in a manner that produces exclusion and a democratic deficit.

### Place-based sustainability movement: United Kingdom

In the UK, place-based, volunteer-led sustainability projects aiming to promote environmental action in communities emerged around 2005. The best known

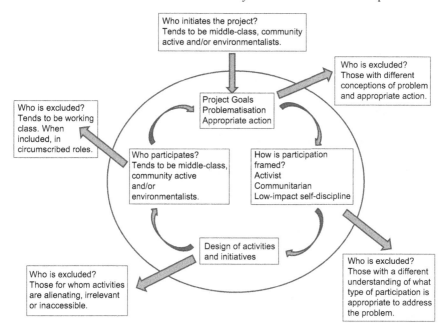

*Figure 9.1* Mechanisms and moments of exclusion from community-based sustainable consumption projects: A feedback cycle.

is the Transition Towns "movement," which grew from a single initiative in Totnes, to a global network of similar projects. Transition Towns took climate change and peak oil as its key concerns, addressing these in a range of activities, including local food and currencies, and community energy. Further initiatives based on the principle of finding local solutions to environmental problems emerged concurrently, including community energy initiatives, low-carbon community projects, and food-growing projects. Collectively, these amount to a loose coalition of initiatives, and form a movement in the sense that they all attempt to stimulate change in place-based communities. The case study outlined here is an example of a place-based sustainability project, Congleton Sustainability Group (CSG).

## Methods

The empirical work for this case study was conducted in April 2012. The main form of data collection was qualitative interviews with the chairman, four co-ordinators, and six less-active participants. Documentation associated with CSG was also part of our analysis, including the website, the Facebook page, back issues of the newsletter, and a series of resources aimed to promote sustainable living produced by the group. We analyzed datasets qualitatively, looking for the framing of sustainability problems and proposed solutions.

*Who participates?*

Congleton has a highly active voluntary sector. As a geographically distinct market town, surrounded by countryside, it has a reputation for community action and events. The town is, to some extent, a community of two halves: one part of the population has above-average educational qualifications and good employment prospects in the nearby knowledge industry. Residents of the social housing estate, where unemployment rates are high, are more likely to have basic school-leaving qualifications.

The Congleton Sustainability Group (CSG) was initiated by the Congleton Partnership, an explicitly non-political voluntary group representing key stakeholders in the town (emergency services, local councillors). The leader of CSG argued that environmental issues were poorly represented in the town strategy and that there was a need for a sub-group on environmental issues. Individuals and organizations around the town with an interest in the environment were invited to join the group; later, like-minded volunteers were attracted to get involved. CSG had a formal structure (chairman, treasurer, and secretary) and included representatives from a number of local environmental organizations. The group was predominantly made up of (ex-) professionals: mainly retired people who had worked in the local knowledge industries.[2] Members were using CSG as a network for their connected interests, as they were frequently engaged elsewhere as volunteers or community organizers, rather than actively engaging in collective work.

*Mechanisms of exclusion and inclusion*

Clearly, the methods of recruitment to the group, and its status as a subsidiary initiative of the Congleton Partnership, had an impact on who got involved in CSG activities at the outset. Logically, the people involved at the beginning set the agenda of the group for the longer term, framing group activities, and delineating who participates. In order to avoid association with the politics and practices of more radical forms of environmentalism, CSG framed their activities in opposition to two common framings of environmental action: promoting radical political change, and dwelling on doom-and-gloom narratives of environmental apocalypse. As the group stated on its website:

> A group of us has grown so tired of the negative portrayal of "Sustainability"— sandals, whole nuts and mucky mulches in the garden—that we have banded together to create the Congleton Sustainability Group, part of the Congleton Partnership. (CSG, 2014).

CSG positioned itself as part of the active community sector in Congleton, which is known for providing opportunities for action:

> [CSG] has been formed by people interested in finding lots of… community opportunities to address the impact of climate change on Congleton (CSG, 2014).

The group characterized its activities as fun and money-saving. While this framing of the problem of, and solutions to, climate change may seem innocuous, it is also exclusive, in particular marginalizing activist forms of participation. Inevitably none of the members interviewed espoused a radical green identity in the context of the group. Further, such strong "apolitical" framing resulted in group activities which avoided any form of perceived radicalism or deep green intent.

Instead, the group's identity was clearly aligned with a sense of professionalism. Given that most group members came from middle-class, professional backgrounds, this is hardly surprising. A professional identity played out in a number of practices in the group. For instance, the group had a formal management structure, and meetings were held in a local company's boardroom. On joining the group, one volunteer, Anna, reported on the leader's (Peter) assessment of her potential:

> Peter... asked what I did [for work]... So Peter was clever in the way an employer would be, he assessed what skills I had and he decided how he was going to allocate his jobs...

In effect the group leader ran CSG as a manager would a company. This professional approach also produced formal project management practices. One interviewee explained that after the group responded rather negatively to an idea she had about producing food for free, she wrote a formal plan for the venture, drawing on her business planning skills. She found that by mobilizing this ethic of professionalism she was able to garner support for her project. Professional practices require skills widespread among the participants of CSG. They are also highly exclusive, with even the location of meetings (the boardroom) likely to deter all those that do not define themselves as "professionals."

*Goals, processes, and outcomes*

The ethic of professionalism, and avoidance of radical identities, led to a series of activities characterized by the group as "sensible solutions." These typically encourage low-effort changes to townsfolk's lifestyles, often with financial benefits. As volunteer Chris, put it: "[We're not] saying you have to fundamentally change the way that you live, but be more informed... when you make choices." Initiatives, including a "top tips" leaflet, and a Watt Watch program (where people are encouraged to record and reduce their energy use) emphasize saving money (and energy) through incremental behavior changes. The logic here fits clearly into the low-impact self-discipline framing of participation, implying that townsfolk should reduce their demand for energy in order to facilitate a government-led, low-carbon transition.

Not surprisingly, given their emphasis on non-radical solutions, CSG did not challenge either government or business structures; indeed, they clearly saw both as having an important role in a transition to a low-carbon future. This runs counter to both activist and communitarian notions of participation, which tend to start with the belief that governments and businesses are causing environmental problems. Quite the contrary, CSG's professionalism encouraged an entrepreneurial orientation, exemplified by their discussions about developing their successful apple juice project to be run "on a commercial footing." In an activist or communitarian context this would likely have provoked concern about the potential for conflicts of interest. This orientation also narrows the field of potential participants: CSG activities appeal to environmentalists who believe in incremental change, and people interested in the benefits of such change (for instance to save money on energy bills).

There was an implicit assumption in much of the group's activity that people are over-consuming energy, which fails to recognize that some Congleton residents experience the ill effects of fuel poverty, and would therefore benefit from increasing consumption. There was limited evidence of the group taking into consideration residents' financial concerns, likely because those that ran the group (middle-class, educated professionals) were less likely to experience, and therefore prioritize, financial difficulties. For instance, the barrier to townsfolk engaging in local food production and consumption was seen to be availability and accessibility rather than cost, and initiatives aimed to increase the former, rather than to decrease the latter.

Many of the activities of the group are, therefore, aimed at wealthier townsfolk. A more substantive example of this is the group chairman turning down an offer to use a shop's premises. The group had aspirations to open a shop to sell and promote local produce. However, the premises offered were located in the less wealthy part of town: near the social housing estate. The group felt that products for sale would be too expensive for residents of the estate. This is symptomatic of an understanding of the relevant publics for CSG action: those who can afford to pay a premium for green alternatives.

The dominance of middle-class, professional volunteers in CSG is eminently predictable given the goals and processes outlined here, and the framing of the group's activities as non-radical and professional. While the group only set out to intentionally exclude "radical" environmentalists, its marked inclusion of professionals is likely to have given CSG an exclusive image. The professional identity it espoused is particularly problematic, as it excludes people who are not able to engage in the practices and understandings of professional life (typically the working classes).

### The eat-local movement: Canada

The local food movement[3] in Canada is barely two decades old but has had significant impacts on popular culture and urban and rural landscapes across the country. These shifts are evidenced by recent developments of local food policies at federal, provincial, and municipal levels; by increased marketplace activity (both inside and outside conventional food supply chains); and by the rise in the number of food-related voluntary associations and in memberships. This is a case study of actors who advance local food systems under the auspices of community-building and environmental protection.

## Methods

Data were collected in 2013–14 using interviews and participant observation within state, market, and civic spheres. Fifty-seven leaders of the food movement were interviewed and 12 food-related events were observed; we conducted nine interviews with government employees, and 24 from individuals in both the market and civic spheres. Data were collected in three cities: Victoria, BC; Edmonton, AB; and Toronto, ON. The purpose of the interviews was to understand what prompted participants' leadership role in the food movement, how they envisioned mobilizing others, what their ideal food system was, and what barriers and opportunities influenced the likelihood of achieving that ideal.

## Who participates?

Local food consumers are politically liberal members of the middle class[4] (Guthman, 2008; Johnston, 2008; Baumann et al., 2017). Less is known about who participates in the leadership of this "movement." Of our 57 interviewees, the vast majority are women (only 14 men), almost all are well-educated (only four participants do not have at least a university degree), and most are white (only six non-white participants).[5] These individuals participate because they want to make a better world, locally. For some, this is because they felt upset about the quality of food being consumed and its impact on health. For example, Marina, who works in the non-profit sector in Toronto, explains what motivated her involvement:

> I couldn't believe the parents of my kids' friends would have a meal for their kids on their way to their activities and it would be a sandwich in the back of the car. That was it! In my family, we always sat together.

Marina's comments reflect a general characteristic of those who participate: local food leaders imbue middle-class food consumption practices with moral correctness and tend to denigrate the type of food eaten (e.g., orange juice from concentrate, processed foods) and the rituals around food consumption (e.g., eating in the back of a car) that are more typical of the working classes. While Marina wanted to advance health, other leaders sought to improve local food security, the environmental impact of food production, and community cohesion (see Kennedy, 2016 for more details).

## Mechanisms of exclusion and inclusion

Almost all interviewees described their ideal food system as a place where everyone eats local food, yet they do not envision everyone having a role in realizing that food system. Participants struggled to imagine people with different values and tastes engaging in local food movements. For instance, Anya, a woman in her 20s who works for a local food farm and delivery company in Toronto, explains:

> Obviously every day you have to make those choices multiple times a day. I think the idea of learning how to grow your own food is a very powerful experience that I think once people do it something kind of clicks and you understand more.

Like the CSG members who neglect to acknowledge poverty in their community, Anya pictures people who share her capacity to choose what to eat each day. This vision obfuscates those who feel little agency when choosing what, how often, or how much to eat, and assumes the experience of growing food is universally transformative.

Food leaders celebrated the big-tent diversity of the food movement. However, this diversity was limited to variation in age and political orientation. Very few participants envisioned diverse social classes working together to localize the food system. When interviewees envisioned a role for the working classes, it was as beneficiaries of healthier (non-processed, whole) foods, not as collaborators. Below are examples of how age and political diversity are supported in the food movement. The first excerpt is from a woman who works in the city government in Toronto:

> Kids get excited about food. People of our older generations have knowledge that they can share and knowledge that comes from other countries and cooking. Food seems to be this great way that you can respect and honor the knowledge that you do have and the assets that you do have in your community and to be able to sort of bring them up.

A man who works in the civic sector in Toronto has witnessed political polarization fade in the local food context:

> You can rebuild communities around food because whether a Conservative, Liberal, this or that or the other thing, we all understand food and all have stories and memories and connections around food.

In contrast to this diversity, working classes are almost entirely excluded by aligning participation with consumption of food that requires the economic and cultural capital of the middle classes. Similar to CSG, where professionalism (a middle-class characteristic) was an implicit requirement for participation, here taste is a requirement. Indeed, when food leaders imagined the working classes becoming engaged in local food initiatives it was after they overcame the barrier of education—in other words, it was not the cost of local food that was seen as prohibitive but a lack of appreciation for "good" food.

Further, in the same way CSG members saw government and corporate entities as important allies, so too did local food advocates. For example, Chelsea, a manager of a farmers' market in a mixed-income neighborhood in Edmonton articulates her vision of the different stakeholders in the local food movement, a vision that does not include working-class individuals:

> Food is one of those issues that crosses all sectors and needs solutions and needs a systems way of thinking and in order to get a systems thinking, you need to be engaging the top decision makers in all three levels of government and top business leaders and the top thinkers in the community.

It is unlikely that state and corporate actors are going to push for a food system that pays workers a fair wage, that challenges subsidies to large agri-business, or that challenges the commodification of food. By actively including these actors and inadvertently excluding people with lower socio-economic status, the local food movement is shaping the goals and potential outcomes of the movement.

The mechanisms of exclusion in the food movement are inadvertent. By failing to imagine other relationships to food—for instance, one based on necessity rather than tastes for "authentic" foods—food leaders create conditions that exclude the working class. There is awareness that the food movement is ethnically white and a desire to diversify the movement in that regard. However, working-class individuals are, if ever discussed, referred to as beneficiaries of a food movement rather than partners in the transformation to a more just and sustainable food system.

*Goals, processes, and outcomes*

The choice to pursue the inclusion of some entities (e.g., state and corporate actors) and to view working classes as outsiders (or possible beneficiaries) in the pursuit of a localized food system is accompanied by particular ways of framing participation. Specifically, we see that most local food leaders promote engagement as either the low-impact self-discipline (exhorting consumers to eat better) or the communitarian form (developing community-based assets to support local food) and their objectives for change follow suit. For example, Mimi, a social entrepreneur from Toronto believes people would make better food consumption choices if the state had stricter labeling policies:

> [We need] labeling laws that are for people's health and not for the food corporation bottom line. If they want to sell their crap, they still can do it but I would put a tax on junk food. If you have to pay a tax on food, then there is a tax and every time you buy garbage, you are aware as a citizen that you are going to pay a tax because it is going to help pay for people's health later on that is damaged by those products.

While Mimi is adopting an antagonistic stance toward food corporations, it is only because they are acting as a barrier to an individualized style of food system reform that will allow her community to eat "better." Mimi envisions advancing health and nutrition by making some "unhealthy" foods (also foods more typical of working-class tastes) more expensive.

Participants often saw individual food consumption patterns as the most substantial barrier to realizing the ideal food system. Thus, several people aspire to encourage "people to grow as much of their own food as they [can], using whatever resources are available to them." As Mimi expressed, the villain is big industry but the process for defeating the villain is circumvention, not confrontation—by encouraging people to make "better" food choices. For example, a participant from the civic sphere in Victoria says:

> [In my ideal world], people would go meatless and have meat only on Friday, instead of just a meatless Friday. I mean we're horrified. Don't talk to us about the meat and the fish industry.

People are drawn to local food to make their communities more resilient or enjoyable. In pursuit of these goals, participants tend to idealize middle-class food tastes and see working-class tastes as a problem to be solved. The food leaders we spoke with wanted the eat-local movement to be inclusive. Yet this imagined inclusivity did not encompass participants from across the socioeconomic spectrum, but rather people of diverse ages or political ideologies. Many worked toward their goal of a better food system through low-impact self-discipline and communitarian forms that excluded actors who would choose more radical (activist) approaches. Like the case of CSG above, the primarily middle-class leadership of the eat-local movement is most comfortable pursuing goals that work with, rather than against, the interests of the state and market. They perceive promoting low-impact self-discipline (in the form of modifying food consumption choices) and communitarian (in the form of building community-based local food assets) approaches as most effective to circumvent corporate control of the food system.

### The zero-waste movement in India

Waste management has emerged as a key civic and environmental issue in India, as municipal infrastructures are unable to cope with the increasing amounts of waste produced in cities, making it the primary domain for middle-class[6] civic involvement (Mawdsley, 2004). While many middle-class campaigns around waste are focused on cleaning up streets, the past decade has seen a growing zero-waste movement (ZWM) that is pushing households to change consumption and disposal practices, bringing this movement into the domain of sustainable consumption.

### Methods

Data for the case study are based on a qualitative study of community-based, zero-waste initiatives conducted in Bangalore in 2011–13. It involved interviewing 38 individuals who participated in neighborhood-based, zero-waste initiatives.

Organizational representatives from social enterprises and non-profits (n = 10) who supported zero-waste initiatives through service provision and expert knowledge were also interviewed (for more detail see Anantharaman, 2014).

*Who participates?*

Bangalore's ZWM is largely composed of middle-class individuals similar to what has been documented in other Indian cities (Srinivasan, 2006). Middle-class movement participants fall into four categories: local leaders, city-wide leaders, "sustainable consumers," and organizational representatives. Local leaders set up and supervise zero-waste initiatives. These leaders, mostly women, run awareness campaigns to educate their neighbors on ZWM principles, supervise workers, and liaise with service providers. They embody the communitarian form of participation in that they see community coordination as key to solving civic and environmental problems. Some have also become involved in disseminating zero-waste practices to other localities and in influencing municipal policies, emerging as city-wide leaders. "Sustainable consumers," on the other hand, are individuals who participate in these initiatives through individual behavior change. These rank-and-file members have different levels of commitment to the ZWM, and are largely framed as beneficiaries of the movement. Finally, these community-based initiatives are supported by a network of organizations and businesses.

Interviews revealed that motivations for involvement in the ZWM are diverse. For many leaders (10 out of 18), involvement in zero-waste was an extension of civic involvement. To elaborate, many middle-class neighborhoods in Bangalore are home to Residents' Welfare Associations (RWA) dedicated to improving civic amenities. These associations and networks provide the community and social infrastructure for waste management initiatives to spread and establish. As Sneha, explained:

> I have been active in my local RWA for several years, tackling various issues such as bad roads and garbage dumping. Waste was one of our biggest problems and we needed creative solutions beyond just cleaning up or trying to get the waste pick-up service to do a better job. That is when I started hearing about home-based composting and segregation of waste, and decided to give that a try in my apartment complex.

For others (6/18), their foray into community work was directly related to their environmental consciousness. According to Lalitha:

> My family comes from the village, and from childhood I have always had a consciousness about waste. The village model is a closed system where all waste is recycled and reused. This has always been in the back of mind, especially as I see how different things are here in Bangalore. So for me I started off by composting at home, by myself. But as I got more connected, I have become more active in my community, helping others start composting at home too.

For individuals like her, waste became a domain to express concern and care for the environment. Lalitha also bicycles and grows organic food, and her involvement in the ZWM was a part of her ecological orientation.

Finally, a small subset of middle-class actors (4) became involved in zero-waste initiatives out of social justice concerns. These individuals, whose prior work involved labour organizing and charitable activities, entered the movement with the explicit goal of making sure that middle-class initiatives did not dispossess Bangalore's waste-engaged poor.

## Mechanisms of inclusion and exclusion

The ZWM was led by middle-class individuals who, along with organizational representatives, played a central role in identifying the scope of the "waste problem" and devising suitable solutions. These leaders managed to gain authority and were recognized as experts in waste management despite the fact that most of them lacked any formal training in environmental or public health issues. The source of this authority and the way in which it serves as a mechanism of exclusion signifies the class politics of civic activism in Indian cities. Middle-class property owners, emboldened by formal participation schemes constituted by the government that privilege elite voices in urban governance, have come to see themselves as guardians of clean, green, and world-class cities (Coelho and Venkat, 2009; Ellis, 2012). Additionally, being educated and well-resourced, they are able to acquire information on environmental and civic issues from the Internet and deploy this information to gain credibility. In contrast, informal sector waste workers, who actually do most recycling in Indian cities, are easily framed as having vested interests and incapable of making informed decisions that contribute to the common good (Anjaria, 2009). Consequently, the waste-engaged working classes are often excluded from deliberations on how to manage waste. This mechanism of excluding working-class participation is partially subverted because middle-class individuals depend on the working classes (Schindler, 2014). Most middle-class households have domestic workers who are responsible for cleaning and disposing waste. Working-class people sweep streets, collect and transport garbage, and reclaim recyclables from garbage dumps, subsidizing the functioning of Indian cities. Working-class and lower caste people thus become included in zero-waste projects as executors: zero-waste initiatives need domestic workers, garbage collectors, and waste-pickers to segregate waste, operate composting systems, and transport recyclables (Anantharaman, 2014). Workers are included in the execution stage, while lacking voice in the planning stages of these projects.

## Goals, processes, and outcomes

Zero-waste activities emerged first in response to Bangalore's garbage-induced public health and aesthetic problems. Frustrated by the government's inability to deliver reliable services, communities turned to composting and recycling as viable solutions. Indeed, for many middle-class zero-waste practitioners, their involvement starts and stops with these community initiatives. They remain focused on changing waste disposal behaviors in their immediate localities, sticking to communitarian forms of participation.

Other actors, building on successes with small-scale efforts in their neighborhoods, have convened a city-wide zero-waste movement. For these individuals, engagement in zero-waste discussions online and offline, and coming into contact with environmental organizations like the Global Alliance for Incinerator Alternatives (GAIA), have turned what started as a civic endeavor into one that has explicit environmental goals. Zero-waste practitioners have educated themselves on the environmental impacts of dumping and incineration, learning about climate change and water pollution. Some individuals visited landfills in the periphery of the city and witnessed the degradation of land and soil first-hand. Through continued engagement, these individuals developed environmental subjectivities, and some embraced more activist identities:

> The more I got involved in all this, the more I realized that just cleaning up my street or just getting some households to change their behavior won't do. We need to change how the government manages waste from just a dumping mode to one where there is mostly recycling and composting. And for that we also have to hold the companies that produce all this waste accountable. You have heard of Extended Producer Responsibility? That has to be implemented here.

As the quote demonstrates, individuals who started off as neighborhood leaders soon looked to play a more prominent role in municipal waste governance. Now interested in greening the city as a whole, they sought to set up zero-waste systems that went beyond their individual streets or apartment complexes to cover entire localities. These activists began to identify service providers to collect recyclables and operate composting plants. Through all of this, zero-waste activists were largely oblivious of the fact that Bangalore is home to a sizable waste-engaged informal sector that collects, sorts and diverts over 1000 tonnes of recyclable material every day. Indeed, middle-class activists initially turned to private companies to develop their zero-waste infrastructures, ignoring the informal sector. These plans to privatize waste reclaiming could have displaced several hundred waste-pickers in Bangalore, demonstrating how sustainability initiatives shepherded by individuals oblivious to poor and working-class interests can actively harm these groups by failing to account for their lived realities.

Becoming increasingly cognizant of these threats, organizations representing informal sector waste-pickers built connections with middle-class zero-waste groups in order to protect waste-pickers' livelihoods. Indeed, following other social movements that recognized that rebranding social justice movements as environmental movements can help garner middle-class support, informal sector organizations adopted "green" language and imagery to establish ecological legitimacy. This resulted in a perceptible shift in the goals pursued by the ZWM. Instead of prioritizing public-private partnerships with corporate entities, zero-waste activists began to partner with waste-pickers to set up waste collection and sorting centers. Some middle-class individuals who started off in the communitarian form of participation have, flouting convention, embraced activism in support of waste-pickers. Conversations with labour organizers and environmental activists pushed these individuals to advocate for the rights of communities living near landfills, protest Waste to Energy projects, revise the city's waste management rules, and assist waste-pickers in obtaining occupational identity cards through legal activism.

Nevertheless, while many middle-class activists have become more supportive of the concerns of the waste-engaged working classes, the latter are still under-represented within the ZWM. The decision-making procedures of the ZWM, which rely on consensus building and ad-hoc relationships with political elites, most often exclude waste workers. Waste workers are usually represented by one or two organizational representatives, who might themselves be middle class. This means that even if working-class voices are represented, this inclusion is indirect and in circumscribed roles. Thus, while the goals and outcomes of the movement may have evolved, the ZWM remains locked into a form of participation where waste workers are viewed largely as beneficiaries and executors.

## Discussion

With governments in many national contexts moving from a regulatory to a facilitating role, community-based sustainable consumption will likely continue to play a prominent part in environmental governance. Given arguments that non-representative initiatives can perpetuate social injustice, we used three case studies to ask, *Who participates in community-based sustainable consumption projects and through what forms of participation? What are the mechanisms of exclusion and inclusion? And, how are these mechanisms related to the goals, processes, and outcomes of sustainable consumption projects?*

In each case, we found that the leaders and initiators of projects played a central role in defining the problem to be addressed, the scope of the project, and therefore participation more broadly. In the English case, movement leaders explicitly critiqued the "activist" form of participation from the outset, seeing sustainability as a behavioral and managerial challenge. In Canada, movement leadership problematized food consumption habits and industrialized production practices, but ultimately sought to motivate behavioral changes reflecting middle-class tastes. The form of participation most frequently observed in both these cases was "low-impact self-discipline," though communitarian forms were also evident. In Bangalore, a movement that initially involved only low-impact self-discipline and communitarian participation broadened to include activist forms as new entrants into the movement's leadership challenged the ways in which waste issues were initially problematized. This last case is rather promising, given that the initial framing of the case was reworked into a more radical mode, suggesting the potential for new ideas and new publics to be included in some contexts.

With respect to mechanisms of exclusion, in the **activist** form, only some actors were recognized as having the authority and expertise to speak for the "common good" and in India these actors were largely middle class. Most individuals interested in activism feared group activities becoming "too political," thereby alienating less radical, middle-class constituents. In the process, they likely alienated other progressive movements. In the **communitarian** form, a primary mechanism of exclusion was the tendency to homogenize community identity, rendering working-class populations invisible. When designing initiatives, organizers inadvertently failed to take into account the fact that participation in valued activities relied on economic, educational, and cultural capital. In the Canadian examples, those trying to expand local production did so because they felt this was the primary barrier to a localized food system. However, evidence suggest barriers include cultural tastes, costs, food skills, availability, and leisure time (Guthman, 2008; Alkon and Agyeman, 2011; Schoolman, 2016). When working-class actors were included in community initiatives, they were seen as beneficiaries of the movement (Canada) or in circumscribed execution roles (India). In the **low-impact self-discipline** form of participation, leaders aimed to tell people in their communities how to live better, designing activities that promoted healthier, more sustainable, and eco-friendly lifestyles. This required an agreed-upon standard of what it means to live well; we found that across our cases this ideal reflected middle-class values and tastes. It also overlooked distinctly working-class barriers to living well, in this way excluding their participation.

In sum, the manner in which activities and efforts were designed was intimately shaped by the middle-class people who took leadership roles in these movements. The forms of participation that ensued contributed to the consolidation of project goals and outcomes appropriate and desirable for project leaders, in the manner of a feedback cycle (Figure 9.1). This cycle unintentionally excluded working-class participants, as the goals, problem and solution framing, and the activities themselves were designed to the leaders' tastes.

Given the feedback cycle identified above, the sustainability and social justice outcomes achieved by these initiatives are mixed. Clearly, the more community action that takes place, the more extensive the participation in sustainable consumption governance. This is in itself a positive step, and we celebrate the energy and enthusiasm of the volunteers involved in these projects. However, there are also more negative outcomes. As Bulkeley and Fuller (2012) point out, in low-carbon community projects there is little recognition of the possibility of exclusion, either as a result of structural inequality, or through marginalization in decision-making processes. This lack of recognition of the possibility of exclusion is very much apparent in our cases, particularly in the English context. When the possibility for injustice is not acknowledged, that possibility is heightened. Our cases point to injustices such as:

- Groups gaining authority in the community, and speaking for a broader community that they do not represent (all three cases);
- An entrenchment of issues relating to both environment and community being understood as the province of the middle classes (all three cases);

- Local inequalities being reinforced by a failure to recognize the diversity of voices involved in communitarian projects (UK and Canada); and
- Working-class people being oppressed by "community" action because their interests are not being taken into account (India).

In most cases, these injustices seem to be produced by a lack of attention to equity issues when framing these initiatives. Consequently, we posit that when community-based sustainable consumption initiatives explicitly think about questions of inclusion and exclusion, some of these injustices can be circumvented. This would require movement leaders to consider how to problematize sustainable consumption and community problems from the outset, how to frame participation, and how to deal with conflict.

Mainstream environmentalism has long been the bastion of white and/or middle- and upper-class populations. Environmental organizations like the Sierra Club are beginning to recognize that this lack of diversity is problematic both in and of itself and because it limits who supports their agendas, and they are working on improving their grassroots organizing and outreach capacities. Sustainable consumption projects could follow this lead and implement "best practices" in community organizing, which include community mapping, applying asset-based approaches, and cultivating leadership from within marginalized communities. Similarly, movements should question taken-for-granted authority and expertise: in the domain of sustainable consumption, it is not just the well-off who have good ideas. The quotidian, pro-environmental practices of the working classes and the poor are also key to any sustainability transition. Thus, considering the normative basis of sustainable consumption would be a necessary first step to creating more inclusive projects. Reflecting both principles of justice and equity and evidence of past successful social movements (Scott, 2008), it is likely that by representing a more diverse public, community-based sustainable consumption projects will better serve the environment they strive to protect.

Our case studies depict a feedback cycle driven by the appeal of community-based sustainability projects to the middle class and the tastes for engagement forms these people bring with them. When middle-class individuals dominate groups, the groups develop identities and sensibilities that in turn attract other middle-class members. Even when projects lack an explicit intention of being exclusive or apolitical, they become so through this feedback cycle. In this way, potentially transformative community-based sustainability initiatives can normalize and legitimize existing inequities in access to resources *and* to participation in decision-making, resulting in community action that fails to fully represent or include the community.

## Notes

1. Middle class is a complex term that lacks a singular definition. We provide context specific definitions in each of our cases, but in general, we follow Bourdieu (1984) as we take "middle class" to refer to a large social group that leverages significant

cultural capital and moderate socioeconomic capital to accrue privilege and assert power by influencing which tastes are deemed markers of social status. Additionally, we recognize that the term operates as much as a cultural construct as a sociological category, in that the discourses around the term "middle class" are as important to its definition as income or consumption practices.

2. Note that in this case the strong emphasis on "professionalism" is a clear signal of a middle-class aesthetic, as by definition professionals are educated, relatively wealthy, and in possession of the cultural signifiers associated with being middle class. While respondents did not self-identify as middle class, they articulated a clear identity of professionalism, entrepreneurialism, and "sensible," non-radical action, which is symptomatic of a form of environmentalism associated with corporate sustainability.

3. We use the term "movement" loosely, noting that these actors are engaged in efforts to reorganize patterns and systems of production and consumption along lines of sustainability.

4. Consumers across the class spectrum consume locally produced food from home gardens, but the deliberate sourcing of food of local provenance through the use of food labels and shopping at farmers' markets is a middle-class phenomenon (Johnston and Baumann, 2007).

5. In this case, we operationalize class traditionally, noting the participants' high levels of education, professional employment, or time available to volunteer in a strongly middle-class domain ("authentic" local food).

6. India's middle class has been characterized using socio-economic markers such as income and consumption profiles, and sociological criteria like occupation, education levels, linguistic, caste, and religious backgrounds. We follow Fernandes and Heller (2006) to characterize the middle classes as a "class in practice" (i.e., a social group that deploys its cultural and social capital to distinguish itself from the poor and to assert its claim to speak for public good). Middle-class civic politics in urban India have a well-documented illiberal nature, which contributes to the further marginalization of the poor and working classes in the public arena.

# References

Aiken G. (2012) "Community transitions to low carbon futures in the Transition Towns Network (TTN)", *Geography Compass* 6: 89–99.

Alkon, A.H. and Agyeman, J. (2011) *Cultivating Food Justice: Race, Class, and Sustainability.* Boston, MA: MIT Press.

Anantharaman M. (2014) "Networked ecological citizenship, the new middle-classes and the provisioning of sustainable waste management in Bangalore, India", *Journal of Cleaner Production*, 63: 173–83.

——— (2016) "Elite and ethical: The defensive distinctions of middle-class bicycling in Bangalore, India", *Journal of Consumer Culture.* http://doi.org/10.1177/1469540516663441

——— (2018) "Critical sustainable consumption: A research agenda", *Journal of Environmental Studies and Sciences.* https://doi.org/10.1007/s13412-018-0487-4

Anjaria, J.S. (2009) "Guardians of the bourgeois city: Citizenship, public space, and middle-class activism in Mumbai 1", *City & Community* 8(4): 391–406.

Baumann, S., Engmann, A., Kennedy, E.H., and Johnston, J. (2017) "Organic vs. local: Comparing individualist and collectivist motivations for 'ethical' food consumption", *Canadian Food Studies*, 4(1): 68–86.

Baviskar, A. (2011) "Cows, cars and cycle-rickshaws: Bourgeois environmentalism and the battle for Delhi's streets", in, edited by Amita Baviskar and Raka Ray, 391–418. *Elite and Everyman: The Cultural Politics of the Indian Middle-classes*. New Delhi: Routledge.

Bennett, E.A., Cordner, A., Klein, P.T., Savell, S., and Baiocchi, G. (2013) "Disavowing politics: Civic engagement in an era of political skepticism", *American Journal of Sociology* 119(2): 518–548.

Bourdieu, P. (1984) *Distinction: A Social Critique of the Judgement of Taste*. Harvard University Press.

Bulkeley, H. and Fuller, S. (2012) *Low Carbon Communities and Social Justice*. [Online]. Available at: https://www.jrf.org.uk/sites/default/files/jrf/migrated/files/low-carbon-communities-summary.pdf

Cabinet Office. (2007) "Helping out: A national survey of volunteering and charitable giving", Prepared for the Office of the Third Sector in the Cabinet Office by the National Centre for Social Research and the Institute for Volunteering Research.

Chatterton, P. & Cutler, A. (2008) *The Rocky road to a real transition: The transition towns movement and what it means for social change* [Online]. Available at: http://trapese. clearerchannel.org/resources/rocky-road-a5-web.pdf [Accessed].

Coelho, K. and Venkat T. (2009) "The Politics of civil society: Neighbourhood associationism in Chennai", *Economic and Political Weekly* 44: 358–67.

Congleton Sustainability Group. (2014) *Sustainability* [online, accessed 04/07/2014]. Available at: http://www.mybeartown.co.uk/congleton_sustainability.htm

Connors, P. & McDonald, P. (2011) "Transitioning communities: Community, participation and the transition town movement", *Community development journal*, 46, 558–572.

Creamer E. (2014) "The double-edged sword of grant funding: A study of community-led climate change initiatives in remote rural Scotland", *Local Environment*: 1–19.

Defra. (2005) *Securing the Future: Delivering UK sustainable development strategy*. Available at: http://www.sustainable-development.gov.uk/publications/pdf/strategy/SecFut_ complete.pdf

Eliasoph, N. (1998) *Avoiding Politics: How Americans Produce Apathy in Everyday Life* (1 edition). Cambridge, UK; New York, NY, USA: Cambridge University Press.

Ellis, R. (2012) "A world class city of your own!': Civic governmentality in Chennai, India", *Antipode* 44(4): 1143–60.

Evans D. (2011) "Thrifty, green or frugal: Reflections on sustainable consumption in a changing economic climate", *Geoforum* 42: 550–557.

Fernandes, L. & Heller, P. (2006). "Hegemonic aspirations", *Critical Asian Studies*, 38(4), 495–522.

Fong, E. & Shen, J. (2016). "Participation in voluntary associations and social contact of immigrants in Canada", *American Behavioral Scientist*, 60(5-6), 617–636.

Grossmann, M. and Creamer, E. (2016) "Assessing diversity and inclusivity within the Transition Movement: An urban case study", *Environmental Politics*: 1–22.

Guthman, J. (2008) "Bringing good food to others: Investigating the subjects of alternative food practice", *Cultural Geographies* 15(4): 431–437.

Hauxwell-Baldwin, R. (2013) *Tackling Climate Change through Community: The Politics and Practice of the Low Carbon Communities Challenge*, PhD Thesis, University of East Anglia.

Horton D. (2003) "Green distinctions: The performance of identity among environmental activists", *The Sociological Review* 51: 63–77.

Isenhour C. (2012) "On the challenges of signaling ethics without the stuff: Tales of conspicuous green cnti-consumption", in, Carrier, J.G. and Luetchford, P.G. (eds.) *Ethical Consumption: Social Value and Economic Practice*. Berghahn Books, 164–180.

Johnston, J. (2008) "The citizen-consumer hybrid: Ideological tensions and the case of Whole Foods Market", *Theory and Society*, 37(3), 229–270.

Johnston, J. and Baumann, S. (2007) "Democracy versus distinction: A study of omnivorousness in gourmet food writing 1", *American Journal of Sociology*, 113(1), 165–204.

Kenis, A. (2016) "Ecological citizenship and democracy: Communitarian versus agonistic perspectives", *Environmental Politics* 25: 949–970.

Kenis, A. and Mathijs, E. (2014) "(De)politicising the local: The case of the transition towns movement in Flanders (Belgium)", *Journal of Rural Studies* 34: 172–183.

Kennedy, E.H. (2016) "Environmental evaporation: The invisibility of environmental concern in food system change", *Environmental Sociology*, 2(1):18–28.

Kennedy, E.H. and Bateman, T. (2015) "Environmental civic practices: Synthesizing individual and collective sustainable consumption", in, Huddart-Kennedy, E., Cohen, M., and Krogman, N.T. (eds.) *Putting Sustainability into Practice: Applications and Advances in Research on Sustainable Consumption*, 47–66.

Kennedy, E.H., Johnston, J., and Parkins, J. (2017) "Small-p politics: How pleasurable, convivial, and pragmatic political ideals influence engagement in eat-local initiatives", *British Journal of Sociology*.

Kitchen, S., Michaelson, J., Wood, N., et al. (2006) *2005 Citizenship Survey: Active Communities Topic Report*. London: Department for Communities and Local Government.

Lee, C.W., McQuarrie, M., and Walker, E.T. (2015) *Democratizing Inequalities: Dilemmas of the New Public Participation*. New York: New York University Press.

Maniates, M.F. (2001) "Individualization: Plant a tree, buy a bike, save the world?", *Global Environmental Politics*, 1(3), 31–52.

Mawdsley, E. (2004) "India's middle-classes and the environment", *Development and Change* 35(1): 79–103.

Middlemiss, L. (2011) "The power of community: How community-based organisations stimulate sustainable lifestyles among participants", *Society and Natural Resources* 24: 1157–1173.

Middlemiss, L. (2014) "Individualised or participatory? Exploring late-modern identity and sustainable development", *Environmental Politics* 23: 929–946.

Newell, P. (2005). "Race, class and the global politics of environmental inequality", *Global Environmental Politics*, 5(3), 70–94.

Perrin, A.J. (2006). *Citizen Speak: The Democratic Imagination in American Life*. Chicago, IL: University of Chicago Press.

Schindler, S. (2014) "The making of 'world-class' Delhi: Relations between street hawkers and the new middle-class", *Antipode* 46(2): 557–73.

Schlembach, R. (2011). "How do radical climate movements negotiate their environmental and their social agendas? A study of debates within the Camp for Climate Action (UK)", *Critical Social Policy*, 31(2), 194–215.

Schoolman, E.D. (2016) "Completing the circuit: Routine, reflection, and ethical consumption", *Sociological Forum*, 31(3), 619–641.

Scott, J.C. (1985) *Weapons of the Weak: Everyday Forms of Peasant Resistance*. New Haven, CT: Yale University Press.

Seyfang, G. (2009) *The New Economics of Sustainable Consumption: Seeds of Change*. Basingstoke: Palgrave Macmillan.

Seyfang, G., Haxeltine, A. (2012) "Growing grassroots innovations: Exploring the role of community-based initiatives in governing sustainable energy transitions", *Environment and Planning C Government and Policy* 30, 381–400.

Shirani, F., Butler, C., Henwood, K., et al. (2015) "'I'm not a tree hugger, I'm just like you': Changing perceptions of sustainable lifestyles", *Environmental Politics* 24: 57–74.

Srinivasan, K. (2006) "Public, private and voluntary agencies in solid waste management: A study in Chennai city", *Economic and Political Weekly* 41: 2259–67.

Szasz, A. (2007) *Shopping Our Way to Safety: How We Changed from Protecting the Environment to Protecting Ourselves.* Minneapolis: University of Minnesota Press.

Taylor Aiken, G., Middlemiss, L., Sallu, S., et al. (2017) "Researching climate change and community in neoliberal contexts: An emerging critical approach", *Wiley Interdisciplinary Reviews: Climate Change.*

# Index

Printed in the United States
by Baker & Taylor Publisher Services